Death Our l

Also by Peter C. Jupp

Mortality (quarterly journal), co-edited with Glennys Howarth

Contemporary Issues in the Sociology of Death, Dying and Disposal, co-edited with Glennys Howarth

The Changing Face of Death: Historical Accounts of Death and Disposal, co-edited with Glennys Howarth

Interpreting Death: Christian Theology and Pastoral Practice, co-edited with Tony Rogers

Death in England: An Illustrated History, co-edited with Clare Gittings

Golders Green Crematorium 1902–2002: A London Centenary in Context, co-edited with Hilary J. Grainger

From Dust to Ashes: Cremation and the British Way of Death Postmodernity, Sociology and Religion, co-edited with Kieran Flanagan

Virtue Ethics and Sociology: Issues of Modernity and Religion, co-edited with Kieran Flanagan

A Sociology of Spirituality, co-edited with Kieran Flanagan

Death Our Future

Christian Theology and Pastoral Practice in Funeral Ministry

Edited by

Peter C. Jupp

✛ EPWORTH

Scripture quotations are from the New Revised Standard Version of the Bible, copyright 1989 by the Division of Christian Education of the National Council of the Churches of Christ in the USA. Used by permission. All rights reserved.

British Library Cataloguing in Publication data

A catalogue record for this book is available from the British Library

978 0 7162 0638 5

First published in 2008
by Epworth
Methodist Church House
25 Marylebone Road
London NW1 5JR

Typeset by Regent Typesetting, London
Printed and bound in the UK by
MPG Books Ltd, Bodmin, Cornwall

Contents

This book is dedicated to my wife Elisabeth
and to our sons and daughters-in-law:
Edmund and Samantha, Miles and Rachel.

Preface

Ebenezer Calvinist Methodist Church no longer stands in the centre of Newport, Monmouthshire. In the nineteenth century Morgan Howell had been one of its outstanding ministers.[1] When he died in 1852, he was no longer at Ebenezer; his funeral took place at Cendl, where he had been ordained and where his first wife had been buried. On their way to Cendl, a first service was held at Penuel Chapel, Tredegar. A. H. Morris in his history of Ebenezer, tells that a sermon was then preached from 2 Corinthians 5.1–2: 'For we know that if the earthly tent we live in is destroyed, we have a building from God, a house not made by hands, eternal in the heavens.' Morris continued, 'After the sermon the deceased's youngest child, a fortnight old, was christened.'

For Christians, we are invited to face death in the conviction that Jesus Christ was raised from the dead and will share this victory with us. Christian tradition equips us for this confrontation with both words and rituals. This book is offered as a resource for Christian ministry in contemporary funerals. *Death our Future* is a successor to *Interpreting Death*, which Tony Rogers and I edited for the Churches Funeral Group in 1997. That book, sent to its publisher Cassell in 1996, was published just after the death and funeral of Diana, Princess of Wales. Different contributors to this volume may hold contrasting estimates of the effect of the Diana events on British funeral customs. For me, the effect of the mix of all the sacred and secular ingredients in the Princess's funeral was to set a precedent for all sorts of families from then on to seek a greater say in their funeral arrangements.

In retrospect, the Diana event was only the most public of the many pressures that had over 20 years been building up for change and reform in the style of British funerals. In the 1980s a number of scandals in cemeteries and crematoria had drawn media attention. A succession of disasters – transport, terrorist and sporting (especially that at the Hillsborough football stadium) – had stimulated new forms of public mourning. This made for good television, particularly to a public that had followed the Northern Ireland tragedy for over 20 years. But, as older ministers and funeral directors know, signs of change were already apparent in 'ordinary' funerals before the eighties. Funeral congregations began to prefer popular and secular music, which spoke of human relationships and identity far more strongly than the traditional religious hymns. These not only celebrated love, loyalty and separation but spoke of virtues that survived death.

This book is offered to enable everyone called to conduct Christian funerals to provide a better service. It discusses the key changes in British funerals over the last ten years. Its sets the funeral in the changing context of death, bereavement and funeral organization. Its material is organized in five sections: modern death and bereavement, theologies of death and the afterlife, the disposal of the dead, funeral liturgies, regional cultures.

Modern death and bereavement

The first section – Chapters 1–6 – focus on issues of modern dying and bereavement. Geoffrey Rowell introduces the Christian vocation to help people prepare for death, pointing out tensions between traditional doctrines and contemporary beliefs and highlighting the importance of Christ's resurrection. Peter Jupp assesses recent changes in the role and work of the different groups involved in funeral organization, the processes at work and consequences for Christian ministry. Sudden or violent death, of individuals or of masses, receives much media attention. Such tragedies may come by storm or flood, by sporting or transport disaster or murder. Anne Eyre (Chapter 3) discusses high-profile deaths and the role clergy can play in how people and communities cope. Meanwhile, in an era when infant mortality is low, the deaths of children put great pressure upon their families. For each family member death holds different meanings and senses of loss. Ann Dent (Chapter 4) discusses the deaths and funerals of children, and demonstrates the pastoral needs that clergy and lay ministers are called upon to address. And the deaths of the majority? Nearly three-fifths of us die in hospital, and for Mark Cobb (Chapter 5) hospitals are 'major features on the landscape of death'. The relationship between hospitals and their patients is shifting from the passive towards the participatory. Cobb explores the hospital context of ministry to the dying and bereaved, and the need to attend to both the theological and psychological challenges of the task. And after death? In Chapter 6, Christine Valentine discusses how we may minister to bereaved people more effectively, contributing an analysis of the various theories of grief and bereavement that researchers and counsellors have developed over the last decades. Conscious that the dominance of psychological and medical frameworks has reflected the decline in religious belief and its role in making sense of death, she encourages ministers to see bereavement theories as a resource for pastoral support.

Theologies of death and the afterlife

The second section (Chapters 7–9) addresses theologies of death and the afterlife. Peter Jupp (Chapter 7) traces the course of continuity and change in Christian beliefs about the afterlife, with developments set against the basic conviction of Christ's resurrection from the dead. The next two chapters discuss contemporary debates about the mode of the afterlife and its location. In Chapter 8, Douglas Davies assesses the range of concepts available in beliefs about the resurrection of the body and the immortality of the soul. His own survey of attitudes to the afterlife informs his analysis, issues critical in a society where 30 per cent do not believe in afterlife and where traditional beliefs in bodily resurrection are rare. In Chapter 9, Paul Badham examines contemporary concepts of Heaven and hell, about which 'there is probably no area of Christian thought where the gulf between contemporary and traditional belief is so great'. He analyses four ways with which Christians may integrate their hope for Heaven within their overall understanding of reality. Both chapters challenge those in funeral ministry to ponder on the preconceptions which their congregations bring to the funeral.

The disposal of the dead

Issues of theology and belief also feature in the third section of the book (Chapters 10–14), which concentrate on the issue of the disposal of the dead. Parallel chapters by Leonie Kellaher (Chapter 10) and Hilary J. Grainger (Chapter 11) set cremation and burial in historical and contemporary contexts. Facilities for the disposal of the dead must cater for both secular and religious needs, within the constraints set by local authorities (the providers of most cemeteries and crematoria). Kellaher examines how people interact with graves and cemeteries and to graves. She shows how the role of the dead in the life of the livings can still be strong. Grainger addresses the 'oft-vexed relationship' between crematoria and Christian ministry by analysing cremation's history and architecture. Crematoria are symbols of social change and of modernity. Both these chapters suggest ways in which Christian funeral ministry can be made more meaningful in these secular surroundings. Kevin McGinnell and John Lampard discuss respectively the theologies of burial and cremation. McGinnell (Chapter 12) outlines how the historical Christian choice for burial is theologically rooted in the incarnation and resurrection of Jesus. This involves our own baptisms and our hopes for resurrection. He outlines the part that burial grounds can play in both the life of faith and secular life: in memory and in hope. Lampard (Chapter 13) reflects on the failure of the Churches to think theologically about cremation. The basic issue for Lampard is that the choice between burial and cremation is not equal. He argues for cremation to be seen as a preparation for burial, and offers ways in which churches might take both the theology and the use of cremation more seriously. Meanwhile, environmental issues challenge all contemporary arrangements for burial and cremation. Peter Owen Jones (Chapter 14) asserts that green burial is the only way both for Christian churches and for all those concerned for the environment. He discusses secular competition over ceremonies for the rites of passage, believing that green burial resonates with a new sense of the sacred.

Developments in funeral liturgy

The fourth section of the book (Chapters 15–19) analyses liturgical developments. Clergy conduct the majority of funerals. What are the liturgical resources at their disposal? How may popular beliefs and new models of funeral be balanced with orthodox doctrines and integrity? How may clergy accommodate the growing wish of families to be involved in planning and participation? Trevor Lloyd (Chapter 15) discusses the wide-ranging consultation that moulded *Common Worship* (2000). In a chapter strong on practical help for pastors to address the needs of bereaved people, he assesses ten years of Anglican liturgical development. Tony Rogers (Chapter 16) analyses how Catholic funerals have advanced since the *Order of Catholic Funerals* (1990). Like Lloyd, he presents funeral rituals as part of a series of staged rites. In a Catholic context, funerals increasingly need to take on board the circumstances of individual deaths, cater for the marginally religious within funeral congregations and give practical help to those unfamiliar with Catholic liturgy. Paul Sheppy (Chapter 17) analyses the strengths and weaknesses of recent liturgies from Baptist, Methodist and United Reformed Churches. He, too, is concerned for stages rites and discusses how these Free Church texts offer 'a menu of provisions'. In the context of contemporary popular belief, he analyses Free Church hesitancies about praying for the dead and shares his concern about our use of Scripture in addressing contemporary funeral congregations. John Nankivell (Chapter 18) presents a complete contrast. Orthodox liturgies have been little changed since the eighth century. The Church Fathers are not remote figures but daily involved. Their liturgies stress the burial and the resurrection of the body for which the open coffin stands a powerful symbol and music plays a vital role. Brian Parsons (Chapter 19) analyses the role of music in the average British funeral. He maps out the changes, particularly over the last 20 years, linking them to the funeral reform movement and to consumer demand and technological innovation. He discusses how clergy may better cope with tensions between secular and religious choices.

Regional characteristics in funeral ministry

The fifth section of the book (Chapters 20–23) looks at the demands of four major regions within the UK. This section was prompted by Hugh James' excellent book, *A Fitting End: Making the Most of a Funeral* (2004), which alerted me to regional characteristics and the effect of local culture and conditions upon behaviour and expectations at funerals. Mia Hilborn (Chapter 20) writes from her experience as pastor and hospital chaplain in London, where so many different ethnic cultures seek to celebrate their identities at the end of life. She assesses how city ministers meet the practical demands of poor or isolated people at the end of life. Derek Murray (Chapter 21) examines Scottish funeral traditions and points out the significance of the Scottish Reformation upon funeral customs and orthodoxies. Now under the impact of modernity, demographic change and growing secularity, he charts how the old customs are changing and how ministers may have to accommodate new funeral preferences. Keith Denison (Chapter 22) discusses the lasting advantages and constraints of the disestablishment of the Welsh Church. He outlines the challenges posed for clergy who serve wide areas of countryside or dense urban populations, and the increasing need to be bilingual. The 'old funeral communities' can still be found. He shows how Welsh clergy face the challenge to their faithfulness to Christian tradition where bereaved families want to exercise secular or personal preferences in funerals. Godfrey Brown (Chapter 23) commences his chapter with Northern Ireland's experiences of 'The Troubles'. He discusses the similarities and contrasts between Catholic, Church of Ireland and Protestant funeral traditions. Former funeral traditions have often broken down in the urban areas, but there are marked contrasts with the countryside. He recounts his experience of 'celebrity funerals' to discuss the responsibilities of clergy alongside the needs and demands of grieving communities and the responsibilities of clergy

The Edinburgh Festival of 2002 included a play about 9/11. Nine young American actors and actresses recounted their experience when the terrorists' planes struck. Some were lost in buildings and had to grope through darkness towards safety. Others found themselves in the street, running through dust and crowds, the crowds not knowing in which direction safety lay. Others were below ground on the Subways, struggling to reach fresh air. All were unaware of the nature of what had happened, or of its implications.

At the end of the play, I approached some of the actors and asked them why their script had ended so, as I thought, abruptly. The last line had been, 'There are no words.' There had been no attempts at interpretation, only the raw experiences retold. 'But you are actors,' I tried to say courteously, 'your gift is words and the conveyance of meaning. Language is given to us to explain the apparently inexplicable. Why did you not interpret? You can't end with "There are no words."' The actor with whom I spoke replied, simply, 'There are no words. We are telling the story, not of other survivors, but of ourselves. These nine stories are what happened to the nine of us.'

Later, I came across the words of the Welsh poet-priest, the late R. S. Thomas, 'The greatest language . . .' Note the reference to Jacob's ladder, down which the angels of God travelled, bringing God's word for the world and doing God's work within it.

The greatest language
The world has experienced,
And it is as though tongue-tied
Before the challenge.
Of Stalin, Hitler and Pol Pot.
The adjectives are tired,
The verbs indecisive, only the facts
Remain fresh, sprouting out of the
Ground manured by victims

Vocabulary is no longer the ladder
Angels descend and ascend on.[2]

Howell was a Calvinist, a Dissenting minister witnessing to an industrial urban community. Thomas was an Anglican, a universalist, ministering to rural parishes as well as the international audience of a Nobel
nominee. Each man sought to respond to the Gospel according to the
lights, experiences and dominant beliefs of their day. Meanwhile, the
shape of mortality and the forms of human hope have continued to
change. In our own day, how are we to interpret disaster? How are we
to help each other cope with death? The responsibility of those who
conduct Christian funerals abides: to set each death within the death
and resurrection of Jesus Christ; to choose vocabularies and rituals from
the Christian armoury and beyond with which to give personal support
to individuals and communities in their specific needs; and to address
the challenges that mortality poses for all societies. This book is offered
by its authors as an aid in this calling.

Notes

1 A. Morris, *The Story of Ebenezer Church, Newport, Monmouth*, Newport:
W. Jones, 1916.
2 Copyright the estate of R. S. Thomas, *Collected Later Poems 1988–2000*,
Tarset, Northumberland: Blood Axe Books, 2004. Reproduced with permission.

Acknowledgements

Many people have played a part in the making of this book. I have been hugely reliant upon the willingness and enthusiasm of all the contributors, all of whom are experts in their fields. They have shared their time and their expertise and have distilled their wisdom and experience into far smaller chapters than I would otherwise have wished. They have patiently honed their compositions to fit my Procrustean demands. I thank them all.

For additional help along the way, I thank Barry Albin, Paul Badham, Mohammed Kassamali, Leonie Kellaher, David Miller, Robert Murray, David Nesbitt, Brian Parsons, Brian Thornton and Archbishop Kallistos Ware. I am grateful to continuing conversations on funeral issues with colleagues on the Burials and Cemeteries Advisory Group in the Ministry of Justice, the Council of the Cremation Society of Great Britain and members of the Death and Life Group at the University of Durham.

I thank my former colleagues in the Chaplaincy team at Peterborough and Stamford Hospitals NHS Trust, Peter Brett, Sheelah Clarke, Linda Elliott, Richard Higgins, John Minh, David Parkes and Brian Thornton, whose ministry to the dying and bereaved has been a model for me. I am grateful to the staffs of the libraries at Durham University (Cathedral and Special Collections), Edinburgh (University and New College), the Reform Club, the Wellcome Institute of the History of Medicine, and the Laxton library at Peterborough District Hospital. The editing process has been smoothed from time to time by the enjoyable hospitality of Jon and Chris Steele, St John's College Durham, Launde Abbey and of Karen Perschke and Christophe Pelletier at La Bagatelle Restaurant in Edinburgh.

Edith Coole, a member of Westgate Church, Peterborough, and formerly on the staff of the Methodist Publishing House, first volunteered nine years ago to proof read for me. I am especially grateful to her for her watchfulness and her precision.

Natalie Watson first suggested three years ago that I might edit a book on funeral ministry for Epworth Press. Several friends whose books she had edited recommended her. Thus encouraged, I submitted my proposal on All Saints' Eve 2006. On the same day, Pope Benedict consigned Limbo to the discard heap of out-of-date theologies of life beyond death. He thus illustrated how theologies about life after death in Christ continue to evolve, as we humans and believers seek to reconcile the expanding boundaries of human knowledge with our expanding experience of God's knowledge and love of us.

I am grateful to Mary Matthews at SCM-Canterbury Press, Peter Andrews our proof-reader, and to Natalie Watson, now Commissioning Editor at SCM Press, for their help and ready responses to every enquiry.

My wife Elisabeth has been a continual source of encouragement.

Peter C. Jupp

Contributors

Paul Badham is Professor of Theology and Religious Studies at the University of Wales, Lampeter, and Director of the Alister Hardy Religious Experience Research Centre. He is also Vice-President of the Modern Churchpeople's Union and Patron of Dignity in Dying. His publications include *Christian Beliefs about Life after Death: Immortality or Extinction?* and (with Paul Ballard) *Facing Death*.

A. W. Godfrey Brown is a retired minister of the Presbyterian Church in Ireland. He lives in Ballycastle, County Antrim, where he served as minister from 1964 to 2001. Dr Brown was Moderator of the General Assembly in 1988–89, and served as Convener of its Public Worship Committee from 1975 to 1982.

Mark Cobb is a clinical director and Senior Chaplain at Sheffield Teaching Hospitals. He has worked in the community, voluntary and NHS sectors and has specialized in palliative and supportive care. He is an honorary lecturer in the Faculty of Medicine at the University of Sheffield and has published in the fields of chaplaincy, spiritual care and bereavement.

Douglas J. Davies is Professor in the Study of Religion at Durham University's Department of Theology and Religion, and Director of the Durham Centre for Death and Life Studies. His recent theological and anthropological research and publications include *The Theology of Death* (2008), *Bishops, Wives and Children* (2007, with Matthew Guest), *Encyclopedia of Cremation* (2005, with Lewis Mates), *A Brief History of Death* (2004), *Introduction to Mormonism* (2003), and *Death, Ritual and Belief* (2002). He is currently working both on woodland burials and on the role of emotion in religious identity. He is a D.Litt of Oxford and an Honorary Dr Theol. of Uppsala University.

Keith Denison was an Exhibitioner at Downing College, Cambridge, and holds a Doctorate in Philosophy from Cambridge University. He is

Canon Residentiary of St Woolos Cathedral, Newport, and Diocesan Director of Education in the Diocese of Monmouth. He is a member and past Chairman of the Liturgical Commission of the Church in Wales, and a member of the Churches' Funerals Group.

Ann Dent has worked in palliative care and bereavement with adults and children for 30 years, in service provision, education and research. She has been chair of the Child Bereavement Network and the Bereavement Research Forum. She is currently chair of Bristol Bereavement Forum, and patron of The Compassionate Friends and Cruse Bereavement Care (Bristol). Dr Dent has written many papers on dying and bereaved children and has co-authored several books on sudden child death.

Anne Eyre is an independent consultant specializing in trauma and disaster management. She works with a range of organizations developing psycho-social planning, training and response strategies for major emergencies. Dr Eyre belongs to a number of national and international research and practitioner organizations specializing in disaster management. In 2006 she was awarded a Winston Churchill Travelling Fellowship and travelled to New York to examine community support after disasters. Contact details: <anne.eyre@traumatraining.com>.

Hilary J. Grainger is a Dean of the London College of Fashion, University of the Arts, London. A leading authority on the late Victorian architect Ernest George and the architecture of British crematoria, her book *Death Redesigned: British Crematoria – History, Architecture and Landscape* was commended as the best reference book published in 2006 by the Chartered Institute of Library and Information Professionals. Professor Grainger is a member of the Council of the Cremation Society of Great Britain.

Mia Hilborn is Hospitaller and Head of Spiritual Health Care and Chaplaincy Team Leader at Guy's and St Thomas' NHS Foundation Trust, London, and Assistant Curate, North Lambeth Parish. She was formerly Paedriatric and Free Church Chaplain, St Bartholomew's Hospital and the London NHS Trust; and was formerly a United Reformed Church minister in London and Nottingham. She is married to David, and has two children.

Peter Owen Jones grew up in Kent. He spent his early working life on the land, then moved up to London, working in the advertising industry. He was ordained in 1992, and with the support of the Diocese of Ely set up the Arbory Trust, a woodland burial site in Cambridge, in 2000. He is now a non-stipendiary minister in Sussex. He has written several books and currently earns his living presenting religious documentaries for the BBC.

Peter C. Jupp is a United Reformed Church minister. As Director of the National Funerals College, 1992–7, he co-edited *The Dead Citizens Charter*. With Glennys Howarth, he founded the International Conference on the Social Context of Death, Dying and Disposal in 1993 and the (now quarterly) journal *Mortality* in 1996. He has co-edited several books in death studies, and written *From Dust to Ashes: Cremation and the British Way of Death* (2006). He is Chairman of the Cremation Society of Great Britain. With a team based at Durham University, funded by a Leverhulme Research Award, he is now researching the development of cremation in Scotland.

Leonie Kellaher is Emeritus Professor at London Metropolitan University. As a social anthropologist, her research over a decade or more has focused on the social significance of places in contemporary Western society where the remains of the dead are buried, placed, scattered, strewn, or, as ashes, reserved for later disposal. Those who visit and work in cemeteries, as well as the public and professionals responsible for arrangements for ash disposals, have largely informed the research and its findings.

Dr John Lampard is a retired Methodist minister who has been involved in death studies for 20 years. He holds a doctorate from London University in funeral liturgies, he was a member of the Liturgical Committee which produced the 1999 *Methodist Worship Book*, and is vice-chair of the ecumenical Churches' Funeral Group. His book *Go Forth Christian Soul: The Biography of a Prayer* (2005) is a study of prayer for the dying.

Trevor Lloyd, former Archdeacon of Barnstaple, served on the Church of England's Liturgical Commission from 1981 to 2002, chaired the Commission's Pastoral Rites and Funerals Groups and the steering group responsible for the passage of the new rites through the Synod. His son Peter died in 1985 at the age of 13. Since 1991 he has chaired

Children's Hospice South West, which in 2007 opened its second hospice just outside Wraxhall.

Kevin McGinnell is a priest of the Diocese of Northampton and Episcopal Vicar for Education and Formation. Monsignor McGinnell is one-time vice-chair of the Churches' Funerals Group. He is Chair of the Joint Liturgical Group and chair of the English Language Liturgical Consultation.

Derek Murray is a native of Edinburgh. He holds an MA from the University of Edinburgh, a BD from London University, and a PhD from the University of St Andrew's. After many years in the Baptist ministry in Scotland, he became wholetime chaplain at St Columba's Hospice, Edinburgh, in 1987, and retired in 2001. He has written *Faith in Hospices* (2002).

John Nankivell is a Shropshire man of Cornish descent. He graduated in chemistry and theology and spent two years studying in Greece. He worked for 30 years in schools and colleges in the Birmingham conurbation, finishing his teaching career as Principal of Joseph Chamberlain College in central Birmingham. He was ordained deacon in 1989 and was made priest in 2000 to serve as the Orthodox parish priest in Walsall.

Brian Parsons worked as a funeral director in London from 1982 until becoming the editor of *Funeral Service Journal* in 2005. Dr Parsons is author of *The London Way of Death* (Sutton Publishing, 2001), *Committed to the Cleansing Flame: The Development of Cremation in Nineteenth-Century England* (2005) and, with Hugh Meller, the fourth edition of *London Cemeteries: An Illustrated Guide and Gazetteer* (2008).

Tony Rogers is currently a parish priest in Cambridge and vicar general of the Diocese of East Anglia. Monsignor Rogers has previously served as Secretary to the Roman Catholic Bishops' Conference of England and Wales, Department for Christian Life and Worship, and was involved in the publication of the British edition of the *Order of Christian Funerals*. He co-edited *Interpreting Death* with Peter Jupp.

Geoffrey Rowell is Bishop of Gibraltar in Europe and was formerly Chaplain, Fellow and Tutor in Theology at Keble College, Oxford, of which he is now an Emeritus Fellow. He chairs the Churches' Funeral

Group, and among his many books and articles are *Hell and the Victorians* (1974) and *The Liturgy of Christian Burial* (1977). He has served on the Liturgical and Doctrine Commissions of the Church of England and on the Inter-Anglican Standing Committee for Ecumenical Relations.

Paul P. J. Sheppy is a Baptist minister in pastoral charge of a congregation in central Reading. Dr Sheppy is also a Fellow of the Centre for History and Heritage at Regent's Park College in the University of Oxford. He has written extensively on funeral liturgies and is a trustee of the Joint Liturgical Group of Great Britain and of the Churches' Funeral Group. He is a member of Societas Liturgica and is a regular contributor and participant at its biennial congresses. His current research interests are in the general area of liturgical theology and he is currently writing a textbook for publication in this field.

Christine Valentine is currently based at the University of Tokyo where she has been interviewing Japanese people about losing a loved one, and how continuing relationships between the living and the dead emphasise caring and reciprocity. Dr Valentine will compare the findings with those obtained from interviews previously conducted in the UK for her PhD in which continuing relationships were similarly found to encompass caring and reciprocity. These findings extend understandings of bereavement in the Western context and form the basis of her recent book *Bereavement Narratives: Continuing Bonds in the 21st Century*.

I

Introduction

GEOFFREY ROWELL

The philosopher Martin Heidegger famously described human life as *Sein zum tode* – 'being towards death'. Death constitutes the horizon towards which we live, wittingly or unwittingly. So every human being moves towards death, the end, the final moment of human life and existence. The obituary columns of middle-brow newspapers record human lives, their shaping and purpose, and make judgements upon them. Popular newspapers are more selective. If they have no formal obituary columns they devote acres of space to the deaths of celebrities, and what an earlier generation would have called 'horrid murders'. What we say of someone at the end of his or her life enables us to reflect on the whole of that life, not something yet to be fulfilled. Collections of obituaries, gathering together the bizarre and eccentric alongside the dutiful and compassionate, remain popular, providing appropriate presents for birthdays and Christmas.

The ultimate obituary is, in the words of the *Dies Irae* (Day of Wrath), the 'book exactly worded, wherein all hath been recorded, thence shall judgement be awarded'. The Last Judgement was the judgement of God, the definitive verdict on human life and indeed on human death, for, as works such as the *Ars Moriendi* (the art of dying well) and the Catholic *bona mors* (prayers for a good death) remind us, a good life should conclude with a good death. In a Protestant context, last words were important, for they could reveal whether or not dying people indicated by their piety that they belonged to the elect; hence the frivolity of the last words attributed to William Pitt the Younger, 'I think I could eat one of Bellamy's veal pies.'[1] At the end, the judgement of God was seen as both the definitive judgement of the good and evil of the world, the judgement of the nations at the Last Day, and the judgement of each human life at the moment of death. St John of the Cross, the sixteenth-century Spanish mystic, characterized both the content and the manner of that searching judgement of the individual by the God revealed in Jesus Christ, in the powerful words, 'at the evening of life you will be examined in love'.[2]

For Christians, death is transformed by the fact that God in Christ has himself known death. As Christ's dying is interpreted by Karl Rahner, 'death, as the manifestation of sin, was changed in him into a revelation of grace'.[3] Or, as the seventeenth-century Puritan divine Richard Baxter puts it in his hymn, 'Lord, it belongs not to my care, whether I live or die':

Christ leads me through no darker room,
   Than He went through before,
And He who would the Father seek,
   Must enter by that door.[4]

For the Christian, the death and resurrection of Christ is central to the understanding of death and of the funeral liturgy in which those who have departed are commended to God.[5] Subsequent chapters in this collection describe how contemporary social changes in and pressures on funeral practice lead to frequent tension between what the Christian Church wishes to affirm in and through its funeral liturgy and what is asked for by those whose relative is being buried or cremated. As John Lampard makes clear in his contribution, the fact that cremation is now the method of disposal in the majority of funerals has not been matched by theological reflection on the part of the Churches.

There is another tension, highlighted in different ways in the chapters by Douglas Davies and Paul Badham, between the theology of resurrection as professed by the Churches and exemplified in their funeral liturgies, and what is popularly believed. The immortality of the soul, despite the resurrection theology of the Church, remains very much a popular belief. It needs, however, to be remembered on the one hand that earlier traditional expositions of Christian eschatology developed an elaborate theology of the 'intermediate state' between death and resurrection which enabled much to be said about the soul,[6] and on the other that in the late medieval period (particularly the thirteenth century) 'the soul took on so many properties of the body that it in effect became a sort of body'.[7] Alongside this we might place Austin Farrer's comment that Christian philosophers reflecting on the destiny of the soul 'are happy to lean on the old biblical hope of bodily resurrection – that if we are to receive a life hereafter from the hand of omnipotence, it will be through a renewed instrument, a "spiritual body", taking over the rhythms and registrations of the perished body in such a way . . . as to preserve a personal continuity'.[8] As I have myself argued in a number of places, Christian eschatology was historically by no means a neat and tidy systematic theology.[9] A traditional pattern may have been established which tried to set in relationship a theology of the death of the individual and a theology of resurrection at the Last Day. As Frederick Paxton reminds us, 'neither Judaism nor paganism was a monolithic, unchanging system . . . the complex of beliefs about the state of the soul in the afterlife reveals a layering of old and new conceptions'.[10]

The uncertain foundations on which the Christian eschatological picture was built meant that questions were always being posed, not least through the enduring experience of death and dying. The body which had once been alive is now dead, inert and decaying. The life, the breath, is no longer there. 'The dust returns to the earth as it was, and the breath returns to God who gave it' (Ecclesiastes 12.7). Yet the body needs to be treated with reverence. From a Christian perspective there is something more than a little disturbing in the sight of Hindu mourners smashing the charred skulls of cremated relatives on funeral pyres at Varanasi, or seeing the knives laid out for dismembering bodies to be fed to the vultures at sky-burial sites in Tibet. For Christians the body is, as David Brown describes it, 'a sacrament in ordinary',[11] and Caroline Walker Bynum notes that 'the deep anxiety we feel about artificial intelligence and organ transplants, about the proper care of cadavers, about the definition of death . . . connects us more closely than most of us are aware to a long Western tradition of abstruse discussion of bodily resurrection'.[12]

Many of the complex and varied issues discussed in this book are topics which have had to be addressed by the Churches' Funeral Group, of which I have been the chair since 1997. The Group consists of a membership drawn from the major Churches in England and Wales, together with representatives from the funeral directing and cemetery and crematorium services and those concerned with legislation. The Group has thus had to consider issues relating, for example, to the reuse of old graves; memorialization; the disposal (and division) of ashes; embalming in relation to woodland burial and the recent European Union biocides directive; the burial of foetal remains; the appropriate funeral rites for body parts of children (sometimes no more than microscopic slides) retained by hospitals without parental consent; alternatives to cremation such as 'resomation', the liquidizing of bodies to a slurry to be returned to the earth as nutrient, with its clear ecological credentials; the provision of the liturgies of the main Churches for use at crematoria; memorial services; interfaith issues; and many more. The changing culture in which funerals now take place has made the work of the Group more rather than less important, and part of the Group's remit has been to alert the Churches to the changes taking place and press for a proper consideration of how the Churches should respond to those changes.

This book is to some extent part of that raising of awareness and consideration. Behind the particular specialist discussions of the death of children, death in the context of disaster, new approaches to the psychology of bereavement, and the contrasting ways of handling death in various regions of the United Kingdom lies the liturgical and pastoral ministry of the Christian Church to the bereaved and to the dying in a changing context.

In a moving book, *Death and the Family,* published over 30 years ago, Lily Pincus, who founded the Institute for Marital Studies at the Tavistock Institute, wrote of her hope 'that our society may relearn that death is an essential part of life, and free discussion of the processes of grief, mourning, and bereavement may contribute to a changed, more accepting attitude in the community'.[13] In the course of this book Pincus quotes some lines of Rainer Maria Rilke:

To each, O Lord, give his own death;
A dying issues from the very life
In which he knew of meaning, love and pain.[14]

Writing from the Jewish tradition, Pincus writes how the death of her own husband led her to reflect on the importance of understanding those whose lives have been shaped by 'the meaning, love and pain' they have experienced. To understand their responses to bereavement, we therefore, have to understand not only something of their relationship with the deceased, but also something of their life history, and especially of their earlier attachments and losses, which inevitably affect their attitude toward the present loss.[15] Sensitivity to that story is demanded from all called to stand with and alongside others in their grief and in their loss.

But the Christian pastor and the Christian theologian have also to speak of the larger story within which those individual stories are set. The late Dr Murray Cox was a remarkable Christian psychotherapist who spent much of his professional life in the challenging context of forensic psychiatry at Broadmoor Hospital. In his book *Mutative Metaphors,* co-authored with Alice Theilgaard, a Danish psychotherapist, he cites the question of the theologian, J. S. Dunne, 'What kind of a story are we in?' for 'The greater story that encompasses the story of [our] life "cannot be avoided".'[16] 'Religion', Cox comments, 'looks at the large story *sub specie aeternitatis,* "in the light of eternity".' In other words, religion asks 'What, in the long run, is this all about?' It also asks eschatological questions about the 'final things': 'What will you do when the end comes?' (Jeremiah 5.31). Cox cites the words of Robert Graves from his poem 'To Juan at the Winter Solstice', 'There is one story, and one story only/That will prove worth your telling.'[17] For the Christian that is 'when the Word behind the larger story became flesh'. It is out of that mystery of embodiedness, of incarnation, which reaches from a birth into a dying, that prayer is made. As Cox and Theilgaard put it about both death and the situations of death and resurrection in life which anticipate our dying, 'At his proximity to "the great void" man so often questions himself about that which "reasonably" enables him to say: "Call me when my life shall fail me"' (*Anima Christi*).[18] Amid the changing cultural patterns that are today shaping funerals and the context of our dying and the ways in which we remember and memorialize those who have gone before us, the challenge for the Churches, both pastorally and liturgically, is to find the way in which the life-giving, sustaining and transforming mystery of the God who freely chooses to enter into our dying and to know it from the inside may become that source of grace that enables human beings to know the possibility that 'it is in dying that we are born to eternal life'.[19]

Notes

1 The alternative patriotic last words were variously stated as 'Oh, my country! How I love my country!'; 'Oh, my country, how I leave my country!'; or simply, 'My country! oh, my country!', *Oxford Dictionary of Quotations,* 2nd edn, Oxford: Oxford University Press, 1956, p. 369, entries 18–21, William Pitt (1759–1806).

2 Kieran Kavanaugh OCD and Otilio Rodriguez OCD, 'Sayings of Light and Love' §57, *The Collected Works of St John of the Cross,* Washington, DC: ICS Publications, Institute of Carmelite Studies, 1973, p. 672.

3 Karl Rahner, *On the Theology of Death, Quaestiones Disputatae,* 2, Freiburg: Herder; London: Burns and Oates, 1961, p. 78.

4 Originally published in Richard Baxter, *Poetical Fragments: Heart Imployment with God and Itself: The Concordant Discord of a Broken-Healed Heart,* London, 1681.

5 See Jupp, this volume, chapter 7.

6 E.g. in W. Greswell, *A Commentary on the Order for the Burial of the Dead considered as a Manual of Doctrine and Consolation to Christians,* Oxford: J. G. & F. Rivington, 1836, II, pp. 120–47.

7 David Brown, *God and Grace of Body: Sacrament in Ordinary,* Oxford: Oxford University Press, 2007, p. 416, citing C. W. Bynum, *The Resurrection of*

the Body in Western Christianity, 200–1336, New York: Columbia University Press, 1995.

8 Austin Farrer, *Faith and Speculation: An Essay in Philosophical Theology*, London: A & C Black, 1967, p. 157.

9 G. Rowell, *Hell and the Victorians: The Nineteenth-Century Debates about Future Punishment*, Oxford: Clarendon Press, 1973.

10 Frederick S. Paxton, *Christianizing Death: The Creation of a Ritual Process in Early Medieval Europe*, Ithaca and London: Cornell University Press, 1990, pp. 19ff.

11 David Brown, *God and Grace of Body: Sacrament in Ordinary*, Oxford: Oxford University Press, 2007. Brown notes that in adapting George Herbert's phrase 'Heaven in Ordinary' as a subtitle for his book, he is concerned to emphasize that all the world should be seen as sacramental and cites Thomas Traherne's lines, 'Thou has given me a body,/Wherein the glory of thy power shineth . . . For God designs thy body, for His sake,/A temple of the Deity to make', pp. 4, 12, citing Traherne, 'Thanksgivings for the Body' in A. Bradford (ed.), Thomas Traherne, *Selected Poems and Prose*, London: Penguin, 1991, lines 42–3 and 462–3.

12 Bynum, *The Resurrection of the Body*, p. 17.

13 Lily Pincus, *Death and the Family: The Importance of Mourning*, London: Faber & Faber, 1976, p. ix.

14 R. M. Rilke, *Studenbuch*, Leipzig: Insel Verlag, 1928, p. 86, cited in Pincus, *Death and the Family*, p. 13.

15 Pincus, *Death and the Family*, p. 14.

16 J. S. Dunne, *Time and Myth: A Meditation on Storytelling as an Exploration of Life and Death*, London: SCM Press, 1973, cited by Murray Cox and Alice Theilgaard, *Mutative Metaphors in Psychotherapy: The Aeolian Mode*, London and New York: Tavistock Publications, 1987, p. 242.

17 Cox and Theilgaard, *Mutative Metaphors*, pp. 5, 247, citing Robert Graves, *Collected Poems*, London: Cassell, 1961.

18 Cox and Theilgaard, *Mutative Metaphors*, p. 248. The *Anima Christi*, 'Soul of Christ, sanctify me', is a prayer often attributed to St Ignatius Loyola who used it at the beginning of his *Spiritual Exercises* but which probably dates from the early fourteenth century.

19 The concluding words of the prayer 'Lord, make me an instrument of your peace', commonly attributed to St Francis of Assisi, but now generally thought not to be by him but emanating from a Franciscan context.

2

The Context of Christian
Funeral Ministry Today

PETER C. JUPP

Introduction: the centrality of Christ's death and resurrection for Christian ministry

The passion, death and resurrection of Jesus Christ are central to the Gospels, to the Church and to Christian ministry. The Gospels describe Jesus' growing awareness of the significance of his death in God's purposes (Mark 8.29–31). Between one-third and one-fourth of the four Gospels is devoted to the passion and resurrection narratives. St Luke's account of the day of Pentecost following the first Easter sets Jesus' death firmly within the purpose of God: 'this man [Jesus], handed over to you according to the definite plan and foreknowledge of God, you crucified and killed by the hands of those outside the law. But God raised him up, having freed him from death' (Acts 2.23–24).

St Paul became a convert out of his conviction that Christ had met him on the road to Damascus. For him, the resurrection shows how the New Testament fulfils the old, 'As all die in Adam, so all will be made alive in Christ' (1 Cor. 15.22). Christ's resurrection is to guide our behaviour (Rom. 6.6–11) and our attitude to others (2 Cor. 5.14–16). While our mortality makes us aware of transitoriness and insignificance, the Resurrection promises transformation, forgiveness and eternity with God. The resurrection of Jesus lends strength to those who die, whether in their beds or in the martyr's arena: 'Blessed are the dead which die in the Lord' (Rev. 14.13).

Holy Week is the climax of the Church's liturgical year, holding Christ's passion, crucifixion and resurrection together in the narrative of Jesus' Last Supper and its inauguration of the central Christian ritual of the Eucharist. The Passion events are central to the Creeds. They are the basis of baptism and funerals and critical for marriage vows. Catholic, Orthodox and High Anglican churches have rituals for maintaining a dynamic relationship between the living and the dead. Easter, All Saints' and All Souls' Days, with Remembrance Sunday, are public occasions for remembering the dead.

While burial grounds and crematoria have largely moved into secular hands, the churches' stewardship of their burial places enables them to demonstrate their care for the dead and for those who remember them. Open churchyards signal the eternal hope in which the Church's daily work is set. They signify that dead bodies await a future resurrection in God's time. While few believe today what our forebears believed about the form of life in Christ beyond death, churchyards function as a frame for the Church and the gospel.[1] Open or closed, churchyards still offer resources for Christian ministry not only for burial or for cremated ashes but also for secondary concerns, like wildlife or urban regeneration.

The Christian insistence that this life and this world are not the end, but that there is a life to come in which God will have the last word, relativizes all earthly values and institutions, promising God's judgement, forgiveness and ultimate victory over evil. This underlies the Church's authority in the world's politics. In its ministry to the sick and dying, the Church has helped provide models for nursing, pastoral and palliative care of the terminally ill and for social and ritual support in bereavement. In terms of contemporary ethical debates, the Churches with the other major faiths contribute to discussion on war, euthanasia, suicide and abortion.

In Britain, currents of social and cultural change have affected our lives and institutions and also the British way of death.

The social facts of death and grieving

In the UK, there are about 600,000 deaths each year, that is over 2,300 funerals each working day. Around 54 per cent of us die in hospitals and 18 per cent in nursing or residential homes. One in six of us dies at home. Twentieth-century deaths have increasingly had an institutional setting, a trend accelerated by the 1947 National Health Service (NHS). Ten years later, home deaths first became a minority. The hospitalization of death, with greater access to medical care, has undoubtedly provided a more pain-free experience of approaching death. The downside has been the lack of control and participation for dying people and their families, both as death approaches and when funerals are being arranged. A counter-culture about dying was initiated when the Anglican Cicely Saunders opened her first hospice in 1967. Five per cent of us now die in hospices, and palliative care, both institutional and home-based, has spread widely. This has helped challenge the 'taboo' about death that had characterized the British way of death since 1918.[2]

Of what do people die in the UK? Acute infectious diseases like small-pox, scarlet fever and tuberculosis have greatly diminished. While far fewer children die today, there are still 170,000 miscarriages and 200,000 social terminations. Today death is the culmination of *old* age: three-quarters of all males survive their 65th birthday, and seven-eighths of all females. Men aged 65 today can expect to live another 15 years, women 18.5.[3] Long-term chronic and degenerative conditions characterize dying today, particularly cancer and circulatory and respiratory diseases. While these conditions may prepare relatives for 'the inevitable', they may also exhaust carers' reserves.

This raises several issues for the Churches' contemporary ministry to the dying. First, the hospice movement has revived concepts of 'the good death' to which Churches can contribute a long tradition.[4] Second, the reorganization of the NHS in the 1980s gave far greater effectiveness to the profession of hospital chaplains. Third, resources for Christian ministry to the dying and bereaved have been augmented from the ministry of healing and from bereavement support organizations. Fourth, Christian funeral ministry has responded to the public's growing dissatisfaction with funeral practices since the 1980s. The Churches have themselves been challenged by a growing secularist provision for people seeking non-religious funeral ceremonies.[5]

This whole process has also been informed by increasing Government interest in, for example, death registration, coroners, the Shipman affair, funeral costs and pre-paid funeral plans; by media exposure of specific examples of inadequate funeral directing, cemetery and crematorium practices; and by a funeral reform movement that arose both outside and within the funeral service industries, including the Natural Death Centre[6] and the Charter movement[7]. Television and print media have increasingly devoted programmes to funerals and the dying process, and there have been autobiographical accounts of facing death.[8] All these pressures have begun to restore to dying people and their families a greater awareness, control and participation in the approach to death.

Sources of bereavement support

Gorer reckoned in 1965 that, compared with Victorian times, the British lacked traditional support from family and neighbours in coming to terms with death.[9] While his survey revealed regional differences, old-fashioned, rural or close-knit urban neighbourhoods were more supportive, like the 1961 Cape Wrath funeral witnessed by Billings.[10] With the Hillsborough disaster, 1990s Liverpool revealed that older funeral traditions could be much nearer the surface and could be quickly revived and updated.[11] Yet Gorer's assertion largely holds: today's nuclear family unit has been weakened by centrifugal social forces of family breakdown, longevity, the expansion in paid work for women, and social and geographical mobility. To repair this lack, a host of bereavement support groups has sprung up. Margaret Torrie founded Cruse in 1958.[12] Others now include the National Association of Widows, The Compassionate Friends, SANDS, Road Peace, and the Gay and Lesbian Bereavement Group, some focusing on the illness suffered or on forms of violent or accidental death.

One major change is the attention paid to bereaved parents and children.[13] Stillborns and social terminations are no longer disposed of via the hospital sluice or incinerator, or in unmarked graves. Television deserves some credit for this: in 1982, Esther Rantzen interviewed some mothers whose babies had died many years before but who had never known their burial site. The enormous public response was particularly influential in changing attitudes towards the funerals and memorialization of babies. Certainly 'death sells newspapers' and the media are guilty of some 'policing of grief'.[14] Nevertheless the widespread coverage attending such tragedies as the aircraft bombing above Lockerbie, the Hatfield and Paddington rail crashes, the Dunblane and Hungerford shootings, the Bradford, Heisel or Hillsborough football disasters,[15] the death of Diana, Princess of Wales[16] and the terrorist attacks of July 2005 have all offered the public a wide range of models for behaviour in grief and mourning.[17]

Municipalization: cemeteries and crematoria

Providing land for the dead is largely a local government responsibility. In the UK today, 30 per cent of us are buried, mostly in cemeteries.[18] In England, local churchyard burial had become the norm, following the spreading network of parish churches in the ninth century. The era of public cemeteries began in the 1850s following some notorious church-yard scandals[19] and the rise of the public health movement. The new cemeteries were spacious, non-denominational and increasingly expensive to maintain; as the 2000–1 Parliamentary Select Committee on cemeteries commented, with the 1850s legislation 'the cemetery as a wasting asset was born'.[20]

The virtue of cemeteries is that, like the churchyards they succeeded, they serve a local community, providing a place where bereaved people may use graves to mark and maintain family and religious identities.[21] Meanwhile, their ownership and management are secular, 'for the most part considered sacred only in so far as the site is regarded with respect'.[22] The reuse of old graves may now encourage a new era for burial. In 2007 the Burial and Cemeteries Advisory Group of the Ministry of Justice accepted forms of reuse. This should enable more people in urban areas to choose burial, and more encouragement to Anglican churches to use their churchyards for their original purpose.[23] Meanwhile, a burial counter-culture has emerged, with 'green', 'wood-land' and 'natural' schemes, with over 200 sites opened since the early 1990s. Appealing to environmental values, they signal that the disposal of the dead is increasingly a matter of individual choice rather than communal tradition.

In 1874, cremation was first proposed as a hygienic and inexpensive alternative to burial.[24] Once cremation was declared legal in *Regina v. Price* (1884),[25] local authorities began to explore cremation's economic advantages, and the Cremation Act was passed in 1902. World War One drastically changed British attitudes to death and funerals.[26] Cremation's advantages became particularly apparent to post-1945 secular society. There were 58 crematoria in 1945, and 199 by 1967 when cremation overtook burial, offering advantages to a socially and geographically mobile society.[27]

Seventy per cent of people are now cremated. While most recently built crematoria are privately owned, seven-eighths of the 253 UK crematoria (at 2007) are subject to all the budget constraints facing local councils, some still providing only 20 minutes for services and others a rota system of clergy.[28] With rising consumer pressure, the Institute of Cemetery and Crematorium Management's *Charter for the Bereaved* has, since 1996, effected higher standards of cemetery maintenance and facilities for its users. A York crematorium survey in 1994 showed that only 30 per cent of funerals had first begun at a local church; this figure will have declined. So those leading Christian funerals still need to remember that cemeteries and crematoria are essentially secular contexts.[29] They are community facilities, open to people of all faiths and of none. The newest crematoria have portable religious symbols. In 2005 there was a hullabaloo when Torbay Council removed the cross from its crematorium chapel. Newspapers ran charges and counter-charges as all sorts of local interest groups, political and religious, claimed violations of rights. The cross was eventually replaced. Those conducting funerals at crematoria and cemeteries 'still largely need to come to terms with the fact that they are visiting actors on a stage they do not own, enacting a traditional drama subject to contemporary constraints'.[30]

Commercialism: the changing face of funeral directing

Seventeen years after Page's 'grave misgivings' about British funerals, she analysed the rapid changes in the 'dismal trade'.[31] The 1980s generation of bereaved families was somewhat in awe of the funeral director, whom they regarded as a sort of 'second division clergy'. There were then few coffin or flower brochures and fewer written estimates. Bereaved families anxiously wanted to 'do the right thing', with little clue what that was. Consequently they allowed the funeral director to lay out the range of choices and they followed his (invariably 'his') guidance.

Widespread improvements have been effected by successive pressures: media attention, reform movements, environmental concerns and commercial competition. The American company Service Corporation International (which arrived in 1994) experienced a British management buy-out in 2001 (now named Dignity). The Co-operative Group promoted its consumerist Funeral Service Council (1996–2002). The National Association of Funeral Directors (NAFD) has launched all-party Bereavement Forums within UK, Welsh and Scottish Parliaments. Over the last 20 years, the funeral directing profession has improved its training and made premises much more user-friendly. Computerization has improved efficiency; call centres enable 24–hour contact; more funeral directors are women. Families regularly shop around for telephone quotations; written estimates are almost universal; pre-paid funeral plans are on the increase. The NAFD and the National Society for Allied and Independent Funeral Directors (NSAIF) operate Codes of Conduct. Complaints procedures are widely available, despite the demise of the Funerals Ombudsman Scheme in 2002. More openness about funeral directors' procedures followed TV shows like *Six Feet Under*. Several UK funeral directors have published autobiographies.[32]

Some clergy have yet to learn that, once engaged by a family or executor, funeral directors are technically and legally in charge.[33] Clergy, cemetery or crematoria authorities are their sub-agents. Whether or not ministers are paid for funerals, they are seen and treated as part of the commercial process. They are expected both to prepare and preside carefully and to give value for money. Effective Christian funeral ministry necessitates co-operation with the other professionals involved – funeral directors, cemeteries and crematoria staff and memorial masons.[34]

At the same time, alongside their responsibilities to the staff and bereaved families with whom they work, those leading Christian funerals have to uphold their obedience to the gospel. A balance always needs to be struck between the interests of the dead, the survivors and the Church's doctrines.[35] Different Church traditions will emphasize different perspectives: Kilpatrick emphasizes starting from bereaved families' perspectives[36] while Thewlis is concerned to make the Christian hope real, talking of 'God's mercy *in the context of the dead person*'. Thewlis' advice particularly resonates with me: 'Always mention forgiveness: if you don't know why, there's always someone present who does.'[37]

From traditional service to consumer values

In the 1990s, the social entrepreneurs Nicholas Albery and Josefine Speyer developed a concept of 'do-it-yourself' funerals, modelled upon the Natural Childbirth concept. Their Natural Death Centre encouraged people who wished to die at home, promoted burial, willow and cardboard coffins, and woodland burial sites. Their *Natural Death Handbook*[38] brought their ideas to a wider public. Meanwhile, the British Humanist Association was promoting non-religious funerals.

As purchasers, bereaved families needed empowerment to organize their own styles of funeral. In the 1950s Michael Young founded the magazine *Which?* to help people make more informed choices about their purchases. *Which?* first reported on funerals in 1961, with the first edition of *What to do When Someone Dies* in 1967. The Hennessey Report of 1980 and the OPCS's *A Survey of Funeral Arrangements* in 1987 continued the trend, extended by the Charter movement of the 1990s.

Consumers want value for money. As the 1980s take-over frenzy hit funeral directing, consumer awareness became a marketing tactic. After all, with about 600,000 people dying in the UK each year, profits can be

ensured mainly by providing added value, take-overs producing econ-
omies of scale, or by pre-paid funeral schemes. The biennial *Oddfellows
Survey* analyses regional trends in funeral costs and regularly calculates
the 'top ten' of funeral songs and hymns. In 1994, the Co-operative
movement focused on the treatment of customer complaints and promoted the Funeral Ombudsman Scheme. The Co-operative Group set
up the Funeral Care Forum chaired by Clair Rayner to publish *Funeral
Rights: Who Has the Final Say?*[39] Service Corporation International
(now Dignity) invited the columnist Virginia Ironside to write *Arranging the Funeral You Want.*[40] Wider consumer choice brought increased
profits but also enabled client families to make informed choices about
the range of funeral services on offer. Clergy have also had to learn to
adapt to families' exercising rights for informed choice.[41]

Secularization and personalization

Throughout the last century most Churches have grappled with the
increasingly blunted saliency of their shared religion.[42] Women, benefiting far more than men from the opportunities of modernity, have
increasingly discarded their traditional role as the channel of religious
affiliation. Younger generations have grown successively less familiar
with traditional Christianity. This came home starkly to the broadcaster
Kate Adie after the Bradford football ground fire in 1985, when she
attended 17 funerals in a week:

> What I was totally unprepared for in Bradford, even though I knew
> that my experience was that of millions of fifties children . . . was
> church after church into which came noisy schoolchildren shouting
> 'What's this then? What's a church? Why should we shush?' . . . They
> sat through the service in blank amazement, as if attending a tribal
> ritual in a strange country – which, in effect, they were.[43]

The death in 1997 of Diana, Princess of Wales, produced the most
extraordinary funeral event of modern times. The flowers, the memorial
books and street shrines, the queues with their pilgrimage character,
the relocation of the Princess and Dodi Al-Fayed as 'new stars in the
heavens' showed how traditional beliefs and customs, many at variance
with traditional Protestant culture, were pressed into service to mark
Diana's death.[44] The funeral music reflected both popular culture and
sacred tradition with Elton John's 'Candle in the Wind' and John
Tavener's Eastern Orthodox 'Ode to Athene'.

The Diana 'funeral' privileged the place of the 'biography' at funerals.[45] This trend is now being amplified by the 'memorial service', increasingly being used to complement the Funeral Service[46] when diary priorities restrict mourners' attendance and crematoria time-limits restrict rituals. The memorial service, entitled a 'Celebration', offers an occasion to express appreciation for a life now ended. Its 'lowest common denominator' can appeal to a wide variety of attenders, including those more comfortable with beliefs in immortality than in resurrection; who conceive of the afterlife as family reunion; or who believe death is the end. Yet the memorial service fills a need, offering scope for the personalization of funeral rites so many now seek.

In 1990 Walter wrote of 'the tragedy of the crematorium rose': 'identical rose bushes for . . . us who have struggled to wrest individuality from an impersonal society . . . make a truly appalling last statement. Those rose bushes say one thing: "You failed".'[47] Two decades later, personalization has become a far stronger trend. The Diana event gave people permission to contribute more to their family funerals. People have seized the opportunity. The resources available include personal tributes, choice of music,[48] the display of personal mementos, football club colours on coffins and inscriptions on gravestones.[49] The Northern Ireland troubles from the 1960s[50] and the succession of high-profile disasters in the late 1980s[51] made people aware of the wide variety of resources available to them in funerals and mourning. Personalized funeral tributes have been characterized by Davies as a switch from a traditional focus on 'the prospective fulfilment of human identity' to a contemporary focus on its 'retrospective fulfilment',[52] i.e. to mark the life once lived (and now ended) rather than to celebrate a post-mortem future.[53] This 'retrospective' character is also visible in the trend to remove ashes from crematoria (15 per cent in 1970; 60 per cent in 2005), to be located in family graves or places of significance to the deceased.[54] At the same time, personal choice and funeral trade promotion have encouraged a wider choice of memorials.

Secularization has also given confidence to those without faith. The law first permitted funerals without religious rites in 1880.[55] For the Humanist John Pearce the growth of Humanist funerals has benefited from ineffective clerical ministry.[56] Another form of personalized funeral has been promoted by Anne Barber's Institute of Civil Funerals.[57] With no prayers for the departed (the prospective focus), the non-religious funeral privileges the life now ended (the retrospective focus). Today's non-religious rites not only offer those without faith the opportunity to commit their dead with integrity but benefit from rigorous training programmes which the Churches have not yet matched. In 2007, the humanist Simon Allen estimated there were then 8,000 humanist and 3,000 civil ceremony funerals a year. While this represents less than half of one per cent of the UK's funerals, the continued growth of self-confessional atheism among the young will ensure that this proportion will rise.[58] This will test the optimism of Davie's characterization of British Christianity as 'believing without belonging'.[59]

Afterword

In 1998 the Church of England General Synod staged a debate on funeral ministry.[60] Many speeches commented on the respective merits of rival funeral directing companies. Afterwards, Bishop Geoffrey Rowell, Chair of the Churches' Funerals Group, commented to colleagues, 'We have just spent 40 minutes debating the Churches' funeral ministry. Yet not one speaker has spoken of the central Christian contribution to funerals, our Lord's resurrection from the dead.' For that very conviction is the principal element that gives authority to a Christian funeral and gives to families an existential hope. Unless Christians testify to the resurrection in their lives, their liturgies and at funerals, we are speechless and are of all people to be pitied almost as much as those who have been buried or cremated without hope. This book seeks to empower that testimony.

Notes

1 K. Healey, 'English Churchyard Memorials', *Journal of the Society of Arts*, Vol. 115, 1967, pp. 260–74.

2 D. Cannadine, 'War and Death, Grief and Mourning' in J. Whaley (ed.), *Mirrors of Mortality: Studies in the Social History of Death*, London: Europa, 1981, pp. 187–242; T. Walter, 'Modern Death: Taboo or Not Taboo?', *Sociology*, Vol. 25, No. 2, May 1991, pp. 293–310.

3 G. Howarth, *Death and Dying: A Sociological Introduction*, Cambridge: Polity, 2007, p. 47.

4 E.g., N. L. Beaty, *The Craft of Dying: A Study in the Literary Tradition of the Ars Moriendi in England*, London: Yale, 1970; M. Bradbury, *Representations of Death: A Social Psychological Perspective*, London: Routledge, 1999; J. Woodward, *Befriending Death*, London: SPCK, 2005.

5 J. W. Willson, *Funerals without God*, 6th edn, London: British Humanist Association, 2006.

6 S. Weinrich and J. Speyer (eds), *The Natural Death Handbook*, 4th edn, London: Rider, 2003.

7 The National Funerals College, *The Dead Citizens Charter*, 2nd edn, Bristol: The National Funerals College, 1998; Institute of Burial and Cremation Administration (IBCA, now The Institute of Cemetery and Crematorium Management), *Charter for the Bereaved*, rev. edn, London: IBCA, 1998.

8 See for example, R. Picardie, *Before I Say Goodbye*, London: Penguin, 1998; J. Diamond, *C: Because Cowards Get Cancer Too*, London: Vermillion, 1999.

9 G. Gorer, *Death, Grief and Mourning in Contemporary Britain*, London: Cresset Press, 1965, p. 110.

10 A. Billings, *Dying and Grieving: A Guide to Pastoral Ministry*, London: Hodder, 2002. See also D. Clark, *Between Pulpit and Pew: Folk Religion in a North Yorkshire Fishing Village*, Cambridge: Cambridge University Press, 1982, for an account of a community (Staithes) on the cusp of change between villagers choosing burial and incomers choosing cremation.

11 T. Walter, 'The Mourning after Hillsborough', *The Sociological Review*, Vol. 39, No. 3, August 1991, pp. 599–625.

12 M. Torrie, *My Years with Cruse*, Richmond, Surrey: Cruse House, 1987.

13 See Cobb, Dent, Hilborn and Rogers, this volume.

14 For the criticism of 'policing grief' by the media, see T. Walter, *On Bereavement: The Culture of Grief*, Buckingham: Open University Press, 1999.

15 See Eyre, this volume.

16 T. Walter (ed.), *The Mourning for Diana*, Oxford: Berg, 1999.

17 See T. Cocke, *The Churchyards Handbook*, 4th edn, London: Church House Publishing, 2001, pp. 3–5.

18 J. Rugg, 'Defining the Place of Burial: What Makes a Cemetery a Cemetery?', *Mortality*, Vol. No. 3, November 2000, pp. 259–75.

19 P. C. Jupp, 'Enon Chapel: No Way for the Dead' in P. C. Jupp and G. Howarth (eds), *The Changing Face of Death: Historical Accounts of Death and Disposal*, Basingstoke: Palgrave Macmillan, 2007, pp. 90–104; and *From Dust to Ashes: Cremation and the British Way of Death*, Basingstoke: Palgrave Macmillan, 2006.

20 Environment, Transport and Regional Affairs Committee (ETRAC), Eighth Report, *Cemeteries*, Vols I and II, London: The Stationery Office, 2001, p. xi.

21 D. Francis, L. Kellaher and G. Nyophytou, *The Secret Cemetery*, Oxford: Berg, 2005.

22 Rugg, 'Defining the Place of Burial', p. 264.

23 In the debates on reuse there has been little deployment by the Churches of their traditional belief in the resurrection of the dead. Without serious encouragement, clergy will be unlikely to devote fresh energies to their churchyards despite the pastoral and financial benefits.

24 See Jupp, *From Dust to Ashes*, and B. Parsons, *Committed to the Cleansing Flame: The Development of Cremation in Nineteenth-century England*, Reading: Spire, 2005.

25 S. R. G. White, 'A Burial Ahead of Its Time? The Crookenden Burial Case and the Sanctioning of Cremation in England and Wales', *Mortality*, Vol. 7, No. 2, July 2002, pp. 171–90.

26 A. Wilkinson, *The Church of England in the First World War*, London: SPCK, 1978; J. Bourke, *Dismembering the Male: Men's Bodies, Britain and the First World War*, London: Reaktion, 1995.

27 P. C. Jupp, 'Cremation or Burial? Contemporary Choice in City and Village' in D. Clark (ed.), *The Sociology of Death: Theory, Culture, Practice*, Oxford: Blackwell, 1993, pp. 167–97; H. J. Grainger, *Death Redesigned: British Crematoria – History, Landscape, Architecture*, Reading: Spire, 2005.

28 M. Lessiter, 'Clergy Rota', *Pharos International*, Vol. 64, No. 4, Winter 1998, pp. 26–7.

29 By contrast, a survey of popular attitudes to crematoria in Nottingham conducted in 1989 found that as age increased so did the awareness that crematoria were, in some sense, sacred. See D. J. Davies, 'The Sacred Crematorium', *Mortality*, Vol. 1, No. 1, March 1996, pp. 83–94.

30 P. C. Jupp, 'The Context of Funeral Ministry Today' in P. C. Jupp and T. Rogers, *Interpreting Death: Christian Theology and Pastoral Practice*, London: Cassell, 1997, p. 10.

31 M. Page, 'Grave Misgivings', *Religion Today*, Vol. 2, No. 3, 1986; M. Naylor (formerly Page), 'Opening Geoffrey Gorer's Door: A Personal Overview of Funerals, 1983–2003', *Pharos International*, Vol. 70, No. 3, Autumn 2005, pp. 8–10.

32 These include J. West, *Jack West FD: 60 Years with Funerals*, Ilfracombe: Stockwell, 1988; H. Hodgson, *How to Become Dead Rich*, London: Pavilion Books, 1992; P. Aspinall, *To Shed a Light*, Ampthill, Bedfordshire: NFS Publications, 1998; D. Rymer, *A Reluctant Funeral Director*, London: Minerva Press, 1998. B. Albin's *Don't Drop the Coffin*, London: Hodder, 2003, became the basis of an ITV documentary series and was followed by a series of other titles.

33 B. Parsons, 'Conflict in the Context of Care: An Examination of Role Conflict between the Bereaved and the Funeral Director in the UK', *Mortality*, Vol. 8, No. 1, February 2003, pp. 67–87.

34 Maura Naylor (formerly Page), 'Crossed Wires, Frustrations and Conflicts in Crematoria Funerals', Churches' Group on Funeral Services, *Report of the Day Conference Held at Carrs Lane Church Centre, Birmingham, on Monday 20 October 1991*, pp. 1–17.

35 This can lead to disagreements over the choice of music (Parsons, this volume) and the requests of families or family members for the insertion of 'secular', 'folkloric' or 'sentimental' verses.

36 B. Kilpatrick, *Going Forth: A Practical and Spiritual Approach to Dying and Death*, London: Darton, Longman and Todd, 1997, pp. 72–7.

37 J. Thewlis, 'The Difficult Funeral', *Theology*, January 1997, p. 4.

38 N. Albery, G. Elliott and J. Elliott (eds), *The Natural Death Handbook*, 1st edn, London: Virgin, 1993.

39 The Co-operative Group, Funeral Care Forum, Manchester, 2003.

40 V. Ironside, *Arranging the Funeral You Want*, London: SCI UK, c. 1995.

41 For the effect of consumer values on traditional churchyard arrangements, see T. Cocke (ed.), *The Churchyards Handbook*, pp. 4–6.

42 G. Davie, *Religion in Britain since 1945: Believing without Belonging*, Oxford: Blackwell, 1994.

43 K. Adie, *The Kindness of Strangers*, London: Headline, 2004.

44 See, e.g., T. Walter, *The Mourning for Diana*, Oxford: Berg, 1999; J. Wolffe, *Great Deaths: Grieving, Religion and Nationhood in Victorian and Edwardian Britain*, Oxford: Oxford University Press, 2000, not only sets Diana's funeral in its traditional context but also illustrates the precedents for many of today's 'innovative' customs.

45 Many clergy had for 50 years or more included a short character sketch of the deceased at funerals, according to Thewlis, 'The Difficult Funeral'.

46 D. Gray, *Memorial Services*, Alcuin Liturgy Guides 1, London: SPCK, 2002.

47 T. Walter, *Funerals and How to Improve Them*, London: Hodder & Stoughton, 1990, p. 61.

48 P. Denyer, 'Singing the Lord's Song in a Strange Land' in P. C. Jupp and T. Rogers (eds), *Interpreting Death*, pp. 197–202; see also Parsons, this volume.

49 Cocke, *The Churchyards Handbook*.

50 See Brown, this volume.

51 See Eyre, this volume.

52 D. J. Davies, *Death, Ritual and Belief: The Rhetoric of Funeral Rites*, 2nd edn, London: Cassell, 2002; and this volume.

53 The resulting tensions for Catholics are discussed by McGinnell, this volume.

54 The 'retrospective turn', see Kellaher, this volume.

55 R. Fletcher, *The Akenham Burial Case*, London: Wildwood House, 1974.

56 J. Pearce, 'Where We Are with Secular Funerals', *Pharos International*, Vol. 71, No. 3, Autumn 2005, pp. 8–10.

57 The Institute of Civil Funerals defines a civil funeral as 'a funeral which is driven by the wishes, beliefs and values of the deceased and their family, not by the beliefs or ideology of the person conducting the funeral' (info@iocf.org.uk). The Institute's research indicates that approximately half of all civil funerals contain some religious element (letter from Anne Barber, *Funeral Service Journal*, 123, March 2008, p. 82).

58 S. Allen, 'Rising Secularism in UK Funeral Practice', *Funeral Service Journal*, Vol. 123, No. 1, January 2008, pp. 109–14.

59 Davie, *Religion in Britain*.

60 *Good Funerals*. A background paper prepared on behalf of the ecumenical Churches' Group on Funeral Services at Cemeteries and Crematoria in support of the Southwark Diocesan Synod Motion *Funerals: Business and Vocation*, London: General Synod of the Church of England, 1999 (GS Misc 539).

3

Dealing with Disasters:
Issues for Clergy in Responding to Collective Tragedy

ANNE EYRE

Introduction

The 2004 tsunami – the largest earthquake for 40 years with its 33–foot tidal waves – was an event that unfolded 'like a scene from the Bible'. *Washington Post* reporter and survivor Michael Dobbs was swimming off Sri Lanka:

> As the waters rose at an incredible rate, I half expected to catch sight of Noah's Ark. Instead of the Ark, I grabbed hold of a wooden cata-maran that the local people used as a fishing boat. My brother jumped on the boat, next to me. We bobbed up and down on the catamaran, as the water rushed past us into the village beyond the road.[1]

Incidents of mass death through natural disasters such as pestilence, disease and famine have been around since the beginnings of human-kind, but contemporary experiences of death and dying through major disaster are somewhat different today from what they would have been in biblical times. Although such 'mega events' as the Indian Ocean tsunami, which killed hundreds of thousands of people, are exceptional, the global figures for people killed by disasters remain high, and scien-tists predict that events such as floods and storms will continue to have dramatic and long-term effects on people in the years ahead.[2]

Societies within Britain and Europe are not immune from the negative impact of extreme events caused by climate change. When account is taken also of the continuing threat of 'technological' disasters (such as transport or industrial accidents) and deliberately caused acts of violence (through war and terrorism), the importance of preparing and planning for dealing with the effects of mass death and injury becomes clear. This chapter examines the role of Christian ministers and other faith representatives in this work and the implications for dealing with disasters in practical and spiritual terms following mass traumatic death and bereavement.

Disasters as mass emergencies

For those tasked with planning and responding to the practical consequences of emergencies, disasters are often defined as 'major incidents'. These are events requiring the implementation of special arrangements by one or all of the emergency services for the rescue and transport of a large number of casualties, the involvement, either directly or indirectly, of large numbers of people, and the handling of a large number of enquiries, usually to the police, from the public and the news media.[3]

Examples of such events are the tragedy at Aberfan (1966), the 'decade of disasters' in the 1980s including the Hungerford shootings (1987), the Lockerbie bombing (1988) and the Hillsborough football stadium disaster (1989), as well as rail crashes (such as at Ladbroke Grove in 1999 and Selby in 2001). Over the last 40 years or so members of the clergy have played a significant role in responding to the practical, emotional and spiritual needs of those affected by these and other mass fatality events.[4]

More recently, the working definition of mass emergencies has been revised in legislation and guidance, reflecting the experience in the UK of responding to events around the turn of the twenty-first century such as the fuel crisis, the outbreak of foot-and-mouth disease, floods, fires and terrorist attacks. This chapter includes events having a significant social and communal impact as well as those corresponding to the definition of 'emergencies' within the Civil Contingencies Act 2004, namely:

> An event or situation which threatens serious damage to human welfare in a place in the UK, the environment of a place in the UK, or war or terrorism which threatens serious damage to the security of the UK.[5]

The impact of crises

Technological developments and competitive media agendas offering 'breaking news' mean that today we are likely to become aware of tragic events as they unfold or very soon afterwards. 'Bad news' is 'good news' if it involves human distress and destruction, and images and accounts are rapidly beamed across the world and into people's living rooms. Emphasis is placed on immediacy and sensational headlines rather than concern for those receiving or reacting to the distressing images being portrayed. In this way our personal and collective experience and understanding of disasters have become much more immediate and extensive, with many more people beyond those directly affected as bereaved and/or survivors being aware of and likely to be affected by tragedy. This poses particular challenges for those tasked with preparing for and responding to the spiritual and emotional consequences following sudden, unexpected traumatic death.

These days the effects of collective tragedy extend to virtual communities and those affected much farther away from the direct physical or geographical impact zone(s). After the terrorist attacks on 11 September 2001 in the United States (9/11), books of condolence and special church services were arranged all over world for those who wanted to share their grief or simply show their respects. In the aftermath of such deliberate acts of violence, participating in such rituals may also represent a political response to the explicit goal of the terrorist to threaten the sense of psychological and social cohesion.

For these reasons, responding to disaster involves addressing not only multiple physical loss, witnessed through mass death and physical destruction, but also the collective emotional, political and spiritual dimensions of trauma. Though often less tangible, it is these dimensions that many responders have described as the most challenging aspects of the aftermath and recovery phases.

Pastoral crisis intervention

In the United States, the integration of the pastoral role of clergy with a model of emergency mental health has led to 'pastoral crisis intervention' which seeks to offer 'added value' over and above the traditional non-pastoral approach to crisis intervention. Everly suggests that the pastoral crisis interventionist:

benefits from the ability to use, where appropriate, scriptural education, insight, and reinterpretation, individual and conjoint prayer, a
belief in the power of intercessory prayer, a unifying and explanatory
spiritual worldview that may serve to bring order to otherwise in-
apprehensible events, the utility of ventilative confession, a faith-
based social support system, the use of rituals and sacraments, and in
some religions, such as Christianity, the notion of divine forgiveness
and even a life after death.[6]

A key issue here is 'appropriateness' and the need for faith representatives to be equipped with the requisite skills, understanding, training
and preparedness for responding to the particular circumstances of
disaster. Everly acknowledges that pastoral crisis intervention requires
significant insight in order to avoid pitfalls such as: failing to 'listen' to
the secular needs of a person in crisis, attempting to explain spiritually/
theologically 'why' a trauma occurred, preaching or praying with an
'unreceptive' individual, or attempting to 'convert' the unreceptive individual.[7] In the UK, the meaning of appropriateness in preparing for
emergency response includes not only developing the skills and training
of those offering practical and emotional support but also responding
according to structured and co-ordinated pre-plans rather than 'free-
lancing'.[8]

Planning for disasters

The role of clergy and other faith representatives in responding to disasters started to become more formalized as peacetime civil emergency
management developed over the past 20 years or so. From the 1980s,
clergy found themselves being called upon to minister to those bereaved
and injured in hospitals, mortuaries, assistance centres, and, occasionally, at the scene of incidents.

Guidelines have been developed to assist those planning for and
responding to disasters, including those tasked with meeting practical,
emotional and spiritual needs of those affected directly and indirectly. In
2005 the government issued revised guidelines to help local emergency
planners and responders to understand faith needs in major incidents.
Planners are now strongly encouraged to liaise with local faith groups to
establish what support is available to them from different faith communities.[9] The guidance suggests that every county and unitary authority
should develop its own emergency plan alongside the Churches and

other faith communities. Acknowledging that different arrangements may apply in Scotland, Wales and Northern Ireland, the guidance states:

> In many instances the contact person may be the local Church of England Archdeacon (in England) who is the representative of the faith communities and who will pass information on to others. In some circumstances it may be the local Ecumenical Borough Dean (in London) or Salvation Army representative who acts for the faith communities.

Examples of emergency planning structures and activities across the English regions as well as across the devolved countries are well detailed on the internet, with local and regional government websites providing helpful information for clergy wishing to engage in local planning, training and response. A good starting point for becoming involved is the UK Resilience Website, a news and information service for emergency practitioners run by the Civil Contingencies Secretariat, <http://www.ukresilience.info/>.

Responding to the wounded spirit

Erikson[10] offers us one of the most powerful accounts of the collective impact of disaster on a community. He witnessed the aftermath of the 1972 Buffalo Creek flood which killed 125 people and left homeless 4,000 of the 5,000 who lived there. Returning to the community a year later Erikson writes:

> The whole scene looked as if it had been painted in shades of gray. The children neither laughed nor played. The adults acted as if they were surrounded by a sheath of heavy air through which they could move and respond only at the cost of a deliberate effort. Everything seemed muted and dulled, I felt for a moment as though I was in the company of people *so wounded in spirit* that they almost constituted a different culture, as though the language we shared in common was simply not sufficient to overcome the enormous gap in experience that separated us.[11]

Faith representatives may potentially play a key role in responding to this sense of *wounded spirit*. Perhaps this helps to explain why it is not uncommon after disasters for individuals to gather at places of worship and other locations of religious and spiritual significance. As detailed later, those with direct experience of ministering after collective tragedy have highlighted the importance of acknowledging and addressing the sense of wounded spirit among members, as well as supporting the collective community as part of healing and recovery processes.

In responding to the devastating impact of the 2004 Asian tsunami, volunteers from a County Down church spent two weeks volunteering in the disaster area. Commenting on their contribution, one volunteer said he found that the survivors needed reassurance as well as practical support from the outside world: 'I believe they need support from the outside world by people going in and showing by example to try and put a heart back into their community. They . . . need their spirits lifted.'[12]

Places of worship can remain focal points for many years after an event and a symbolic representation of both the history and future of communities affected by tragedy. Since the Lockerbie bombing in 1988 the Tundergarth Kirk, the tiny Church of Scotland church near the town, has remained a place of pilgrimage for many relatives of the victims.[13] In New York, St Paul's Church next to the World Trade Center became not only the focus for the eight-month volunteer relief effort after the terrorist attacks of 11 September 2001, but also an enduring symbol of ministry in the aftermath of mass tragedy.[14]

Ritual, remembrance and sacred space

The sorts of activities clergy might undertake following a major incident include accompanying family members and offering prayers at the disaster site(s) or scene(s) of death. Clergy may also conduct funerals, plan and deliver memorial and anniversary services and make available churches and other sacred places for private reflection, floral tributes and messages of condolence. Ritual activities following mass death can range from the spontaneous to more organized displays. The public response to the Hillsborough football stadium disaster, where over a million people visited Anfield in Liverpool to lay flowers and grieve collectively, has been analysed as a key example of this.[15] Just as with the growth of DIY roadside memorials after road traffic incidents, such displays illustrate the wish and need for people to have control over the nature and expression of mourning and commemoration. Elsewhere I have discussed further examples of these and practical implications associated with the nature, meaning and functions of community remembrance following disaster.[16]

The growth in alternative approaches to funerals and other rituals, as well as advances in technology such as the internet, reflect a broader trend towards bereaved people and survivors taking ownership of the manner in which they mark and mourn collective loss. New 'virtual memorials' illustrate this. After tragedies like the Columbine School shootings in 1999, the murder of two Cambridgeshire schoolgirls in Soham in 2002, and the deaths of two firefighters responding to a fireworks factory explosion in East Sussex in 2006, much use was made of online 'books' of remembrance as a tool of communal commemoration and for the expression of grief. Similarly, websites set up by the bereaved and survivors after the Asian tsunami in 2004 and the 7 July bombings in 2005 included commemorative pages remembering the victims.

In terms of healing I have argued elsewhere that there are advantages in individuals and communities taking control of their own recovery by having greater control over the organization and ownership of remembrance activities.[17] There is, however, still an important role for official and formal services such as funerals and memorial services. Furthermore, as demonstrated by the frequent invitation for faith leaders to comment on the mood of and impact on communities of tragedy, religious representatives still have a significant contribution to make. So what can we learn from those who have led their own communities through such troubled times in recent years?

Almost within an hour of the Dunblane tragedy, people had taken refuge in the town's largest building, the cathedral. Barr describes how it became one of the few places of sanctuary where people realized they could feel safe to sit in their bewilderment and shock:

Kind arms and hands were held out – without words. People stopped in mid-word to sob. The organ alternated with the piano – played gently so that the silence was not overbearing. Little gestures – packets of tissues on all the pews gifted by the Salvation Army – answered practical needs.[18]

Similarly, Alban Jones recognized the sanctuary that was provided by the Church of St Andrew community after the Soham murders. He concluded:

Churches are an appropriate space at a time of crisis. The buildings belong to the communities they serve and, at times of tragedy, it is fitting that they are opened for prayer and reflection. . . . It is not the age of the buildings that makes them so apt, it is the fact that they are places of worship; places set aside to encounter God.[19]

The Soham tragedy: ministering 'through God's grace'

In 2002 Tim Alban Jones, Vicar of Soham, was honoured with an MBE for his services to the village which had been devastated by the deaths of schoolgirls Holly Wells and Jessica Chapman. He had become a high-profile figure in the town which came under intense media spotlight following the disappearance and murder of the ten-year-olds that summer. The town, and in particular St Andrew's Church, became a focus for national grieving, with thousands of bouquets of flowers, notes and cuddly toys being sent from all over the world. Finally, after coach parties made detours to the church to view gifts left in memory of the children, the local vicar appealed through the media for 'time and space' for the community to grieve. Reflecting on his experiences a year later, he wrote:

> Some people have asked me what strikes me most when looking back over the past 12 months. There are a few moments that perhaps stand out in my memory, but throughout the whole year we have witnessed countless deeds of kindness. There have been innumerable people who have responded with outstanding compassion, love and generous good-will. All these many deeds of kindness and thoughtfulness show that love is stronger than hatred. Ultimately, goodness is stronger than evil.[20]

He reflected further on the implications for ministry of being thrown in 'at the sharp end' of things and the accompanying unforeseen heartbreak and emotional turmoil:

> At such times, our ministry can – through God's grace – be comforting and helpful to those in need, though it is perhaps only after the immediate crisis has passed that we step back and reflect on from where we received our strength. As a Christian, I am acutely aware that anything I can achieve through my own efforts will be of little consequence. It is only through the grace of God that we can hope to accomplish anything of lasting value or true worth.[21]

This would certainly be my experience during the difficult times in Soham, in 2002 and after, when Holly Wells and Jessica Chapman were abducted and murdered by Ian Huntley. It was, ultimately, through God's grace alone that I was able to do anything useful or helpful.[22]

Dunblane: ministering beyond words

On 13 March 1996 a man named Thomas Hamilton walked into a primary school in the Scottish town of Dunblane and shot dead 16 children and their teacher before committing suicide. This remains the deadliest attack on children in recent British history. In the aftermath, religious leaders played an active role in responding both to bereaved families and the broader community. By the Saturday evening the minister of Dunblane Cathedral, Colin Macintosh, had spent days and nights sitting with the inconsolable. The following day he spoke for the first time in public as the Sunday morning service was broadcast live by the BBC. In addressing children at the service, he acknowledged their sadness, confusion and fear and spoke of the inappropriateness of explanations.

At other times during that first week words were not needed. Having been involved in the religious broadcasting transmitted from Dunblane during that time, religious journalist Andrew Barr wrote about a vigil organized for Dunblane Cathedral that Friday:

> Without formality music, prayer and shared silence was planned – no singing – no sermon – no processions. When 6,000 people had joined a queue to enter a building which accommodates 1,000, the minister was anxious, fearing that the majority would feel excluded. Then it became clear that the long line of people had ceased to be a queue. They simply wanted to stand with each other quietly in the streets of Dunblane. That line included some of Scotland's church leaders and there they all stayed for several hours – reported on TV and radio by a slightly puzzled media . . .[23]

Not having answers

Like the minister in Dunblane, Alban Jones recognized he could not provide answers and explanations following major loss. At times of acute crisis, he states, it is not unusual for people to have deep and searching questions about the nature of God, sometimes thinking along the lines of 'How can a loving God let this happen?' Christian theology, he says, is full of attempts to answer this, ultimately unanswerable, question:

Being a Christian does not mean that you have all the answers to the difficult questions that we encounter, especially when tragedy strikes, but it does help us as we seek to walk alongside other people in their pain. In responding to the pastoral needs of people, I feel that what is most important is simply being with them, rather than being able to say the 'right' thing.[24]

Barr reinforces the sentiment that Christianity involves staying with the questions rather than seeking to give answers. He reflects on the themes that were highlighted in the official memorial service after Dunblane and relates them to the reflections of the late Mervyn Stockwood, Bishop of Southwark, in 1980:

When I am asked whether I am a believer, my reply is 'Yes, for two seconds out of three.' How can it be otherwise . . . the traumatic experiences that are part and parcel of human experience are difficult to reconcile with the concept of a loving and purposeful creator. Amen to that.[25]

Ministry as 'being there'

This chapter has examined the role of faith representatives in planning for and responding to collective tragedy. For those who have worked in the midst of disasters and following major loss, the value of simple but fundamental social support, of being alongside, has been recognized as crucial. Ultimately perhaps this is also the most significant role that faith representatives can play; this *is* ministry. Alban Jones comments:

We are trying to minister and help because of our beliefs; our faith informs our actions . . . My ministry, and that of the church family in Soham, was that of 'being there' or 'being available'. The fact that Christian women and men are prepared to travel with the broken and bereaved can be a source of comfort to them; and it can help direct them beyond us to God, the ultimate source of comfort, help and hope.[26]

Reflecting on his experience of broadcasting in the aftermath of the Zeebrugge Ferry Disaster in 1987 as well as Dunblane, Barr invites us all to be alongside others in ministering after collective tragedy. Clergy should embrace the media as a vehicle for ministry:

To those of us, you and me, who stand in the front line when the 'Why' questions come up, don't just leave it to the vicar. A mighty crowd may join you on those occasions. Someone else's answers won't do. Don't turn away from the visual media – look closely at its unblinking eye and listen to the understanding it may or may not nurture in your neighbours. Try to give hospitality to the visual culture of the young. Don't dismiss the power of the spiritual idea in any form, especially when it comes in new or unfamiliar ways.[27]

For details of emergency planning and training opportunities in your area, contact your local authority emergency planning team or Local Resilience Forum and/or see the following website for further information: <http://www.ukresilience.info/preparedness/emergencyplanning. aspx>.

Notes

1 Michael Dobbs, 'It Seemed Like a Scene From the Bible', *Washington Post* Staff Writer, 27 December 2004, p. A01, <http://www.washingtonpost.com>.

2 UN ISDR (UN International Strategy for Disaster Reduction) (2007/01), 'Three European Countries Among the Top Ten Deadliest Disasters of 2006', press release, Geneva: UN ISDR Secretariat, 27 January 2007, <http://www. em-dat.net/documents/pressreleasecred%20jan%202007.pdf>.

3 ACPO, *Emergency Procedures Manual*, London: Association of Chief Police Officers of England, Wales and Northern Ireland, 1999.

4 For details of the needs of people which are generated by these events, the responses to them and further references, see Anne Eyre, *Identifying People's Needs in Major Emergencies and Best Practice in Humanitarian Response*, independent report commissioned by the Department for Culture, Media and Sport, D3/621, October 2006, <http://www.ukresilience.info/publications/ha_literature_ review.pdf>, and Christine Mead, *Journeys of Discovery: Creative Learning from Disasters*, London: National Institute for Social Work, 1996.

5 Civil Contingencies Act 2004, Part 1, para 1.

6 George Everly, '"Pastoral Crisis Intervention": Toward a Definition', *International Journal of Emergency Mental Health*, Vol. 2, No. 2, 2000, pp. 69–71.

7 George Everly, 'The Role of Pastoral Crisis Intervention in Disasters, Terrorism, Violence, and Other Community Crises', *International Journal of Emergency Mental Health*, Vol. 2, No. 3, 2000, pp. 139–42.

8 See note 24 for how to find details of planning and training opportunities in local areas.

9 Home Office/Cabinet Office, *The Needs of Faith Communities in Major Emergencies: Some Guidelines*, <http://www.ukresilience.info/upload/assets/

www.ukresilience.info/faith_communities.pdf>, 2005, pp. 3, 6.

10 Kai Erikson, *A New Species of Trouble*, New York: W. W. Norton & Company, 1994.

11 Erikson, *A New Species of Trouble*, p. 13 (italics added).

12 BBC News, 'Church Group Aids Tsunami Victims', 20 February 2005, <http://news.bbc.co.uk>.

13 BBC News, 'Disaster Town "Moves" On', 31 January 2001, <http://news.bbc.co.uk>.

14 This has been illustrated in the development of an interactive exhibit opened in 2007 for visitors entitled 'Unwavering Spirit: Hope and Healing at Ground Zero', <http://www.saintpaulschapel.org/>.

15 T. Walter, 'The Mourning after Hillsborough', *Sociological Review*, Vol. 39, No. 3, August 1991, pp. 599–625.

16 Anne Eyre, 'Remembering: Community Commemorations after Disaster' in H. Rodriguez, E. L. Quarantelli and R. Dynes (eds), *Springer Handbook of Disaster Research*, New York: Springer, 2006, pp. 441–55; Anne Eyre, 'In Remembrance: Post-Disaster Rituals and Symbols', *The Australian Journal of Emergency Management*, Vol. 14, No. 3, Spring 1999, pp. 23–9. For an example of the community dimension of disaster and the specific role of the clergy and Churches in responding to this aspect, see David Bolton's analysis of the Enniskillen bombing and its aftermath: David Bolton, 'When a Community Grieves: The Remembrance Day Bombing, Enniskillen' in Christine Mead (ed.), *Journeys of Discovery – Creative Learning from Disasters*, London: National Institute for Social Work, 1996, pp. 73–89.

17 Eyre, 'Remembering: Community Commemorations after Disaster'.

18 Andrew Barr, 'Guns and Roses and God?', Media and Theology Project Public Lectures, University of Edinburgh School of Divinity, 1996, <www.div.ed.ac.uk/gunsandroses_1.html>.

19 Tim Alban Jones, 'God Stopped at Soham', *The Guardian*, 7 August 2004, <http://www.guardian.co.uk>.

20 Tim Alban Jones, 'Time Passes Slowly for Those Who Grieve', *The Independent*, from an address by the vicar of Soham on the anniversary of the murder of Holly Wells and Jessica Chapman, 4 August 2003, <http://www.independent.co.uk>.

21 Jones, 'Time Passes Slowly for Those Who Grieve'.

22 Jones, 'Time Passes Slowly for Those Who Grieve'.

23 Barr, 'Guns and Roses and God?'

24 Jones, 'God Stopped at Soham'. Dealing with the media after a disaster can be stressful for any professional. Press officers should be able to advise clergy on dealing with an event generating media interest. Additionally there are general training courses available for clergy on conducting interviews (see, for example, <http://www.commstraining.cofe.anglican.org/2007/cc.php>). For an example of general tips for talking to the media available on the internet, see <http://www.essex.ac.uk/comms/what/mediatips.html>.

25 Barr, 'Guns and Roses and God?'

26 Jones, 'God Stopped at Soham'.

27 Barr, 'Guns and Roses and God?'

4

Before and After the Death of a Child

ANN DENT

The dying and death of a child, at whatever age, is a major crisis for any family. For professionals who visit to offer support, it can be a daunting task, especially for those with little or no experience. Prior to visiting, there may be many anxieties and uncertainties. Is a dying child aware of impending death? Do brothers and sisters understand about death? Should they be given truthful information about their dying sibling, or should they be protected from the illness and eventual rituals such as seeing the dead body and attending the funeral? Do mothers and fathers cope differently? What is the role of the clergy when other agencies may be involved? These are some of the questions this chapter will answer in a bid to guide and help clergy in this sensitive and stressful area of ministry.

Introduction

Fortunately, the death of a child in the UK is now a relatively rare occurrence. It is estimated that around 12,000 children die annually; just over a half are stillbirth and neonatal deaths, 26 per cent (aged 28 days to 14 years) are sudden and accidental deaths, 19 per cent (aged 28 days to 14 years) are deaths from illness and congenital conditions, and three per cent (aged 10–19 years) are deaths such as suicides, murders or from drug abuse.[1]

While we accept the death of the elderly with some equanimity, the death of a child today, whether sudden or anticipated, is viewed as untimely. In former generations, many families were affected by child-death due to infectious diseases, accidents and high infant mortality rates. Nowadays, with improved maternity services, immunization programmes, and better housing and nutrition, children are not expected to die before their parents or grandparents. Such an event upsets the 'normal' sequence of life, when we in the Western world would hope for each child to reach maturity and to lead a full and fulfilling life. Thus Rando wrote:

> The loss of a child through death is not quite like any other loss known. Ask adults what they dread most and the majority will state that, while they worry about the loss of a parent, spouse, sibling or friend, the loss they fear they could never cope with, is the death of their child.[2]

A child's death ends the world in which the parents have lived. No longer can assumptions be made about themselves and the world as they enter a new domain in which they may have little understanding of the child's dying and death and how to react to it. Therefore, it is no easy task for any professional to visit a family where a child is dying, where expectations of the parents have been shattered and all members of the family are faced with the death of a young person.

Each family will work in its own way, from the time of diagnosis to the time when they must surrender any hope of control, to be left with just memories and their grief. Daily, family members have to find inner resources to deal with the changing situation. Some will have support from family and friends; others may feel very isolated and rely on the help of professionals. As no two families will cope in the same way, the suggestions in this chapter are considerations only.

The dying child and the family

The principles of caring for a family when a child is dying are similar to those for an adult. A holistic approach is required to cover physical, psychological, social and spiritual needs of both the dying child and the family. Until recently the last was given scant attention as disease was seen solely as a physical condition. Gradually, psychological and social aspects were identified as affecting the physical and then finally spiritual, to combine the true holistic approach.[3]

As Labun suggests, the spiritual nature of human beings is the total personality which links aspects together, and is expressed through relationships, personal practices and beliefs.[4] Thus each person is a spiritual being having a spiritual dimension. Spirituality, however, may or may not include religious rituals and behaviours. As palliative care has developed, spiritual care, as opposed to religious care, is now not the sole prerogative of one particular profession or individual, as all members of a team bring their own unique skills and personalities. In today's hospital/hospice culture, there are paediatric palliative care teams, whose tasks may include spiritual care as it arises.

Sometimes there can be many professionals involved, thus working as part of a team is essential, so that a family is not overwhelmed and quality care can be maximized. This is easier to achieve in a hospital/hospice setting, where professionals work in the same building, whereas in the community a priest may visit a family without the team's knowledge and work independently. It is therefore suggested that any priest and the palliative care team work together. However, it is recognized that, in the practice of spiritual care, there is a need to maintain and respect confidentiality.

In modern society, the role of the clergy is a tenuous one as not all families will need or want the services of a priest. It may be easier to visit families who are involved in the Church when the parents are already known; but a priest, as part of the caring team, may help family members to voice their feelings, worries and concerns, giving religious guidance or help when required. Spiritual care is offered through an attitude of love and acceptance. Needs are identified by listening, and accepting each person as they are and where they are at any given time. Nonetheless, it is a two-way process as the person receiving care also needs to accept the listener.[5]

The dying child

It would seem that one of the most worrying aspects of visiting a dying child is what to say. There may be anxieties around saying the 'wrong' words and thereby causing more problems, unfamiliarity with a child's concept of death at different ages, or being unaware of what the child knows. Thus it may be easier to talk to the parents and exclude the child. Like adults, children take time to trust people and to build up a relationship. On one occasion, I visited a family whose little girl of eight, dying of leukaemia, was lying on a couch in the sitting room. During the visit, a young curate, unknown to the family and dressed in his black cassock, rushed in. He immediately approached the girl, taking her hands in his. 'We must pray together,' he said earnestly and loudly. The girl looked terrified and her mother was appalled. A well-meaning neighbour, a member of the local church, had approached the rector to ask him to visit the family but without asking the family first.

Research shows that dying children frequently know the nature of their diagnoses and are aware of their life-threatening condition, even when efforts are made to conceal the truth.[6] The openness of family members about the illness increases as a child gets closer to the terminal phase.[7] Parents should be encouraged to give honest information, giving time for assimilation and allowing questions. However painful, parents should encourage their child, wherever possible, to take an active part in choices involving their care.

Mothers and fathers

It is no easy task for parents to maintain a warm and consistent attitude. They can experience anger and despair, and/or feel guilty and be critical of themselves for having negative thoughts about their dying child. Some parents may experience a momentary anger at their children for causing them so much pain. They may be concerned as to what to tell the child and any siblings, wanting to protect them from the truth. Women tend to be more open, in contrast to men who may hide their true feelings in a bid to be strong for the family.[8] A mother and father may not react in the same way:

> My husband was not able to accept it. He won't talk about it. He left us two years ago . . . He felt terribly guilty that it was his gene too . . . I don't blame God or feel guilty; I got this and I deal with it. My husband was angry with God. He just wanted it all to go away, which of course it didn't.[9]

For many parents, they may be too involved with the dying child to see that their other children also have needs.

Brothers and sisters

As adults, we know that death is irreversible, final and universal, but children's grasp of concepts develops gradually in an orderly hierarchical sequence as they mature. Kenyon's comprehensive study of children's understanding of death[10] indicates that, like other concepts, these develop gradually. From her literature search, she found that by three years, children understand death as a changed state. Around five years they grasp that death is universal, but what causes death comes later. Generally, Kenyon found that current measures do not detect a complete understanding of universality, irreversibility, non-functioning and

35

personal mortality until around ten years. However, children's concepts of death are multi-faceted and affected by factors other than age, which include: a child's verbal ability to communicate, past personal experience of death and how it was handled, the family's cultural and religious beliefs, and anxiety and fear of death.[11]

Siblings also need to be given information. They should not be excluded from a child's dying as they too have attachments, share secrets and play together. Too often, they can feel marginalized and neglected. Giving them tasks to perform such as sitting and reading to the dying child, watching television together, helping to give drinks, and fetching and carrying may help them to feel included and important. Although the main focus is on the dying child, siblings too have needs from their parents in feeling loved, affirmed and secure.

After the death, there are many issues for parents to consider at a time when they are emotionally distraught and may need help in dealing with the necessary requirements surrounding the funeral. If children do not know of the death, ideally they should be told by their parents. However, parents may be too overcome with their own grief to be able to deal with the children. In such a case this may fall to professionals, who can either be with the parents when the children are told, or they can find a quiet and private place, explaining first that their parents are very saddened and cannot be with them at the moment. The news should be broken gently with an initial 'warning' that they have some sad news to tell them. A brief but accurate description of the death should be given, with no euphemisms or reference to religious beliefs. All children will react differently depending on their age and personality. Reassuring children that their feelings and reactions are OK, sitting with them, and giving time for absorbing the news will all be beneficial.

The funeral

As Hubert suggests, reverence and ritual of the disposal of remains was, and continues to be, important for family members and others.[12] As Walter describes, the funeral or memorial service is part of survivors 'writing the last chapter'.[13] Sometimes the family will plan the funeral in advance with the dying child, especially involving older children. Essentially, the funeral is a special family occasion, marking the end of someone's life. To exclude children of the affected family, either from contributing to the arrangements or attending the service, is to deny them an opportunity of saying goodbye and being part of a family ritual.[14] In the many workshops I have run nationally for professionals, I have been surprised at how, for many, years later, they still felt angry at being excluded from a loved one's funeral when they were children.

Parents may not realize that children can benefit from attending the funeral. A priest is in an ideal position to suggest that children, as part of the family, can choose to be included in funeral arrangements (if old enough) and be present at the funeral.

In guiding and encouraging parents to include the siblings, children need to know what will happen, who will be there and that some people, including their parents, may cry. It is also all right for them to cry or not. They may want to know what to wear, how to behave and what will happen to the body. In Christ's study,[15] children as young as three had attended their parents' funerals with no ill effects. The major gain was that the death became more concrete. Most parents had wisely asked a relative or friend to take charge and to be available to the child, to leave with the child should they need to do so. After careful explanation, surviving children should be offered choices, such as seeing the body, attending the funeral, putting toys, cards, flowers or letters in the coffin, planning and playing a part at the service. A girl aged 12 when her sister died, wrote:

> I didn't want to go to the funeral . . . I don't know why really – I was just scared. So I stayed at the neighbour's house. Then, when everyone came to our house afterwards, I felt left out – like they all knew something that I didn't. Even now (six years later), it's still on my mind. I wish I had gone.[16]

Perhaps, if someone had taken the time to listen to the girl's fears and had explained the funeral service, she might not be still worrying, years later.

Parents should not be rushed into planning a funeral. There are many options available.[17] As this is such an important occasion, it is essential that parents know the range of options and have an opportunity to make informed choices without haste. This is the last public ceremony they will perform for their child. Therefore it is vital that everything is done to make it a special event so that, over time, the family can feel they have done their very best for the deceased child, without recriminations or regret.

It should be noted that there may be a difference in women's and men's belief in an afterlife.[18] This will affect how the parents may individually respond to or cope with their child's funeral.

The grieving family

For each child who dies, there are many people affected. The death is like a stone dropped into water causing a 'death ripple' effect.[19] This extends from the bereaved family – to include parents, siblings and grandparents, to others in the extra-familial setting. It may touch friends of the dead child, colleagues of parents, neighbours, teachers, health professionals and possibly many others. In other words, a whole community is affected. The death will hold different meanings for each member of the bereaved family,[20] for each is a separate being who had a unique relationship with the child who died, whether positive or negative. Where surviving children are involved, it is important to understand what death means to them and how they will react.

Bereaved siblings: reactions at different ages

It is only in recent years that we have come to realize that children grieve and need support in bereavement. As one mother commented about her surviving children:

> I still can't get over how as parents you just expect them to cope and unwittingly give them the message not to intrude and just to get on with their own lives. If only I could have my time again, I'd explain much more, right from the beginning, bringing it into normal everyday conversation.[21]

Under the age of two, a bereaved child is likely to be affected by the main carer's reactions. Because the parent is upset, irritability, crying, eating and sleeping disturbances are not uncommon and can add to the anguish of the parents.

From two to five years, although they may use the word 'death', children have not fully grasped that it is irreversible. They tend to see death as a sleep or departure and may constantly ask questions about when the deceased is returning. They have not the language capacity to describe their emotions or ask for what they need. At this age children are very involved with their own basic physical needs such as eating, sleeping and excreting, so may show curiosity in what will happen to the body of the child. Because they believe in the power of 'magical' thinking, they may believe that they have caused the child to go away, thus harbouring a sense of guilt.

38

From five to nine years, children begin to realize that death is permanent but that it happens to others, not to themselves. They may have a preoccupation with the rituals surrounding death, so, if excluded, may imagine things far worse than the reality. They require simple, honest explanations to avoid ambiguity.[22] During adolescence the full concept of death will be understood. A young person at this age has to cope with many physical, social and psychological changes, so these factors combined with the death of a sibling may leave them feeling confused and insecure. They may react by reckless behaviour to prove, mostly to themselves, that they are as invincible as they feel. They are keenly aware of their peers for companionship and support, so may well withdraw from their parents.[23] Research now shows that, sadly, many bereaved siblings express feelings of being left out, ignored and isolated within the family.[24] 'I hated our house, but they would come over and say: "Be with your mother. Try to help her." They just never understood. I didn't have enough strength to help her. I needed all my energy to go to school' (10-year-old boy).[25]

The bereavement literature suggests that sadness, anger, guilt, irritability, feelings of being alone, bodily discomforts, sleep disorders and loss of appetite are common to both bereaved children and adults.[26] In Dent's studies parents reported their surviving children being 'clingy', needing more attention, showing off, having sleep disturbances, being aggressive, withdrawn and unable to concentrate. Yet, as Worden suggests, most disturbed forms of behaviour are short-lived and cease without intervention. It is only when a child has persistent difficulty in talking about the dead sibling, exhibits aggressive behaviour that becomes worse and destructive, and when anxiety persists so that a child becomes more 'clingy' and/or develops school phobia, that professional intervention may be necessary.[27] Riches and Dawson suggest that the primary role of health professionals is in helping parents manage their own grief so that they feel nurtured and supported. In so doing, there is more likelihood that they will be able to support and nurture their surviving children.[28]

Bereaved parents

Soon after the death, many fathers are likely to put their energies into practical issues, by supporting their partners, controlling their emotions, rationalizing the death and finding practical activities to divert their grief.[29] Some fathers prefer to release their pain in private. A father, in reply to his wife's comment that he didn't show any emotion after the death of their child, said: 'That's all you know. We've this shed at work and there would be times I would lock myself in and just roar.'[30] Conversely, mothers find it easier to express and disclose their feelings.[31] The differences in grieving may lead to further tensions, so parents may need help in accepting and dealing with these, to avoid a further loss in their lives through separation or divorce.

Coping each day with the pain can be exhausting. Stroebe and Schut proposed the dual process model which suggests that people move between loss and restoration-orientated loss. The latter deals with the new reality, doing everyday activities required in the changed situation.[32] Bereaved parents will move between a range of coping strategies that include seeking information, allowing support from others, retreating into or trying to control feelings and finding ways of constructing a relationship with the deceased child. The model suggests time away from both types of loss.[33]

For many parents, it is vital that they have a 'continuing bond' with their dead child where 'survivors hold the deceased in loving memory for long periods, often for ever, and that maintaining an inner representation of the deceased is normal rather than abnormal'.[34] To maintain this bond requires 'the paradox of letting go and remaining involved'.[35] Looking at photographs, remembering good times and keeping mementoes may all help to keep the bond alive.

Resources in the form of emotional, informational or practical support have been found to be the most helpful to parents.[36] However, arising from uncertainty as to what to say and from lack of experience, would-be supporters tend to fade away, even although they would like to help.[37] Others may make trite comments such as: 'You can always have another baby' or 'You'll soon get over it.' This is of no help to grieving parents. Many parents talk of the importance of having people who will listen to their story, which may help them to sort out their confused feelings.[38] These listeners may be sensitive friends, professionals involved during the illness, befrienders (e.g. Cruse – Bereavement Care) or support groups of parents whose children have died (e.g. The Compassionate Friends). As with the time before the death, it is important to establish what help exists so that support can be co-ordinated in the best way for the family, with their consent and approval.

For many parents, coping with the death is in some way transforming. It opens them to new experiences and part of themselves that they did not know existed.[39] Sometimes parents attribute this change to a sense of empowerment when they realize they have survived. As one mother describes: 'I was always waiting for someone to give me permission, and here I am very much in charge. Even how I treat my kids has changed. I've learnt to listen better. Sometimes when I see how much I've changed, I almost don't recognize myself.'[40]

For me, to be involved with a family where a child is dying or has died gives a sense of privilege. Families deserve the very best support we can give them, so that they can heal and go forward with courage and strength. Children in the family will be the adults of tomorrow. Recognizing their needs and helping them through this trauma may help them later in their lives to deal with other inevitable losses. Supporting is demanding and emotional work at both personal and professional levels. Thus it is important for all carers to recognize their limitations, to know when they have moved out of their depth and to seek help and support for themselves.

Notes

1 Office for National Statistics, mortality statistics for causes of death, *Review of the Registrar General on Deaths by Cause, Sex and Age in England and Wales*, London: Office for National Statistics, 2002.

2 T. Rando, 'The Unique Issues and Impact of the Death of a Child' in T. A. Rando (ed.), *Parental Loss of a Child*, Champaign: Research Press, 1986, pp. 5–43, 6.

3 D. Stoter, *Spiritual Aspects of Health Care*, London: Mosby, 1995.

4 E. Labun, 'Spiritual Care: An Element in Nursing Planning', *Journal of Advanced Nursing*, 3, 1988, pp. 314–20.

5 Stoter, *Spiritual Aspects of Health Care*, p. 16.

6 M. Bluebond-Langner, *The Private World of Dying Children*, Princeton: Princeton University Press, 1978.

7 Bluebond-Langner, *The Private World of Dying Children*, p. 184.

8 P. R. Silverman, *Never Too Young to Know*, New York: Oxford University Press, 2000.

9 Silverman, *Never Too Young to Know*, pp. 124–5.

10 B. Kenyon, 'Current Research in Children's Concepts of Death: A Critical Review', *Omega Journal of Death and Dying*, 43, 2001, pp. 63–91.

11 B. Davies, *Shadows in the Sun: The Experiences of Sibling Bereavement in Childhood*, Philadelphia: Brunner/Maxel, 1999.

12 J. Hubert, 'Dry Bones or Living Ancestors? Conflicting Perceptions of Life, Death and the Universe', *International Journal of Cultural Property*, Vol. 1, No. 1, 1992, pp. 105–27, 111.

13 T. Walter, 'A New Model of Grief: Bereavement and Biography', *Mortality*, 1996, pp. 7–27, 14.

14 M. E. Lauer, R. K. Mulhern, B. J. Bohne and B. M. Camitta, 'Children's

Perceptions of their Sibling's Death at Home or Hospital: The Precursors of Differential Adjustment', *Cancer Nursing*, No. 8, 1985, pp. 21–7.

15 G. Christ, *Healing Children's Grief: Surviving a Parent's Death from Cancer*, Oxford: Oxford University Press, 2000.

16 Davies, *Shadows in the Sun*, p. 121.

17 A. Dent and A. Stewart, *Sudden Death in Childhood: Care of the Bereaved Family*, Edinburgh: Butterworth/Heinemann, 2004, Appendix 10.

18 D. J. Davies, 'Contemporary Belief in Life after Death' in Peter C. Jupp and T. Rogers (eds), *Interpreting Death: Christian Theology and Pastoral Practice*, London: Cassell, 1997, pp. 138–9.

19 J. Jordan, D. Kraus and E. Ware, 'Observations on Family and Development', *Family Process*, No. 32, pp. 425–40.

20 J. Nadeau, *Families Making Sense of Death*, London: Sage, 1998.

21 M. Hitcham, 'Direct Work Techniques with the Siblings of Children Dying from Cancer' in S. Smith and M. Pennells (eds), *Interventions with Bereaved Children*, London: Jessica Kingsley, 1995, pp. 24–44, 25.

22 See Christ, *Healing Children's Grief*, and Davies, 'Contemporary Belief in Life after Death'.

23 Davies, 'Contemporary Belief in Life after Death'.

24 G. Riches and P. Dawson, *An Intimate Loneliness: Supporting Bereaved Parents and Siblings*, Buckingham: Open University Press, 2000.

25 H. Sarnoff Schiff, *The Bereaved Parent*, New York: Souvenir Press, 2000, p. 89.

26 A. Dent, L. Condon, P. Blair and P. Fleming, 'A Study of Bereavement Care after Sudden and Unexpected Death', *Archives of Disease in Children*, No. 74, 1996, pp. 522–6; and A. Dent, 'Support for Families Whose Child Dies Suddenly from Accident or Illness', PhD thesis, School of Policy Studies, Bristol University, 2000.

27 J. W. Worden, *Children and Grief: When a Parent Dies*, London: The Guildford Press, 1996.

28 Riches and Dawson, *An Intimate Loneliness*, p. 115.

29 A. Hazzard, J. Weston and C. Guttares, 'After a Child's Death: Factors Related to Parental Bereavement', *Journal of Development and Behavioural Paediatrics*, Vol. 13, No. 1, 1992, pp. 24–30.

30 Riches and Dawson, *An Intimate Loneliness*, p. 149.

31 J. Duncombe and D. Marsden, 'Workaholics and Whinging Women: Theorizing Intimacy and Emotion Work – the Last Frontier of Gender Inequality?', *Sociological Review*, No. 43, 1995, pp. 150–70.

32 See Eyre, this volume.

33 M. Stroebe and H. Schut, 'Meaning Making in the Dual Process of Coping with Bereavement' in R. Neimeyer (ed.), *Meaning Reconstruction and the Experience of Loss*, Washington DC: American Psychological Association, 2001, pp. 55–75.

34 P. Silverman and S. Nickman, 'Children's Construction of Their Dead Parents' in D. Klass, P. Silverman and S. Nickman (eds), *Continuing Bonds: New Understandings of Grief*, Washington DC: Taylor & Francis, 1996, pp. 73–86. See also chapter 2.

35 P. R. Silverman and S. L. Nickman, 'Concluding Thoughts' in Klass et al.,

Continuing Bonds, p. 351.

36 F. Thuen, 'Social Support after the Death of an Infant Child: A Long-term Perspective', *Scandinavian Journal of Psychology*, Vol. 38, No. 2, 1997, pp. 167–87.

37 D. R. Lehman, J. H. Ellard and C. B Wortman, 'Social Support of the Bereaved: Recipients' and Providers' Perspectives on What Is Helpful', *Journal of Consulting and Clinical Psychology*, No. 52, 1986, pp. 218–31.

38 Nadeau, *Families Making Sense of Death*.

39 Silverman, *Never Too Young to Know*.

40 Silverman, *Never Too Young to Know*, p. 211.

5

Death in Hospital

MARK COBB

Introduction

It is only in relatively modern times that medicine has been able to intervene in the fatal sequence of events that can unfold as a result of infection or injury or the faults and dysfunctions of our bodies. It is now widely expected that medicine can defy death and that our inevitable mortality can be postponed. Hospitals are the site where these longings are often fulfilled, but they are also the place where most people will face death. Thus death for many takes place within an ordered clinical context where experts are on hand to preserve life and minimize the risk of dying. When death cannot be avoided it is therefore accompanied by medical procedures and rituals in an institution that contains and manages dying on behalf of society.

The hospital context shapes the experience of death for many people and provides a clinical language, meaning and process. This is the setting in which family and friends may learn about and witness the death, where the dead body will be subject to post-mortem procedures and storage, and where the bereaved will receive the property of the deceased and the certification required to proceed with a funeral. But the hospital is also a community of people who are trained in caring, who have experience in dealing with death and bereavement, who are sensitive to the beliefs and practices of individuals, and recognize that the spiritual and pastoral dimension can be an important aspect of care for some patients.

In this chapter I shall outline the ways in which people come to die in hospital and the consequences this may have for those who minister to the dying and their carers and for those who lead funerals. In particular I shall aim to describe what takes place in hospital in terms of end-of-life, post-mortem and bereavement care so that ministers who prepare family and friends for a funeral may have a better understanding of how their ministry relates to the hospital context.

Dying in hospital

Most people can expect to live well into their late seventies or early eighties. Consequently around a half of all deaths occur among people aged between 65 and 84 years, with around a third of all deaths occurring in people aged 85 years and over. The majority of deaths will occur in hospital and the most common causes are conditions related to the circulatory system which include heart attacks (myocardial infarction) and strokes (a disruption of blood supply to the brain).[1] The prevalence of these conditions is age related and rises significantly after the age of 45. One in four people will die from a cancer, which represents the second most common cause of death and is predominantly a disease of older people. The most prevalent cancers are lung, prostate and colorectal cancers in men, and breast, lung and colorectal in women. Behind these aggregated mortality figures are significant differences according to age and sex. For example, deaths in children are mainly due to accidental injury and poisoning as well as cancer.[2] Deaths in young men are more likely to result from accidental injury or poisoning (including a significant proportion of suicides) whereas deaths in young women (half those of young men) are more likely to result from cancer.[3]

Deaths in hospital take place in diverse circumstances and settings, but the majority of people will die on a hospital ward as a result of a deteriorating condition or physiological decline which is either responding poorly to treatment or where it has been decided, ultimately by the clinician-in-charge, that death should no longer be postponed. Medical consumerism and inflated expectations of cure and healing have led to death becoming seen as a medical failure by many rather than a natural and inevitable event. Postponing death and being kept alive is a real option in many cases, but what is technically possible is not always in the best interests of a person, and the burdens of the treatment are not always outweighed by the benefits. Consequently, the withholding or withdrawal of life-prolonging treatment has become a focus of much ethical and legal debate.[4]

Most deaths in hospital are uneventful and are indicated by the absence of vital signs of breathing and a heartbeat. Body temperature and colour remain for a while and the person can appear to be asleep. Unconscious patients who have been receiving intensive care and respiratory support from a ventilator may show no outward signs of death until such support is removed. In addition, a patient with irremediable damage to the brain may suffer brain-stem death before full biological death, a condition in which brain-stem reflexes, including respiratory movements, are absent. People who die from the cessation of the heart will also stop breathing, and either of these functions may be shown on a monitor providing a visual and audible indicator of activity. The external cause of a death resulting from trauma may be more apparent. For example, people who have been critically injured in a road traffic accident may have obvious signs of blood loss and damage to their bodies. The sight of a relative or friend in such a condition can be very distressing to people and they may require skilled support.

There are many initiatives in hospitals aimed at ensuring good care of the dying and the bereaved. The influence of the modern hospice movement has been particularly significant, and people who are dying from an advanced progressive illness may often receive care in hospital that is based upon palliative care principles and practices. Palliative care is attentive to the whole person and is sensitive to the spiritual dimension alongside the physical, social and psychological dimensions of being human.[5] Wards may also follow care pathways in the last days or hours of life which provide a framework to enable the optimum care of the dying and the support of those significant to them.[6] The healthcare team may also consult with specialist palliative care professionals in the hospital who may assess the patient and provide advice and support.

Ministry in hospital

Medieval hospitals aimed to care for the body and the soul, and this religious heritage is evident in today's hospitals through the role and function of the hospital chaplain and in the facilities of chapels and prayer rooms. The NHS aims to respect the beliefs and practices of its users, and it recognizes that 'meeting the varied spiritual needs of patients, staff and visitors is fundamental to the care the NHS provides'.[7] The responsibility for this provision rests with hospital chaplains[8] who work with a network of volunteers and community-based ministers of religion to meet the varied needs of those within the hospital.[9] Chaplains are usually salaried NHS staff who undertake specialist training and continued professional development in healthcare chaplaincy. They provide care and support to people whose spirituality is framed within traditional religious forms and who belong to religious communities, as well as to those with spiritual needs who have no association with traditional religious practices or communities. In most acute hospitals there is provision for chaplaincy 24 hours a day, and referrals can be made to hospital chaplains by patients, their carers and staff, and their own ministers. Nevertheless hospital chaplains welcome the contribution and support that a patient's minister may be able to provide and which can continue an existing relationship of pastoral care.

Ministry to the dying and bereaved[10] in hospital begins with establishing a pastoral relationship, or reconnecting to one that has existed outside of hospital. The setting for this relationship has many challenges, not least in terms of access and privacy, but once these have been negotiated a minister may seek to be a supportive companion to the dying and bereaved, a representative of the community of faith, a sign of God's love, a person prepared to encounter the sacred in the midst of suffering and death, and a liturgist or authorized minister of the rites and sacraments of the Christian community.

Fine-tuned communication skills and well-developed pastoral practice are essential to the critical situations in which people are dying, but equally important, ministers must be skilled in the interpretative art of pastoral theology. In hospital, people face suffering, pain, hopelessness, peace, love and death. It is in this context that the minister stands in the space between the particular life-stories of individuals seeking support and the Christian story. The minister is therefore located in a place of dialogue in which connections can be formed, meanings explored and new ways of relating to the human and the divine can be fostered and fashioned.[11] Pastoral theology provides ministers with a way for our experiences of humanity and God to interrelate in a critical and creative way in order that our knowledge and understanding of both can be enriched and deepened.[12]

Facing death can be no less a difficult personal experience for ministers than for anyone else, but if they are to seek to support the dying and bereaved then they will need to attend to both the theological and psychological challenges of this task. This means attending to the difficult questions of theodicy and the place of suffering in our world, the value of human beings, the meaning of death, the divine love from which we cannot be separated, the meaning of forgiveness and the hope of the resurrection. To do this we must take our lived and encountered stories, bring them into dialogue with the foundation texts of pastoral practice[13] and be prepared to engage in a continuing theological work-in-progress. Equally, ministers must develop the self-awareness to recognize the psychological impact that caring for the dying and bereaved has upon them, their motivation for such ministry, the fears it raises in them, and their weaknesses and blind spots in pastoral practice. For these reasons, access to support and some form of supervision by an experienced colleague can provide a necessary and safe space for ministers to explore their own distress, prejudices and doubts, to reflect theologically on experience and to continue developing and learning about ministry.[14]

The care of the deceased person

When someone has died in hospital there are a number of practical issues that must be addressed, including the preparation, removal and storage of the body prior to the funeral, the certification of the cause of death, and the return of any property the deceased person had on the ward. These practices are informed by guidance, established clinical procedures and statutory regulation. Prior to this, at the time of death there is the opportunity for family and friends to spend time with the dead person, and to say prayers and support each other. A hospital chaplain is usually on duty to attend in such circumstances if requested.

Before a body is removed from a ward it is customary for nurses to carry out Last Offices.[15] This is a practice in which the final form of care is provided to the person who has died. This usually involves closing the person's eyes and straightening the limbs, removing external equipment from the patient, such as a syringe driver or catheter (where the cause of death is known), washing, dressing the patient in a clean gown, and wrapping the patient in a clean sheet. Wards and units may offer more specific care and support developed around particular needs. For example, when a baby has died around the time of birth or during pregnancy, parents and those significant to the parents are given as much time as possible to be with the dead baby, and opportunities may be provided to take photographs of the baby and prints of his or her hands and feet.[16] A hospital chaplain can provide rites of naming, blessing and commendation, and the chaplain can also assist in making funeral arrangements.

Mortuaries

Mortuaries[17] are the facilities and services in hospitals where dead bodies are safely stored, post-mortem examinations carried out and where bereaved relatives and friends can see and spend time with the person who has died unless subject to the instructions of the Coroner.[18] The place where a deceased person can be visited in hospital is generally known as a viewing room or chapel of rest. These are rooms which provide a comfortable environment in which to spend time with the deceased person and which generally are devoid of any religious arti-facts or symbols unless specifically requested. Appointments can usually be arranged at the earliest opportunity, subject to the availability of staff. However, this facility is only available while the dead body is in the care of the hospital, and separate arrangements are required to visit a deceased person when they have been released to a funeral director.

A mortuary service usually prepares and presents the body of the per-son who has died for viewing and is sensitive to the particular religious and cultural requirements of relatives. Where particular needs cannot be met in the mortuary, for example, the facility for ritual washing, then mortuary staff will usually offer to make arrangements with a funeral director or religious community who can meet this need. A deceased person can also be released to any responsible person who undertakes safe custody of the body prior to a lawful funeral. This may be a parent in the case of baby or child, a partner in the case of an adult, a repre-sentative of a religious community or, most commonly, a funeral director.

Organ donation

The current law and guidance was established following inquiries into the practice of removing and retaining organs at the Bristol Royal Infirmary,[19] Alder Hey Hospital[20] and the report of the Retained Organs Commission.[21] In England, Wales and Northern Ireland the removal, storage, use and disposal of dead bodies, organs and tissue are now regulated by the Human Tissue Authority (HTA) according to the Human Tissue Act 2004 (there is separate legislation in Scotland – the Human Tissue (Scotland) Act 2006). In particular, guidance issued by the HTA covers organ, tissue or cell donation, the donation of whole bodies for anatomical examination, and post-mortem examinations.

In their lifetime, competent adults and children can record consent to donation through the Organ Donor Register. If no decision was made in the case of a child, then a person with parental responsibility for the child can consent to organ donation. For an adult, or a child with no parents, consent can be sought from someone close to them in a qualifying relationship (for example, spouse, civil partner, sibling or longstanding friend). In addition, an adult may nominate one or more people to represent them after death in relation to providing consent to donations.[22]

Donation to a medical school

Anyone who wishes to donate their body or part of the body for ana-tomical examination in a university medical school or anatomy labora-tory must complete and sign a specific consent form for this purpose while they are alive and competent to do so. The death is certified and registered in the usual way and the body is preserved to allow the anatomical examinations to be carried out. Once completed, the body is disposed of in accordance with the deceased person's wishes, with separated body parts buried or cremated with the body from which they were removed.[23] Medical schools may also hold an annual memorial service for relatives and friends of those who have donated their bodies.[24]

Post-mortem examinations

The majority of deaths in hospital are certified by a doctor, and relatives can proceed to have the deceased person transferred to a funeral direc-tor and the death registered prior to a funeral. There are two circum-stances in which post-mortem examinations can be carried out. The first, with the prior consent of the deceased person, is the consent of their nominated representative or the consent of a person in a qualifying relationship, following a request by a doctor in hospital, in order to gain a better understanding of the cause of death and to enhance future medi-cal care. Specific consent must be obtained to store and/or use tissue (including blocks and slides). The second is when a post-mortem is ordered by a coroner, in which case consent is not required.[25] Approxi-mately 0.5 per cent of deaths are subject to a hospital post-mortem examination and 20 per cent of deaths are referred to the coroner, of which just over three-quarters are certified following a post-mortem.[26] Following this, the death can usually be registered and a funeral arranged. If a coroner decides that a death does not result from a natu-ral cause, an inquest may be held to establish who has died, when and where the death occurred, and the cause of death. When this informa-tion is established the death can be registered and a funeral arranged.

Hospital funerals

In some circumstances a hospital takes responsibility or assists with making funeral arrangements for patients who have died, because rela-tives cannot be traced, or they cannot afford to pay and do not qualify for Social Fund Funeral Payments, or because they are unwilling to take responsibility for funeral arrangements.[27] A hospital bereavement officer usually makes the arrangements following sensitive enquiries with any family and friends, or, where there are none with carers. Particular attention is paid to the religious preferences of the deceased person, and a hospital chaplain is usually consulted in more complex cases. The funeral is provided by a funeral director under contract to the hospital, and a hospital chaplain leads the service where this is appropriate to the known religion of the deceased person, unless the person was known to a minister in the community.

Hospitals that care for children and provide maternity services may offer to assist with or make funeral arrangements designed to meet the particular needs of parents whose baby has died. It is usual practice for hospitals to arrange and pay for the funerals of stillborn babies (i.e. a baby born dead after reaching the legal age of viability of 24 weeks gestation). Babies who die during pregnancy and before the legal age of viability, for example ectopic pregnancies or intra-uterine foetal deaths, may be buried or cremated, and hospitals will make funeral arrangements according to the wishes of parents. Hospitals will also provide a funeral when parents choose not be involved, and will also arrange for the dignified disposal of foetal tissue.[28]

The care of the bereaved

The care and support of bereaved people is an inevitable aspect of the work of hospitals, and healthcare professionals receive training in this important role. However, in most acute wards and units, bereavement support is limited to the time around death and the immediate needs of survivors. Hospitals have had to make provision for the administrative duties related to death, but it is only recently that the NHS has been recommended to develop sensitive, responsive and professional bereavement services.[29] Consequently, national advice has been issued to improve services, and these recognize the important role of hospital chaplains and the provision of spiritual care.[30]

A bereavement service provides the link between the hospital and the next-of-kin to support communication of advice and information, decision-making, planning and the co-ordination of activities that follow when a person has died in hospital. People who are bereaved may have no prior experience of dealing with death or its consequences, and a hospital bereavement service can guide them through the process. This may include dealing with issues such as organ donation, the certification of death, post-mortems, the involvement of the coroner, liaison with the mortuary service and funeral directors, and options of follow-up support from agencies and healthcare professionals in the community.

Memorial services are sometimes organized by hospital wards and units for bereaved relatives and friends. These are likely to be in relation to specialist areas such as oncology or neonatology, or in relation to particular types of death such as road traffic accidents or pregnancy loss. Services are usually planned with the involvement of bereaved relatives and they can take a wide range of forms, from the religious to the secular.[31] Finally, the impact upon hospital staff of dealing with death needs acknowledgement and routine inclusion within accessible support systems. These may include staff support groups and counselling, supervision and mentoring, and staff training and development.

Conclusion

Hospitals are major features on the landscape of death and they shape the experience of death for the majority of people. The relationship between hospitals and those they care for is shifting from the passive to the participatory as patients become more critical and informed consumers of health care. Consequently, issues around death are reflecting more the concerns, values and desires of the public. Evidence of this can be found in the debates around withholding and withdrawing treatment, the legal recognition of proxy decision-makers,[32] the procedures for retaining and disposing of human organs and the provision of funerals for babies who have died in early pregnancy. In some cases advances in medical technology and science have driven change; in other cases it has been the ethical and legal arguments which have been refined or revised, often in response to the former. The results are that hospitals can intervene more at the threshold between life and death, the public require more respect and dignity for the human corpse, and people who are bereaved expect professional support to be available to them. All of these issues have implications for religious communities, their ministers and those engaged in pastoral practice; and in turn they all inform, question and stimulate the ongoing theological and pastoral tasks of the Church.

Notes

1 National Statistics, *Mortality Statistics: Review of the Registrar General on Deaths in England and Wales, 2004*, London: Office for National Statistics, 2006.

2 See Dent, this volume.

3 Madhavi Bajekal, Velda Osborne, Mohammed Yar and Howard Meltzer (eds), *Focus on Health: 2006*, London: Office for National Statistics, 2006.

4 British Medical Association, *Withholding and Withdrawing Life-Prolonging Medical Treatment*, Oxford: Blackwell Publishing, 2007.

5 National Institute for Clinical Excellence, *Improving Supportive and Palliative Care for Adults with Cancer*, London: NICE, 2004.

6 John Ellershaw and Susie Wilkinson (eds), *Care of the Dying: A Pathway to Excellence*, Oxford: Oxford University Press, 2003. See also Hilborn, this volume.

7 Department of Health, *NHS Chaplaincy: Meeting the Religious and Spiritual Needs of Patients and Staff*, London: Department of Health, 2003.

8 Mark Cobb, *The Hospital Chaplain's Handbook*, Norwich: Canterbury Press, 2005.

9 See Hilborn, this volume.

10 Bill Kirkpatrick, *Going Forth: A Practical and Spiritual Approach to Dying and Death*, London: Darton, Longman and Todd, 1997.

11 Charles Gerkin, *An Introduction to Pastoral Care*, Nashville: Abingdon Press, 1997.

12 Emmanuel Y. Lartey, *Pastoral Theology in an Intercultural World*, Peterborough: Epworth, 2006.

13 Gordon Oliver, *Holy Bible, Human Bible*, London: Darton, Longman and Todd, 2006.

14 Peter Hawkins and Robin Shohet, *Supervision in the Helping Professions*, Maidenhead: Open University Press, 2007.

15 Lisa Dougherty and Sara Lister (eds), *The Royal Marsden Hospital Manual of Clinical Nursing Procedures*, 6th edn, Oxford: Blackwell, 2004, chapter 21.

16 Judith Schott and Alix Henley, *Pregnancy Loss and the Death of a Baby: Guidelines for Professionals*, London: SANDS, 2007.

17 Department of Health, *Care and Respect in Death: Good Practice Guidance for NHS Mortuary Staff*, London: Department of Health, 2006.

18 The Coroner is an independent judicial officer who enquires into the cause of the death of those reported to him or her.

19 Ian Kennedy (chair), *Learning from Bristol: The Report of the Public Inquiry into Children's Heart Surgery at the Bristol Royal Infirmary 1984–1995*, London: The Stationery Office, 2001.

20 Michael Redfern (chair), *The Royal Liverpool Children's Inquiry Report*, London: The Stationery Office, 2001.

21 Margaret Brazier (chair), *Remembering the Past, Looking to the Future: The Final Report of the Retained Organs Commission, including the Summary Accountability Report for 2003/2004*, London: Department of Health, 2004.

22 Human Tissue Authority, *Code of Practice: Donation of Organs, Tissue and Cells for Transplantation*, London: Human Tissue Authority, 2006.

23 Human Tissue Authority, *Code of Practice: Anatomical Examination*, London: Human Tissue Authority, 2006.

24 Eric Tinker, 'An Unusual Christian Service: For Those Who Have Donated Their Bodies for Medical Education and Research', *Mortality*, Vol. 3, No. 1, 1998, pp. 79–82

25 Human Tissue Authority, *Code of Practice: Post-mortem Examination*, London: Human Tissue Authority, 2006.

26 National Statistics, *Mortality Statistics: Review of the Registrar General on Deaths in England and Wales, 2004*, London: Office for National Statistics, 2006, Table 21, p. 74. For the hospital chaplain's work in this regard, see Hilborn, this volume.

27 Department of Health, *When a Patient Dies: Advice on Developing Bereavement Services*, London: Department of Health, 2005, pp. 18–20.

28 Human Tissue Authority, *Code of Practice: The Removal, Storage and Disposal of Human Organs and Tissue*, London: Human Tissue Authority, 2006, Appendix B.

29 Ian Kennedy (chair), *Learning from Bristol: The Report of the Public Inquiry into Children's Heart Surgery at the Bristol Royal Infirmary 1984–1995*, London: The Stationery Office, 2001, p. 440.

30 Department of Health, *When a Patient Dies: Advice on Developing Bereavement Services*, London: Department of Health, 2005.

31 See Eyre, this volume.

32 Department of Constitutional Affairs, *Mental Capacity Act 2005: Code of Practice*, London: The Stationery Office, 2007, chapter 7.

6

Contemporary Perspectives on Grief and Bereavement

CHRISTINE VALENTINE

Introduction

This chapter explores recent developments in academic perspectives on grief that reflect the changing nature of contemporary British society. This exploration aims to provide those who minister to bereaved people with a framework for approaching this task more effectively. It highlights a shift in focus from interpreting grief as an inner psychological condition to an appreciation of the diverse and profoundly social nature of the way people grieve, including the continuing bonds forged between the living and the dead. In so doing, the chapter assesses the contribution of theorists who have been influential in representing grief as an internal process of 'relinquishing ties' with the deceased in order to 'move on' in life. This assessment draws attention to the way some bereavement counsellors have translated such theory into universally applicable, prescriptive, stage models of grief. It identifies how, in an increasingly culturally diverse society, this approach is proving inadequate to reflect the complexity and diversity of grief. Finally, recent perspectives that take account of social factors and seek to address the challenges posed by this changing socio-cultural context are discussed, together with their implications for those who minister to dying and bereaved people.

Psychological approaches

Until relatively recently the scientific and rationalist values of modernity provided the framework for engaging with mortality to construct a particular culture of grief.[1] Such a culture has been dominated by psychological and medical frameworks, reflecting the decline in religious belief and its role in making sense of death.[2] The discourses associated with these frameworks are rooted in a scientific paradigm that is concerned with reducing the variety of human experience to measurable data from which generalizations, models and prescriptions can be developed.[3] Reflecting a social context of liberal democracy or a secular society of private individuals, grief has been constructed as a condition of the individual psyche. Psychological studies of bereavement have developed universal theories from the individual 'grief reactions' of Westerners, mainly widows. These have focused on defining the symptoms of grief and identifying its healthy and its pathological forms.[4]

In the hands of bereavement counselling services, the prescriptive use of theories that their proponents intended as *descriptive* has promoted a universal stage model approach. It is thus important to acknowledge the epistemological gap that has arisen between theory and practice in order to do justice to the work of the theorists. Kübler-Ross's stages of dying, Bowlby's attachment theory and its development by Parkes are considerably more nuanced, reflective and open to further development than is represented by the prescriptive models attributed to them. Indeed, Parkes has continued to explore the wider social implications of attachment theory.

Elisabeth Kübler-Ross's five stages of dying – denial, anger, bargaining, depression and acceptance[5] – have been subject to widespread misapplication to bereavement as well. The final stage of acceptance, in particular, has been promoted as the desired outcome for everyone.[6] However, Kübler-Ross's observations and understandings arose out of and therefore reflect the institutional context in which dying occurred.[7] In spite of her insistence that not all people experience all stages, nor were they necessarily linear, such qualifications as well as context have been lost to a prescriptive application of her ideas.

Kübler-Ross was one of the first to challenge what has been identified as the post-war denial of death in which care for the dying tended to be synonymous with protecting people from their dying. Her work in identifying the grief experienced by those who were about to die represented a crucial step in drawing attention to the problems encountered by a marginalized group of people and their needs as living human beings. In the UK a similar challenge to the denial of death was made in relation to the experience and treatment of bereaved people, by the sociologists Gorer and Marris, and the psychiatrists Bowlby and Parkes. However, the sociological perspectives of Gorer and Marris failed to penetrate the prevailing psychological discourse of relinquishing ties with deceased loved ones.[8]

Bowlby's contribution to bereavement theory was based on his observations and understandings of the responses of hospitalized children to maternal deprivation, from which he developed his attachment theory.[9] His work with Parkes led him to recognize the striking similarities between such responses and spousal bereavement. According to Bowlby, the capacity for healthy grieving depends on the extent to which a child's instinctive need for attachment is met sympathetically, rather than treated as something to be outgrown as soon as possible. An unsympathetic response to such behaviour only increases a child's 'separation anxiety', creating an insecure sense of attachment that becomes restimulated in the bereavement situation.

Grief is thus conceptualized as a special case of separation anxiety, biologically programmed and shaped by childhood. If such childhood shaping has produced an unbearably high level of separation anxiety, this can predispose the bereaved person to 'pathological' forms of grieving. These Bowlby represented as either denial of loss or inhibited grieving, or else a prolonged attempt to recover the lost person or chronic grieving.[10] Such 'abnormal' grief was defined against that of 'normal' grief, which consisted of four phases: numbing; yearning, searching and anger; disorganization and despair; and reorganization. Grief has thus been normalized as a predictable process that runs a 'natural course', in which emotional expression is perceived as crucial to facilitating recovery. Such recovery was defined in terms of relinquishing one's attachment to the deceased in order to be able to form new attachments.

Bowlby's work on the nature of human attachment allows an appreciation of the extreme pain that may accompany bereavement. It provides insight into why some people are more emotionally resilient than others in the face of loss. His focus on early, formative environmental factors represents a movement away from the psychoanalytic emphasis on the child's fantasy world to take into consideration children's actual experience. However no account is taken of the social context in which the bereaved person lives or the nature of his or her relationship with the deceased person. Rather, his phase model approach still emphasizes the internal world of individualized grief and has served to promote a prescriptive model of the 'grief reaction'.

This changed emphasis was further developed by Parkes who built on Bowlby's attachment theory in relation to 'pathological' forms of grieving. In studies of predominantly young widows, he identified three forms of atypical grief reactions: chronic, delayed, and inhibited.[11] He constructed normal grief as a 'process and not a state' which 'involves a succession of clinical pictures which blend into and replace one another ... '[12] These pictures include numbness, pining, disorganization and despair, and 'It is only after the stage of disorganization that recovery occurs.' In professional discourse, Parkes' ideas have been used prescriptively to construct a fixed sequence through which every bereaved individual must pass in order to 'recover'. His original focus on the experiences of young widows has been lost.

The construction of grief as a private, internal condition of the individual, with healthy and pathological forms, has medicalized and professionalized bereavement. Indeed, Engel likened grief to a disease and a syndrome, thinking this would facilitate its scientific study and improve its medical management by making it easier to diagnose and treat.[13] Lindemann's 'symptomology' of grief has provided a classic description of grief reactions.[14] However, the promotion of 'expert' models and technical jargon has distanced us from an experience that is integral to life. Such distancing has disempowered ordinary people, leaving the bereaved without sufficient social support. For example, teachers have been found to lack confidence in their capacity to respond to bereaved pupils.[15] Rather, this was for the counselling professionals and incompatible with the role of 'teacher'. Where such support has been forthcoming, bereaved people have reported how this was a time-limited offer, with the expectation that they should soon be 'back to normal'.[16]

Incorporating the social

In attempting to understand why some people failed to follow the 'normal' pattern of grieving, psychologists began to recognize the significance of social factors in shaping the way people grieve. Initially these were conceptualized as 'vulnerability' or 'risk' factors and treated as 'complicating variables', such as age, gender, relationship to deceased person, type of death, response of family and friends, beliefs of the bereaved person. Yet such a reductionist approach to the social context in which people live their lives only serves to reinforce the separation of bereavement from the ordinary business of living. It fails to appreciate how these so-called 'risk' factors are integral to a person's identity or the inherently social nature of the self.

However, Parkes has since theorized grief as a 'psycho-social transition' (PST),[17] in which he acknowledges the intimate relationship between personal and social realities. Rather than focusing on the 'grief reaction', the PST model emphasizes the impact that bereavement has on our 'assumptive' world or the 'taken for granted' reality that we construct in relation to others. In this, Parkes echoes the approach of the sociologists Berger and Luckmann[18] and their emphasis on the way we construct, affirm and maintain our sense of reality and identity by engaging with others through language and social activities. We then take our socially constructed world for granted, unless something happens to call it into question, such as the loss of someone we love. This perspective appreciates the profound and painful nature of the change wrought by the loss of loved ones and helps to explain the loss of identity and sense of unreality that bereaved people may feel.

Further models have been developed, reflecting Parkes' emphasis on the need to adapt to changed reality. Some of these have tried to account for the individuality and diversity of grief and encompass social and spiritual dimensions as well as psychological and behavioural.[19] The most recent and influential of these is Stroebe and Schut's 'dual process' model (DPM),[20] which moves away from representing bereavement as a linear process of stages or phases to offer a more dynamic and flexible model that allows for individual, social and cultural differences. As such, the DPM promotes a dynamic, regulatory coping process of 'oscillation' between 'loss-orientation' and 'restoration-orientation', by which bereaved people at times 'confront' and at other times 'avoid' their loss. Some people and certain cultures may emphasize one or other of these orientations, while others oscillate between the two according to their own personal rhythm.

Though acknowledging the influence of culture, these models still prioritize individual psychology and bereaved people's personal resources in relation to the 'work' or 'tasks' that need to be accomplished to achieve resolution.[21] Parkes highlights the need for successful 'grief work' in order to make the necessary psychological adjustment and adaptation to the 'real' world in which the deceased person no longer exists. Yet this perspective does not take account of the diversity of world-views and 'alternative realities' in which death is not necessarily final for all bereaved people. Rather, grief may involve transforming one's relationship with the deceased person and incorporating him or her into one's life in a way that allows one to go on living.

The DPM similarly places more emphasis on individual psychology than social context, identifying core features that characterize 'healthy adjustment'. It implies that grief has a time scale. As a time-bound process of 'oscillation' between the demands of the living and the dead, it does not fully capture the way that for some people the deceased may become a permanent part of their day-to-day lives. For example,

Littlewood's study of a group of widows reports how these women 'were expressing the ability and desire to conduct an ongoing relationship with the person they knew to be dead'.[22] These women had no intention of 'resolving' their loss or giving up their attachment to their dead husbands. So for them, the notion of moving between facing and avoiding their loss or of moving between grief works and coping tasks does not really fit; nor does the notion of adjustment to the 'real' world without the deceased. In terms of the literature, they had adopted a position of 'chronic' grief. Yet they were not expressing any belief or hope that their husbands would return to them or 'avoiding the reality' of their deaths.

Continuing bonds

Such challenges to the conventional wisdom have replaced the relinquishing ties discourse with that of continuing bonds. This perspective sits more easily with Roman Catholic and Orthodox than Protestant traditions, as represented by the belief in the 'community of saints' where a dynamic relationship with the dead was maintained and made plausible.[23] Rather than death as finality and the task being one of internal adjustment to the 'reality of death', this new approach challenges the boundary between the living and the dead. It recognizes how people's relationships may survive death and how significant others continue to influence those they leave behind. The focus is placed on how bereaved people make sense of, and manage the changed nature of their relationship with deceased loved ones. Bereavement is thus conceptualized as an ongoing process of negotiation and meaning-making.

The concept of 'continuing bonds' was originally coined and presented as an alternative model of grief, which challenged the modernist view of relationship as 'instrumental'.[24] This includes the idea that people only have a limited amount of energy for any particular type of relationship. So, to have a new relationship, one must give up the old. Such a mechanistic view of human behaviour insists on separateness, views dependency as negative and fails to appreciate the importance of connection and intersubjectivity. Yet recent qualitative studies have revealed how new ties do not necessarily displace old. Widows may remarry while still retaining a relationship with their dead husband.[25] Adopted children may still feel and foster a connection with their biological parents alongside their relationship with their adoptive parents.[26]

The diversity of grief

Recent anthropological and sociological perspectives have drawn attention to the increasingly diverse and fragmented nature of contemporary Western societies. The use of informal interactive methods of research has allowed researchers to adopt a more inclusive focus and engaged stance that attempts to enter the social world of participants and integrate the overlapping aspects of the experience of death.[27] In contrast to traditional methods in which the researcher remains separate from the field of study, this approach is revealing the complexity and diversity of bereavement, which may incorporate dying, death, mourning, memorialization, and religious, spiritual, ethical and practical issues. It has revealed the limitations of the stage theory approach that focused on the individual grief reaction to the exclusion of the way bereavement is lived out in people's day-to-day lives.

A shift in focus from the 'symptomology' of the 'grief reaction' to the utterances of self-reflecting individuals has revealed the experience of death and bereavement as integral to life rather than a condition to be treated. This is not to minimize the extreme pain, suffering and disruption the loss of a loved one can generate. Rather, following the current trend in the field of health and illness, it is to focus on the way and the extent to which this 'becomes embodied in a particular life trajectory'.[28] Thus there can be no 'formula' for grief, since how people grieve cannot be separated from the way they live the particularity of their individual lives.

This more culturally sensitive perspective has drawn attention to the variety of ways in which bereaved people maintain relationships with dead loved ones. A psychological approach bases such relationships on an inner representation of the deceased loved one with whom the bereaved person interacts.[29] This perspective locates the experience in the mind of the bereaved person and implies that it is 'imaginary' rather than 'real'.[30] However, by adopting a sociological perspective that emphasizes the way people construct and make sense of the world in which they live, then it is no longer a question of what is 'real', but how people act in relation to what they take to be 'real' and meaningful for them.

This approach has revealed how the dead may retain a social presence and significance in the lives of the living and how this may be experienced as sensory and material.[31] Thus the dead have been found to live on in a social as well as 'inner' sense, in terms of exercising agency in the lives of the living.[32] Studies of elderly widows reveal the way husbands may continue to have agency in their wives' lives, providing companionship, support, advice, direction and meaning. Such agency and presence may be experienced not just in the mind but via the senses, such as hearing the sound of a dead husband's footsteps.[33]

Sociological studies have drawn attention to the role of 'memory-making' in creating a space for deceased loved ones that is comfortable to live with. Walter[34] has highlighted the value of engaging with others to construct a biographical narrative in order to locate the dead in the life of the living and restore a sense of meaning and continuity. Francis *et al*. have focused on memorialization and visits to the cemetery as one of the key sites within which an ongoing relationship with the dead may occur.[35] Hockey and Kellaher have explored how continuing bonds are forged and sustained in relation to practices around cremation and the disposal of ashes.[36] In particular, the practice of removing cremated remains from crematoria has been found to offer bereaved people more scope to create highly personalized spaces for deceased loved ones.

Such a perspective represents a profound shift away from the modernist search for universal laws to postmodern celebration of difference. It has produced an increased focus on the personal and the individual, as well as the broader cultural and social dimension of experience. This focus has revealed the extent to which people are forging 'continuing bonds' with dead loved ones. In a culturally diverse society, it has revealed the extent to which bereaved people may pick and mix images and ritual forms to fashion their own personalized memory-making activities and spaces that reflect the unique character of deceased loved ones and their relationship with them.[37]

Implications for supporting bereaved people

This chapter has drawn attention to a growing mistrust of expert models and how the notion of a grief process that must run its natural course does not capture people's lived experience. Rather, bereaved people have reported that, because grief is so individual, the extent to which others could really understand was limited.[38] However, they have also conveyed how isolating, disorientating and overwhelming grief can feel. Thus, being able to share one's thoughts and feelings with another can help to 'piece' things together again.[39] As indicated, conversational remembering has been found to facilitate the construction of a memory of the deceased with which the survivors can comfortably live.[40]

In trying to make sense of their experience, bereaved people have been found to appreciate an approach that was empathic and non-judgemental, and acknowledged the individual nature of grief.[41] Such a stance places those in a supporting role in a far more complex and emotionally demanding position than that of being able to offer a route map. It means being an 'explorer' and 'companion' rather than an 'expert',[42] and listening carefully and respectfully, without imposing one's own values and assumptions.[43] As conveyed by Dent,[44] it means accepting the limits of the help that one can offer rather than attempting to find solutions. What one *can* provide is a non-judgemental, reflective space. This takes time that may not be readily available amidst the demands and pressures of contemporary living.

This is not to suggest that explanatory models are of no value. If used eclectically rather than prescriptively they can provide useful insight into adjustment to loss. However, models over-simplify, giving the impression of order where none may exist. They can therefore be no substitute for engaging with the bereaved individual's personal struggle to make sense of his or her loss. Indeed it has been argued that imposing a model of grief may discourage bereaved people's attempts to find meaning in their experience.[45] Rather, those who support or minister to bereaved people need to strike a balance between providing explanations where appropriate, while respecting and affirming the bereaved person's own style of grieving and methods of coping.[46]

Notes

1 M. Stroebe, W. Stroebe and R. O. Hansson (eds), *Handbook of Bereavement.: Theory, Research and Intervention*, Cambridge: Cambridge University Press, 1993; J. Hockey, 'The View from the West: Reading the Anthropology of Non-western Death Ritual' in G. Howarth and P. C. Jupp (eds), *Contemporary Issues in the Sociology of Dying, Death and Disposal*, Basingstoke: Macmillan, 1996, pp. 3–16; C. Valentine, 'Academic Constructions of Bereavement', *Mortality*, Vol. 11, No. 1, 2006, pp. 57–78.

2 T. Walter, *The Eclipse of Eternity: A Sociology of the Afterlife*, Basingstoke: Macmillan, 1996.

3 N. Small and J. Hockey, 'Discourse into Practice: The Production of Bereavement Care' in J. Hockey, J. Katz and N. Small (eds), *Grief, Mourning and Death Ritual*, Buckingham and Philadelphia: Open University Press, 2001, pp. 97–124.

4 E. Lindemann, 'Symptomology and Management of Acute Grief', *American Journal of Psychiatry*, Vol. 101, 1944, pp. 141–8; C. M. Parkes, *Bereavement*, 1st edn, New York: International Universities Press, 1972; I. Glick, C. M. Parkes and

R. S. Weiss, *The First Year of Bereavement*, New York: Wiley, 1974; C. M. Parkes and R. S. Weiss, *Recovery from Bereavement*, New York: Basic Books, 1983; W. Stroebe and M. Stroebe, *Bereavement and Health: The Psychology and Physical Consequences of Partner Loss*, Cambridge: Cambridge University Press, 1987.

5 E. Kübler- Ross, *On Death and Dying*, London: Tavistock, 1970.

6 N. Samarel, 'The Dying Process' in H. Wass and R. A. Neimeyer (eds), *Dying: Facing the Facts*, 3rd edn, Washington DC: Taylor and Francis, 1995.

7 K. Charmaz, *The Social Reality of Death*, London: Addison-Wesley Publishing Company, 1980.

8 P. Marris, *Widows and Their Families*, London: Routledge and Kegan Paul, 1958; P. Marris, *Loss and Change*, London: Routledge and Kegan Paul, 1986; G. Gorer, *Death, Grief and Mourning in Contemporary Britain*, London: Cresset Press, 1965.

9 M. Stroebe, 'Paving the Way: From Early Attachment Theory to Contemporary Bereavement Research', *Mortality*, Vol. 7, No. 2, 2002, pp. 127–38.

10 J. Bowlby, *Loss, Sadness and Depression: Attachment and Loss, Vol. 3*, New York: Basic Books, 1980.

11 Glick, Parkes and Weiss, *The First Year of Bereavement*; Parkes and Weiss, *Recovery from Bereavement*.

12 C. M. Parkes, *Bereavement: Studies of Grief in Adult Life*, 2nd edn, Harmondsworth: Penguin, 1986, p. 27.

13 G. I. Engel, 'Is Grief a Disease?', *Psychosomatic Medicine*, Vol. 23, No. 1, 1961, pp. 18–22.

14 Lindemann, 'Symptomology and Management of Acute Grief'.

15 J. Katz, 'Supporting Bereaved Children at School' in Hockey, Katz and Small (eds), *Grief, Mourning and Death Ritual*, pp. 144–58.

16 G. Riches and P. Dawson, *An Intimate Loneliness: Supporting Bereaved Parents and Siblings*, Buckingham: Open University Press, 2000.

17 C. M. Parkes, 'Bereavement as a Psycho-social Transition: Processes of Adaptation to Change' in D. Dickenson and M. Johnson (eds), *Death, Dying and Bereavement*, London: Sage, 1993, pp. 241–7.

18 P. L. Berger and T. Luckmann, *The Social Construction of Reality*, London: Allen Lane, 1967.

19 For example, S. S. Rubin, 'The Death of a Child Is For Ever: The Life Course Impact of Child Loss' in M. Stroebe, W. Stroebe and R. O. Hansson (eds), *Handbook of Bereavement: Theory, Research and Intervention*, Cambridge: Cambridge University Press, 1993, pp. 285–99; and T. A. Rando, *Treatment of Complicated Mourning*, Champaign: Research Press, 1993.

20 M. Stroebe and H. Schut, 'The Dual Process Model of Coping with Bereavement: Rationale and Description', *Journal of Death Studies*, Vol. 23, 1999, pp. 197–224; M. Stroebe and H. Schut, 'Models of Coping with Bereavement: A Review' in M. Stroebe, R. O. Hansson, W. Stroebe and H. Schut (eds), *Handbook of Bereavement Research*, Washington DC: American Psychological Association, 2001, pp. 375–403.

21 J. W. Worden, *Grief Counselling and Grief Therapy*, 2nd edn, London: Routledge/New York: Springer, 1991.

22 J. Littlewood, 'Just an Old-fashioned Love Song or a Harlequin Romance?

Some Experiences of Widowhood' in Hockey, Katz and Small (eds), *Grief, Mourning and Death Ritual*, pp. 82–93, p. 85.

23 See McGinnell and Nankivell, this volume.

24 D. Klass, P. R. Silverman and S. L. Nickman (eds), *Continuing Bonds: New Understandings of Grief*, London and Philadelphia: Taylor and Francis, 1996.

25 M. S. Moss and S. Z. Moss, 'Remarriage of Widowed Persons: A Triadic Relationship', in D. Klass et al., *Continuing Bonds*, pp. 163–78.

26 S. L. Nickman, 'Retroactive Loss in Adopted Persons' in Klass, Silverman and Nickman (eds), *Continuing Bonds*, pp. 257–72; S. Miller-Havens, 'Grief and the Birth Origin Fantasies of Adopted Women' in D. Klass, Silverman and Nickman (eds), *Continuing Bonds*, pp. 273–92.

27 M. Bradbury, *Representations of Death*, London and New York: Routledge, 1999; E. Hallam, J. Hockey and G. Howarth, *Beyond the Body: Death and Social Identity*, London and New York: Routledge, 1999; E. Hallam and J. Hockey, *Death, Memory and Material Culture*, Oxford: Berg, 2001.

28 A. Kleinman, *The Illness Narratives*, New York: Basic Books Inc., 1985, p. 31

29 S. J. Marwit and D. Klass, 'Grief and the Role of the Inner Representation of the Deceased' in Klass, Silverman and Nickman (eds), *Continuing Bonds*, pp. 297–309.

30 G. Howarth, *Death and Dying: A Sociological Introduction*, Cambridge: Polity Press, 2007.

31 Hallam, Hockey and Howarth, *Beyond the Body*; G. Bennett and K. Bennett, 'The Presence of the Dead: An Empirical Study', *Mortality*, Vol. 5, No. 2, July 2000, pp. 139–57.

32 Hallam, Hockey and Howarth, *Beyond the Body*, p. 155.

33 Hallam, Hockey and Howarth, *Beyond the Body*, p. 158.

34 T. Walter, 'A New Theory of Grief: Bereavement and Biography', *Mortality*, Vol. 1, No. 1, pp. 7–26.

35 D. Francis, L. Kellaher and G. Neophytou, 'The Cemetery: The Evidence of Continuing Bonds' in Hockey, Katz and Small (eds), *Grief, Mourning and Death Ritual*, pp. 226–36; D. Francis, L. Kellaher and G. Neophytou, *The Secret Cemetery*, Oxford: Berg, 2005.

36 J. Hockey and L. Kellaher, *Environments of Memory: Changing Rituals of Mourning and Their Personal and Social Implications. ESRC Report*, 2005.

37 Hallam and Hockey, *Death, Memory and Material Culture*.

38 C. Wright and A. Coyle, 'Experiences of AIDS-related Bereavement among Gay Men: Implications for Care, *Mortality*, Vol. 1, No. 3, November 1996, pp. 267–82.

39 Riches and Dawson, *An Intimate Loneliness*.

40 Walter, 'A New Theory of Grief'.

41 Wright and Coyle, 'Experiences of AIDS-related Bereavement'; G. Riches and P. Dawson, 'Communities of Feeling: The Culture of Bereaved Parents', *Mortality*, Vol. 1, No. 2, pp. 143–61; Riches and Dawson, *An Intimate Loneliness*.

42 Riches and Dawson, *An Intimate Loneliness*.

43 L. Rowling, 'Being In, Being Out, Being With: Affect and the Role of the Qualitative Researcher in Loss and Grief', *Mortality*, Vol. 4, No. 2, July 1999,

pp. 167–81; C. Valentine, 'Methodological Reflections: Attending and Tending to the Role of Researcher in the Production of Bereavement Narratives', *Qualitative Social Work*, Vol. 6, No. 2, 2007, pp. 159–76.

44 See Dent, this volume.

45 J. W. Nadeau, *Families Making Sense of Death*, London: Sage, 1998.

46 Wright and Coyle, 'Experiences of AIDS-related Bereavement'.

7

Changing Christian Beliefs about the Afterlife

PETER C. JUPP

The Jewish context

Jesus and his apostles preached first to Jewish audiences. The Jewish people had been called into being by God. Through successive covenants involving the Exodus, the monarchy, the Exile and Restoration, Jews believed that God assured his nation of a positive future which, from about the sixth century BC, also involved a Messianic figure.[1] As for individual destiny, throughout most of the Old Testament the dead lived in Sheol, a shadowy existence where former mortal status counted for nothing. The hope that the future of Israel might include a restoration of life to the faithful is echoed only in isolated texts, as in Ezekiel's vision in the valley of dry bones. There was 'no explicit reference to the hereafter in the Hebrew Bible'.[2] Judaism only began to extend and develop earlier scriptural themes about life after death in the intertestamental period.

The rabbis sought to develop a doctrine of rewards and punishments but were hampered because of the paucity of scriptural authority for beliefs in bodily resurrection. On this ground the Sadducees rejected resurrection, a situation Paul exploited at his trial in Acts 23. The Maccabaean war experience, however, accelerated the plausibility of the concept of resurrection: 2 Maccabees 6 and 7 speak of resurrection as a reward for the faithful martyrs. By contrast, 4 Maccabees and the Wisdom of Solomon speak of life after death in terms of the immortality of the soul.

Meanwhile, the successive Greek and Roman conquests of the Mediterranean world had introduced concepts of the immortality of the soul to Jewish thought. Into these already conflicting eschatologies involving resurrection, immortality, Messianism and judgement were born Christ and the Christian Church. 'The resurrection of Christ meant that the resurrection of the body became a cardinal affirmation of the Christian faith, and thus eschatology of the immortality of the soul could never entirely dispense with the resurrection at the Last Day.'[3] For Rowell, no coherent eschatology can be derived from the New Testament. As the Church down the ages has sought to articulate its doctrines of life after death in Christ, the relationship of the two eschatologies has proved contentious.[4]

The centrality of Jesus' death and resurrection

The passion, death and resurrection of Jesus Christ are central to the Gospels, to the Church and to Christian ministry. Within the first century, St Paul's conversion by his encounter with the risen Jesus on the road to Damascus proved critical for the spread of Christianity. His letters assess the significance of Christ's death and resurrection in a series of metaphors. Jesus' death and resurrection are variously interpreted as a ransom, a sacrifice, a reconciliation or a victory over the powers of evil and death. They guarantee life after death for all those 'in Christ', his resurrection being the firstfruits of a whole harvest of the dead. Among non-Pauline authors, Hebrews describes Jesus as 'the pioneer of their salvation made perfect through suffering' (Hebrews 2.10).

The New Testament writings illustrate the tension between resurrection and immortality. The Christian dead, especially martyrs, share immediately in the life of heaven (Revelation 7); the dead sleep until the sound of the last trumpet brings the general resurrection (1 Corinthians 15.51–5);[5] eternal life is a present reality for Christians (John 17.3); Christ visited and preached to the dead;[6] death is followed by two judgements, one immediately after death and the second at the end of time (Revelation 20). In successive ages, different Churches and sects have privileged different alternatives, depending upon their understanding of scripture or of the needs of the world.

Until quite recently, Christians have buried their dead – partly because of Jesus' own burial and partly because of their Jewish inheritance. Their seriousness about funeral rites[7] sprang from their conviction that Christ's death and resurrection had supreme consequences for the individual, a hope of life free from guilt and from the fear of death and regularly sustained by the sacraments of baptism and Eucharist, in which the benefits of Christ's death and resurrection were both symbolized and imparted. Christians regarded neither the corpse nor the grave as polluting, because Christ had conquered death and he would raise the dead. The Emperor Julian the Apostate (AD 360–2) cited the Christian treatment of their dead as one of the reasons for their conversion of the Roman Empire.[8]

The first centuries

As Christianity spread around the Mediterranean, its funeral rituals also incorporated local and pagan customs. Four are of particular interest. The Eucharist became Christianity's equivalent of the *viaticum*,[9] the coin placed in the mouths of corpses to pay the ferryman for guiding their souls safely across the River Styx. The practice of giving the Eucharist to the dying was long established by AD 325.[10] Second, while Christians frowned on the frequently drunken pagan feasts celebrated at gravesides, and wary of their implications concerning the state of the departed, Christians began to bring *refrigerium* (refreshment) to the martyrs' tombs as annual memorials;[11] wake traditions and Church discipline have often been at odds.[12] Third, Christians adopted Roman commemoration days, and the Western Church later adopted the month's mind and year's mind, ritual relationships forbidden by the Protestant Reformation. Fourth, the Church also sought to replace the pagan *vestes sordidae* with white clothes. Cyprian protested that Christian mourners should not wear black while their dead already wore white in heaven.[13]

Though the Church lost this last battle, Christian attitudes to the dead in the earlier Christian centuries were frequently characterized by joy and hope, with singing at funerals known from the third century.[14] 'Honour for the dead', said St Chrysostom, 'does not consist in lamentations and moanings, but in singing hymns and psalms and living a noble life', for the departed goes on his way in the company of the angels, even if no one is present at his funeral.[15] Appropriate ritual, clothing and music at funerals perplex Christians today who seek to ensure that their funeral behaviour symbolizes their resurrection faith as well as respects local and family traditions.

For St Augustine, burial was symbolic and practical, but it was not obligatory; for the afterlife depended on God's activity rather than human modes of disposal. About humiliations inflicted publicly on the bodies of martyrs, he wrote, in words that have inspired many funeral reformers:

So many Christian bodies have not received a covering of earth, and yet . . . the whole universe is filled with the presence of him who knows from where he is to raise up what he has created . . . Such things as a decent funeral and a proper burial, with its procession of mourners, are a consolation to the living rather than a help to the departed.[16]

Nevertheless, burial symbolized the hope of resurrection.[17] Bynum has analysed Christian debates about the resurrection of the body.[18] The Patristic writings reflect successive discussions with anxious believers who fretted about the resurrection and about the intermediate state.[19] For St Paul, the dominant metaphor for bodily resurrection was the seed. Being sown as a natural body and raised as a spiritual body carries ideas both of continuity and change.[20] Successive Fathers advanced other metaphors to illustrate how, by God's power, personal identity and physical characteristics could survive death. Augustine, perhaps influenced by the cult of relics,[21] preferred the metaphor of the broken and reassembled statue. His texts fundamentally shaped the medieval discussion.[22]

The development of concepts of heaven and hell, dominant from the first Christian centuries, are summarized by Badham, below.[23] Purgation as a process developed over several centuries.[24] Le Goff dated the final elaboration of Purgatory as a place when he realized that, from c. 1170, narratives of all saints, whatever their holiness, included their visit to Purgatory *en route* to heaven. Le Goff attributed this shift to the rise of cities in the medieval period; the 'threat' of Purgatory strengthened the Churches' influence over human morality behaviour in the changing social context. Bremmer, by contrast, attributes the shift to the Cathar movement which taught that only their sacrament for the dying could guarantee the faithful instant salvation without the fear of hell.[25]

Concern for the welfare of the dead was a major focus for medieval piety. This was shown in deathbed and graveside rituals, in chantry prayers,[26] in obituary lists and Masses for the dead, in month's minds and year's minds, in relics and tomb sculpture, indulgencies and pilgrimages and the observance of All Souls' Day. This concern was paralleled by a heightened medieval emphasis on judgement, which began to supplant earlier themes of hope and joy at funerals, a mood reflected in the thirteenth-century *Dies Irae*. One origin of this change was monastic life, where offices for the dying and the dead were emphasized and extended.

The Protestant Reformation

The Reformation brought sharp changes in attitudes and practices around death. Luther's *A Recantation of Purgatory* (1530) asserted that Purgatory had a financial, not a scriptural basis; as a gift from God to the faithful, salvation could neither be bought nor earned. Henry VIII's rejection of papal authority gave English Reformers their head: prayer for the dead was forbidden and chantries closed. The 1552 Prayer Book omitted all prayer for the dead; there was no commendation of the soul, only the committal of the body. In Scotland, Knox sought to remove from funerals any opportunity to pray for the dead, stripping burial ritual to a minimum in his attempt to outlaw Catholic superstition and idolatry.[27] Yet, in outlawing devotion to saints and relics and prayers for the dead, the Reformers denied the common people a part in death. For Duffy, medieval funerals has been intensely concerned with the notion of community. 'The means of transaction between the living and the dead was charity, maintained and expressed by prayer. The dead . . . remained part of the communities they had once lived in.'[28] Now, 'each generation could be indifferent to the spiritual fate of its predecessor'.[29]

With Purgatory abolished, heaven and hell were placed in sharper opposition. Protestant orthodoxy increasingly emphasized the day of death as the decisive determining point of salvation. This is exemplified in Protestant versions of the *ars moriendi*,[30] two contrasting models of which developed in the seventeenth century. In Puritan tradition, the individual's faith was the greatest support in the face of death. As Richard Baxter wrote, 'Let those that are about you see that you take the life to come as a reality, and that you verily expect to live with Christ in joys for ever.'[31] Such convictions empowered families to articulate deathbed hopes. The second model was the Anglican sacramental tradition, encouraging confession, absolution and final Communion. Jeremy Taylor's *Holy Dying* (1651) was its finest exponent.[32]

Under Protestantism, funerals, forbidden to benefit the dead, shifted more attention to survivors;[33] and funerals were increasingly used to signal the social status of mourners, a practice which spread down the social scale. The Reformation had also brought about the decline of charnel-houses, where old bones had been piled. As long as local populations had remained stable, churchyard space could be continually re-used; but now rising populations and urban development brought overcrowding, especially with the growing popularity of gravestones, from the sixteenth century.[34] On one hand, burial grounds began to acquire a moralizing function, illustrated in the poetic cult of the grave.[35] On another, burial conditions for the urban poor increasingly gave rise to scandals which, with the rise of concern for public health, led eventually to the closure of churchyards in cities and a lesser role for the Church in the disposal of the dead.[36]

Protestant emphases on individual preparation for death came increasingly to stress the concept of immortality of the soul alongside bodily resurrection. From the late seventeenth century, moral discipline was increasingly enforced by the immortality of the soul as much as by the Last Judgement.[37] While the Established Church exercised a controlling interest over morality, Enlightenment thinkers grappled with the doctrine of hell, as an affront to a God of love.[38] Within Enlightenment debates about Christian doctrines of salvation and of judgement, 'natural religion' still allowed for a belief in the immortality of the soul. The Evangelical revival brought other concepts of the afterlife; these challenged older Calvinist convictions that post-mortem prospects for the dead could not be predicted. Evangelical certainties about salvation by faith not only encouraged global mission but also opened up wider views of access to life beyond death, including the reassembling of family groups in heaven. Stories of deathbed piety were one of many tools for conversion.[39]

The nineteenth century

The nineteenth century saw increasing fragmentation both in beliefs about life after death and in arrangements for disposal. From 1660, and despite folk-beliefs about death and the afterlife,[40] Anglican theology and liturgy provided the medium for articulating post-mortem hopes at funerals. Methodists and Catholics were mostly buried in parish churchyards. Anglicans controlled the rite, site, mode and presidency of burial. There were exceptions: Baptists and Quakers, holding scruples about sacraments, provided their own burial grounds. Especially given the high infant mortality statistics, the vast majority of the dead children were given Anglican burial.

The Industrial Revolution was accompanied by a major growth in cities and the growth and prosperity of the middle class. With the inclusion of Ireland within the UK in 1801, Catholics became one-quarter of the UK population. In 1828, Parliament removed many civil disabilities from Nonconformists and in 1829 from Catholics. Both groups sought more burial grounds of their own, to express their denominational identity and theology. From 1820, Nonconformists had begun to form their own private cemetery companies.[41] The Established Church was alerted to the need to reform funerals both by individual reformers and the Church of England Burial Reform Association and the Ecclesiological Society.[42] Yet it was increasingly unable to extend its burial land within cities, and there were scandalous accounts of how extra space was achieved, with public concern exacerbated by body-snatching scandals.[43] The rise of the public health movement, stimulated by cholera epidemics, drew attention to the squalor of urban burial grounds.

Under such pressures, Parliament passed a series of Interment Acts in the 1850s. It closed all burial grounds in towns, both denominational and commercial. It established cemeteries, funded and maintained by local government: the greatest change in the British disposal of the dead for 1,000 years.[44] In Rugg's phrase, cemeteries were 'the industrial mode of disposal'.[45] The new cemeteries were spacious and inter-denominational, owned and managed by secular authorities with no remit for religious interpretations of death or of post-mortem destinies. They broke the traditional link between the physical communities of the living and the dead, the latter now being buried in larger and more distant cemeteries. Anglican influence was further diminished when, in 1880, Parliament extended the rights of Nonconformists and of non-believers within Anglican churchyards.[46]

Christian attitudes were affected in other ways. From 1870 there began a fall in the death rate: public health reforms, better diet and living standards were largely responsible. Between 1850 and 1911, longevity rose from about 40 years to 52 for men and 55 for women. Thus death began to become an event of old age rather than of infancy, and people's preoccupation with the prospect of death began to recede. Meanwhile, the 'Victorian crisis of faith' characterized the second half of the nineteenth century. The intellectual challenges to revealed religion from biblical criticism, geology and theories of evolution undermined old certainties. Jalland noted that faith was more likely to triumph at the deathbed of a loved one in the 1850s than 20 or 30 years later.[47]

Christian beliefs about heaven and hell have always been subject to development.[48] Rowell has charted the process in which the doctrine of eternal punishment posed an increasing dilemma for Victorians. In 1853 F. D. Maurice was deprived of his university professorship for such convictions as 'the real hell was the absence of God from the human soul'.[49] For F. W. Farrer, author of *Eternal Hope* (1878), the 'virtue which has no better basis than fear of hell is no virtue at all'. The higher criticism weakened Protestants' reliance on scriptural foundations for hell[50] and the Baptist Charles Spurgeon warned against this 'downgrade'. A range of alternative views on life after death emerged. Some revived the doctrine of Christ's *Descensus*. Anglo-Catholics offered prayers for the dead. Others promoted social and civic gospels, with social reform as a mark of the kingdom. For Wheeler, such views, academic or popular, reflected a longing for different *kinds* of continuity between this world and the next.[51] This was further developed by the rise of Spiritualism which came from the United States at mid-century[52] and rapidly proved popular with its mediums and séances. The emergent secularist movement immediately realized how Spiritualism, in taking for granted the immortality of the soul, could undermine traditional Christian beliefs both in Jesus' resurrection and in our own.[53] From 1882, the Psychical Research Society,[54] with its elite leadership and scientific research, helped keep the subject under the spotlight until the inter-war period.[55] All this served to weaken credibility in the resurrection of the body.

Traditional beliefs in the resurrection of the body were also challenged by cremation.[56] In 1874, the Cremation Society was founded to promote an alternative to burial. Bishop Fraser of Manchester, like Lord Shaftesbury, recognized that, come resurrection morning, neither dust nor ashes could constrain Almighty God. Few believed that cremation, whatever its economic and hygienic advantages, would be widely adopted. Then in 1884 the trial of Dr Price produced a judicial decision that cremation was not illegal provided no public nuisance was caused.[57] The Churches were thus faced with a fait accompli. Local authorities, having discovered the real cost of the burial responsibilities they had inherited from the Churches in the 1850s, began to turn to cremation. The Cremation Act 1902 set cremation on proper legal and regulated footings, but the dominance of the burial tradition was undergirded by religious, class and economic factors.[58] All were upturned by the Great War.

The twentieth century and beyond

World War One proved an assault on many Christian values and certainties;[59] it changed many attitudes and practices about death. Over 700,000 British soldiers died. The armies of war widows, parents and orphans at home suffered bereavement on a mass scale. Those whose Christian faith had been forged in Sunday School or adult church found their faith severely tested; forms of fatalism and superstition proved ready coping mechanisms. Soldiers' experiences of death and dead bodies challenged traditional beliefs about resurrection. Traditional doctrines of hell and of judgement were among the theological casualties, with clergy seeking to comfort the bereaved with the assurance that those who had died in a good cause had gone straight to heaven. Old Protestant scruples about praying for the dead recognized the worth of what Anglo-Catholics had revived. Spiritualist practices blossomed. By 1918, many people had lost their faith in the traditional concepts of the afterlife.[60]

Immortality now rivalled resurrection. This was confirmed by two heresy trials, within the Church of England about Principal H. D. A. Major, and among Methodists about Leslie Weatherhead. Each denied the resurrection of the body in the traditional sense. When the dust of the controversies settled, their opinions turned out to have become acceptable to many, many people. Second, Spiritualism remained popular: its attraction for a number of leading Anglicans prompted an enquiry by Archbishop Lang. The findings were controversial and publication was delayed.[61] Third, the move from resurrection was accelerated by the development of cremation, a mode of disposal implicitly suggesting that the physical body had no post-mortem future but that the soul survived. Cremation propaganda reinforced this assumption. During the interwar years, local authorities increasingly promoted cremation, a policy that bore fullest fruit after 1945. The 1942–44 Convocation debates saw Anglican bishops favouring cremation more than parish clergy. The former saw cremation as an alternative to burial, the latter preferred to see cremation as a preparation for burial (of the ashes) in consecrated ground. Wartime Convocation debates that had begun with authorizing prayers for cremation services produced a conclusion which announced that 'cremation has no theological significance'.[62]

The Beveridge Report of 1942 articulated the nation's hopes for a welfare state 'from cradle to grave'. With National Insurance in 1946 and National Health Service in 1947 the government's welfare state programme, together with better diet, work, housing and education, accelerated an increasingly healthy society in which longevity was extended, infant mortality decreased and maternal mortality almost extinguished. Infectious diseases were replaced as the primary cause of death, by non-communicable, long-term conditions like heart disease and cancer. Death was increasingly postponed to an older age. As the location of death moved out of the home and into hospitals and other institutions, families grew increasingly unfamiliar with death and with traditional coping strategies.[63] With increasing social and geographical mobility, and increasing secularization, the British preference for cremation had reached 70 per cent by 2006.[64] Meanwhile, fears about dying and resources of bereavement support have been confronted, the former by Dame Cicely Saunders's hospice movement and the latter by the growth of bereavement support groups.

While the correlations are complex,[65] the dominance of cremation in a society which has largely lost its traditional belief in the body's resurrection has privileged the concept of the soul's immortality. Discussing the symbolism of disposal, Davies has written: 'The traditional burial service focuses on the body and its resurrection future . . . The only hope that many can read into the cremation service is the hope of a surviving soul.'[66]

The decline of the Churches' influence has itself contributed to the free-for-all in religious practice and belief. Post-1945 immigration has brought large communities of Hindus, Sikhs and Muslims for whose funeral rituals local authorities have had to make provision. When all religious perspectives are considered valid at law, none can claim uniqueness. The rival claims of the different major faiths are now set alongside a range of beliefs which traditional Christians would have found heterodox, including reincarnation, New Age and spiritualist beliefs. Many of these belief groups privilege sentiments about the inextinguishableness of the human spirit above the immortality of the soul, and look to the renewing of the earth rather than the resurrection of human bodies laid in it. 'Green burial' focuses not on resurrection but on the salvation of the environment. New forms of assertive secularism have offered new rituals for funerals based upon a rejection of religious belief.[67] The growth of conviction that there is no life beyond death has been charted in successive social surveys, like Mass Observations' *Puzzled People* (1947), Gallup's *Television and Religion* (1964) and *Re-using Old Graves* (1995).[68]

In 1976, the Presbyterian John Hick asserted that in the face of the cultural rejection of traditional Christian afterlife beliefs, Christian theology since 1945 had presented a spectrum of disarray. Theologians had made no serious attempt to spell out the content of eschatology in face of the challenge of contemporary secular thought.[69] John Polkinghorne is one of a number of theologians who have now turned their attention to eschatology. Polkinghorne perceives, first, a growing distrust of science and, second, that, despite the Churches' decline, our multicultural society is characterized by a persistence of religion, including a fascination with spirituality. Third, he observed a concern about eschatology arising from the millennium, heightened by the rise of global terrorism that surged with 9/11. To mark the millennium, an interdisciplinary group of scholars met 'to consider, in the light of modern knowledge, the expression of Christian eschatological hope concerning the end of the world and concerning the fulfilment of the divine purpose for creation'.[70] These are by no means the only theologians, conservative or liberal, now reflecting on eschatology. Their work can better empower Christians to articulate our account of the faith that is in us. It will help us explore concepts of resurrection and of spirituality, broaden our approach to both the subject and the reality of death, and enable Christians to understand better the questions and doubts people express. The better that ordinary Christians can articulate the gospel about the death and resurrection of Jesus and contribute to contemporary debates on death and bereavement, the more that those to whom we testify will gain in confidence about life in Christ beyond death.

Notes

1 J. Bowker, *The Religious Imagination and the Sense of God*, Oxford: Oxford University Press, 1978, ch.i.5.

2 D. Cohn-Sherbok, *Judaism: History, Belief and Practice*, London: Routledge, 2003, p. 456.

3 D. G. Rowell, *Hell and the Victorians: A Study of the Nineteenth Century Controversies concerning Eternal Punishment and the Future Life*, Oxford: Clarendon Press, 1974, p. 24.

4 For systematic discussions of the development of these doctrines, see Rowell, *Hell and the Victorians*.

5 In the post-Reformation period, the concept of 'Christian mortalism' was proffered, whereby the soul either slept until the Day of Judgement or was annihilated and then recreated; see N. T. Burns, *Christian Mortalism from Tyndale to Milton*, Cambridge, MA: Harvard University Press, 1972.

6 1 Peter 3.18ff . That 'he went and made a proclamation to the spirits in prison' (1 Peter 3.19) refers to Christ's descent to the dead (as in the Apostles' Creed) is vigorously disputed by scholars. B. Reicke, *The Disobedient Spirits and Christian Baptism: A Study of 1 Pet. III. 19 and Its Context*, Copenhagen: Ejnar Munksgaard, 1946, is the best guide to the debate.

7 D. G. Rowell, *The Liturgy of Christian Burial*, London: Alcuin Club/SPCK, 1977.

8 Rowell, *The Liturgy of Christian Burial*, p. 18.

9 See G. Grabka, 'Christian Viaticum: A Study of Its Cultural Background', *Traditio*, No. IX, 1953, pp. 1–43.

10 See the eighth Canon of the Council of Nicaea, Rowell, *The Liturgy of Christian Burial*, p. 14.

11 Bishop Ambrose forbade this custom in Milan; St Augustine's mother Monica was among those who obeyed. St Augustine, *Confessions*, vi.2.

12 See, for example, R. Grainger, 'Let Death Be Death: Lessons from the Irish Wake', *Mortality*, Vol. 3, No. 2, July 1998, pp. 129–41.

13 Cyprian, *De mortalitate* xx (CSEL. iii.309), cited by Rowell, *The Liturgy of Christian Burial*, p. 23.

14 Rowell, *The Liturgy of Christian Burial*, p. 22.

15 St Chrysostom, *Homily on John*, lxii (on John 11.1–29), cited by Rowell, *The Liturgy of Christian Burial*, p. 22.

16 St Augustine, *The City of God*, Book I, ch. 12 (trans. H. Bettenson), Harmondsworth: Penguin, 1984, p. 21. The rest of the chapter offers resources for contemporary Christian answers to questions by those concerned about unburied body parts.

17 For a contemporary discussion of resurrection versus immortality, see Davies, this volume.

18 C. W. Bynum, *The Resurrection of the Body in Western Christianity, 200–1336*, New York: Columbia Press, 1995. For recent brief discussions, see A. E. McGrath, *A Brief History of Heaven*, Oxford: Blackwell, 2003, pp. 33–8; and P. C. Jupp, 'Resurrection and Christian Thought' in D. J. Davies with L. H. Mates, *Encyclopaedia of Cremation*, Aldershot: Ashgate, 2005, pp. 353–8.

19 Bynum, *Resurrection*, p. 61; see also Rowell, this volume, endnote 12.

20 For a discussion of the factors which led following generations to interpret the resurrection of the body as that of the flesh, see J. G. Davies, 'Factors Leading to the Emergence of Belief in the Resurrection of the Flesh', *Journal of Theological Studies*, Vol. 23, New Series, 1972, pp. 448–55.

21 P. Brown, *The Cult of the Saints: Its Rise and Function in Latin Christianity*, London: SCM Press, 1981. For devotion to relics in the Middle Ages, see R. Finucane, *Miracles and Pilgrims*, Basingstoke: Macmillan, 1977.

22 Bynum, *Resurrection*, pp. 94–5.

23 See Badham, this volume. See also, for example, J. B. Russell, *A History of Heaven: The Singing Silence*, Princeton: Princeton University Press, 1997; C. McDannell and B. Lang, *Heaven: A History*, New Haven: Yale University Press, 1988; A. E. Bernstein, *The Formation of Hell: Death and Retribution in the Ancient and Early Christian Worlds*, London: UCL Press, 1993.

24 For the major discussion, see J. Le Goff, *The Birth of Purgatory*, London: Scholar Press, 1984. For a recent discussion, see J. Bremmer, *The Rise and Fall of the Afterlife*, London: Routledge, 2002.

25 Bremmer, *The Rise and Fall*, pp. 64–9.

26 For a recent discussion, see F. Woodman and J. Middleton-Stewart, 'Purgatory: The Beginning and the End' in B. Brooks-Gordon, F. Ebtehaj, J. Herring, M. H. Johnson and M. Richards (eds), *Death Rites and Rights*, Oxford and Portland, Oregon: Hart, 2007, pp. 117–32.

27 See Murray's comments (this volume) on *The Buke of Discipline*. The Knoxian emphasis was only challenged in the late nineteenth century.

28 E. Duffy, *The Stripping of the Altars: Traditional Religion in England 1400–1580*, New Haven and London: Yale University Press, 1992, pp. 474–5.

29 K. Thomas, *Religion and the Decline of Magic*, Harmondsworth: Penguin, 1971, p. 721.

30 For a full discussion, see Ralph Houlbrooke, *Death, Religion and the Family in England, 1480–1750*, Oxford: Oxford University Press, 1998.

31 In W. Orme (ed.), *The Practical Works of the Rev. Richard Baxter*, 23 vols (1830), IV, p. 439, cited by R. Houlbrooke, 'The Age of Decency: 1660–1760' in P. C. Jupp and C. Gittings (eds), *Death in England: An Illustrated History*, Manchester: Manchester University Press, 1999, pp. 174–201, 180.

32 See Houlbrooke, *Death, Religion and the Family in England 1480–1750*.

33 C. Gittings, *Death, Burial and the Individual in Early Modern England*, London: Croom Helm, 1984.

34 See Gittings, *Death, Burial and the Individual*. For post-Reformation changes in burial practice, see V. Harding, *The Dead and the Living in Paris and London, 1500–1670*, Cambridge: Cambridge University Press, 2002.

35 Robert Blair's 'The Grave', Edward Young's 'Night Thoughts' and Gray's 'Elegy in a Country Churchyard' are the best-known examples of this genre.

36 P. C. Jupp, *From Dust to Ashes: Cremation and the British Way of Death*, Basingstoke: Palgrave Macmillan, 2006, chapter 2. For a London burial scandal, see P. C. Jupp, 'Enon Chapel: No Way for the Dead' in P. C. Jupp and G. Howarth (eds), *The Changing Face of Death: Historical Accounts of Death and Disposal*, Basingstoke: Macmillan, 1997, pp. 90–104.

37 D. G. Rowell, 'Changing Patterns: Christian Beliefs about Death and the Afterlife' in P. C. Jupp and T. Rogers (eds), *Interpreting Death: Christian Theology and Pastoral Practice*, London: Cassell, 1997, pp. 17–29, 23.

38 See P. C. Almond, *Heaven and Hell in Enlightenment England*, Cambridge: Cambridge University Press, 1994.

39 See, for example, R. J. Bell, '"Our People Die Well": Deathbed Scenes in John Wesley's *Arminian* Magazine', *Mortality*, Vol. 10, No. 3, August 2005, pp. 210–23.

40 See, for example, V. Gammon, 'Singing and Popular Funeral Practices in the Eighteenth and Nineteenth Centuries', *Folk Music Journal*, Vol. 5, No. 4, 1988, pp. 412–47.

41 J. Rugg, 'The Origins and Progress of Cemetery Establishment in Britain' in Jupp and Howarth (eds), *The Changing Face of Death*, pp. 105–19; J. Rugg, 'Nonconformity and the Development of Early Cemeteries in England 1820–1850', *The Journal of the United Reformed Church History Society*, Vol. 6, No. 5, 1999, pp. 309–21.

42 See Jupp, *From Dust to Ashes*, chapter 2; and G. Rowell, 'Nineteenth-century Attitudes and Practices' in G. Cope, *Dying, Death and Disposal*, London: SPCK, 1970, pp. 49–50.

43 See, for example, R. Richardson, *Death, Dissection and the Destitute*, London: Routledge and Kegan Paul, 1987.

44 Jupp, *From Dust to Ashes*; C. Brooks, *Mortal Remains*, Exeter: Wheaton, 1989.

45 Dr Julie Rugg, personal communication.

46 R. Fletcher, *The Akenham Burial Case*, London: Wildwood House, 1974.

47 P. Jalland, 'Victorian Death and Its Decline' in P. C. Jupp and C. Gittings (eds), *Death in England*, pp. 230–55, 249.

48 For the Orthodox exception, see Nankivell, this volume. For a full discussion and an assessment of the social and theological conditions under which devel-

opments take place see, for example, C. McDannell and B. Lang, *Heaven: A History*, 2nd edn, New Haven: Yale, 2001; and J. B. Russell, *A History of Heaven: The Singing Silence*, Princeton: Princeton University Press, 1997.

49 Quotations cited by M. Wheeler, *Heaven, Hell and the Victorians*, abridged edn, Cambridge: Cambridge University Press, 1994, pp. 185, 188.

50 For a full discussion, see Rowell, *Hell and the Victorians*.

51 Cited by Rowell, 'Changing Patterns', p. 26.

52 G. K. Nelson, *Spiritualism and Society*, London: Routledge and Kegan Paul, 1969.

53 L. Barrow, *Independent Spirits: Spiritualism and English Plebeians 1850–1910*, London: Routledge and Kegan Paul, 1986.

54 R. Haynes, *The Society for Psychical Research 1882–1982: A History*, London: Macdonald, 1982.

55 J. Hazelgrove, *Spiritualism and British Society between the Wars*, Manchester: Manchester University Press, 2000.

56 For fuller discussions, see Jupp, *From Dust to Ashes*; and B. Parsons, *Committed to the Cleansing Flame: The Development of Cremation in Nineteenth-century England*, Reading: Spire, 2005.

57 S. R. G. White, 'A Burial Ahead of Its Time? The Crookenden Burial Case and the Sanctioning of Cremation in England and Wales', *Mortality*, Vol. 7, No. 2, July 2002, pp. 171–90. Price had attempted to burn the body of his dead son.

58 For the causes of persistence of the burial tradition, see J.-M. Strange, *Death, Grief and Poverty in Britain, 1870–1914*, Cambridge: Cambridge University Press, 2005.

59 For a fuller description of the effect of war upon beliefs, see A. Wilkinson, *The Church of England in the First World War*, London: SPCK, 1978; and 'Changing English Attitudes to Death in the Two World Wars', in Jupp and Howarth (eds), *The Changing Face of Death*, pp. 149–63.

60 Meanwhile, agnosticism was increasingly the mindset of the elite according to A. Hastings, *A History of English Christianity*, London: Fount, 1987.

61 The report was reprinted in *The Christian Parapsychologist*, Vol. 3, Nos 2–3, 1979.

62 For assessments of the Canterbury Convocation debates, see Jupp, *From Dust to Ashes*, pp. 135–41, and Lampard (this volume).

63 After 1958–9, less than half of UK deaths took place at home. By 2008, the proportion was about 20 per cent.

64 Over the last 20 years, interest in burial and in cemeteries has revived. For a full discussion about the persistence and purpose of grave visiting habits, see Kellaher (this volume) and, in particular, D. Francis, L. Kellaher and G. Nyophytou, *The Secret Cemetery*, Oxford: Berg, 2005.

65 Jupp *From Dust to Ashes*, pp. 195–6.

66 D. J. Davies, *Cremation Today and Tomorrow*, Nottingham: Grove Books, 1990, p. 33.

67 For a recent survey of the Humanist funeral movement, see J. Pearce, 'Where we are with Secular Funerals', *Pharos International*, Vol. 71, No. 3, Autumn 2005, pp. 8–10; and S. Allen, 'Rising Secularism in UK Funeral Practice', *Funeral Service Journal*, Vol. 123, No. 1, January 2008, pp. 109–14.

68 For a brief survey, see J. Hick, *Death and Eternal Life*, London: Collins,

1979; D. Davies and A. Shaw, *Re-using Old Graves*, Crayford: Shaw and Sons, 1995.

69 Hick, *Death and Eternal Life*, pp. 92–3.

70 J. Polkinghorne, *The God of Hope and the End of the World*, London: SPCK, 2002, p. xi. See further, J. Polkinghorne and M. Welker, *The End of the World and the Ends of God: Science and Theology on Eschatology*, Harrisburg: Trinity Press International, 2000.

8

Resurrection and Immortality of the Soul

DOUGLAS J. DAVIES

Introduction

Imagine an average funeral service: family, friends, neighbours, work colleagues, some grief-stricken and unaware of liturgical nicety, many attentive, a few dutifully present. As a rite of passage the funeral helps formalize the new social status of widow, widower or 'adult orphan' children, and perhaps influences the psychological state of becoming an invisible parent.[1] For many it is a rite of intensification[2] in which core beliefs are expressed for acceptance, framed by reinforcing emotions, and in which previous experiences are felt anew with memory re-inforced.

What of these beliefs? If our 1995 survey is representative of the British population,[3] just under a third see death as the end, about ten per cent do not know what to think, and just over 20 per cent say that every-thing is in God's hands: an acknowledgement of belief but devoid of detail. Since about half are unbelievers or generally doubtful, how might they respond to services expressing traditional certainties, given that ritual success depends upon an empathy with words and actions?[4] Might some prefer to employ a civil celebrant ready to implement their person-al choice of ceremony or, perhaps, are churches already responding to such changing needs, as chapters on liturgical development in this vol-ume suggest? Again, in a 'standard' congregation, just over a third prob-ably believe that a soul has passed from the deceased, with some 12 per cent reckoning we 'come back as something or someone else', and about eight per cent think that something – resurrection perhaps – may happen to the body. Just how these belief-profiles relate to cremation or burial services is a profound question for pastoral theology, church study groups, prayers and funeral addresses. A final glance at this, notional, congregation will show the significance of gender, with women believing

82

in afterlife ideas about twice as much as do men. In general, Anglicans tend to resemble general public beliefs, though, counter-intuitively, with fewer references made to resurrection. Of Catholics, by contrast, nearly a half emphasize the soul and nearly 20 per cent the resurrection, with only 14 per cent thinking death was the end. While theology, liturgy and 'truth' are not, of course, based on statistics, the Christian goals of evangelism and pastoral care cannot but be interested in such attitudes to resurrection and immortal soul belief in today's complex world.

Tradition

Whether we are simply a body, a compound of a body and soul, or of body, soul and spirit, not only influences notions of what constitutes a human being but also affects Christian belief on how death is overcome by life in the person of Jesus. While contemporary views of life have been deeply influenced by science and technology, especially knowledge of genetics, afterlife beliefs still endure and highlight the fact that human identity is not easily exhausted by available scientific models.

One Christian view agrees with genetics in emphasizing 'embodiment', affirming that we live and die as a body with no possibility of life after death unless it is created anew by God in a process of resurrection. This faith-stance assumes a miracle[5] grounded in God's power, will and 'memory',[6] with God's knowledge of us enabling us to be made again 'from nothing' and still be ourselves – whether over a few days, as with Jesus, or over millennia makes no difference. Christian scientists like John Polkinghorne have used such science-engendered models of memory-bank 'resurrection' to reflect upon how God might recreate new worlds beyond those presently anticipated.[7] A second view of human identity assumes some combination of body and soul or body, soul and spirit. This widespread spirit or life-force theory raises two potential afterlife scenarios. In one the soul departs the body, causing its death, to follow its destiny as a living soul. In the other the soul leaves the body at death, only to be reunited with it in the future act of resurrection. The soul will have had its own experiences during its separation; some speak of its 'sleep', its purification or even of its occupying a 'material' base provided by God to maintain its integrity and identity prior to resurrection: resurrection-reunion yielding a transformed unity of transformed parts. Gregory of Nyssa, for example, thought that the soul kept a kind of note of where decayed body particles had gone so that God could reunite them in the resurrection.[8]

The destiny of Christians has been debated from earliest Christian times,[9] often in terms related to interpretations of Jesus and his human and divine natures. Was he a body only or a body and soul, or even a body, soul and spirit? Did he 'exist' between his crucifixion-death and his resurrection? The text indicating that he was 'put to death in the flesh but made alive in the spirit in which he went and preached to the spirits in prison'[10] itself fostered much debate in Reformation England[11] and still poses questions, as in Sheppy and Nankivell's chapters in this book and in Wright's interpretation that has sought to avoid any soul–body distinction. Wright argues for what he calls the 'transphysical' body of the risen Jesus, one that was the same and yet different from his earthly body.[12] Whatever the eternal engineering of selves, traditional Christian theology bases future existence in the divine will, in God's powerful creativity motivated by love, mercy, forgiveness, and by a kind of commitment to or covenant with humanity, as displayed in Christ's resurrection.

Immortal rights

This divine causation is made problematic if people argue that since they have or are an immortal soul[13] they have a right to eternal life, something made more plausible by the rise of Spiritualism over the last century and a half.[14] It is precisely this 'natural rights' argument that some oppose because of their commitment to the idea of humanity as fallen or sinful and to the corresponding belief in God's grace in conferring a future existence as a gift of love. So, for example, with William Temple: 'Man is not immortal by nature or of right: but he is capable of immortality and there is offered to him resurrection from the dead and eternal life if he will receive it from God and on God's terms.'[15]

In ancient Judaism, the process of dying could be allied with the pains of death, with the soul lingering around the body prior to its departure. Subsequent bodily decay allowed the ultimately clean bones to be gathered to their ancestors, often placed in ossuaries.[16] Resurrection ideas emerged in Israel for a variety of reasons, including God's vindication of the martyred dead, and framed early Christian belief in Jesus' resurrection. His death and resurrection underlay subsequent Christian rites of baptism and Eucharist.

We must stress, however, that while the history of these ideas absorbs the minds of theologians, ordinary believers are affected more by local culture and by their own life and religious experiences rooted in worship and prayer. When believers ponder biblical accounts of Christ's death, resurrection and ascension, these accounts can seem profoundly real and easily come to be read as historical events. Non-believers, those outside doctrinally- and worship-influenced views of life, read biblical narratives differently, more as historical texts open to the interpretation used for the lives and deaths of other historical figures. Critics of an 'historical resurrection' speak of the hope-filled community arising amongst early Christians after Jesus' death. Some use psychological theories of visions or conversion experiences to explain the core of whatever happened.[17] The 'believer'/'non-believer' comparison, therefore, is not so simple, for Christian New Testament scholars also differ over whether or not to accept the resurrection of Jesus and believers' resurrection in a direct and literal fashion.[18] Indeed, 'the New Testament texts say a variety of things that cannot be construed in a single way'.[19] Even Paul's engagement with Corinthian Christians suggests some problems over the resurrection of bodies.[20] Indeed, the important early tradition of the empty tomb left open the question of interpretation. Though readily answered by belief in a transformed resurrection body, it also allows for other insights of faith. For example, Rowan Williams wondered whether John's Gospel account of two angels sitting each side of where Jesus' body should have been was meant to echo the Old Testament image of the two cherubim framing the throne of God in the Jewish temple: a throne the physical emptiness of which manifested the divine presence. On that basis, to 'see' the God of Judah 'is to look into the gap between the holy beings'.[21] While that creative reflection will enhance some Christians' faith, others might find it too speculative.

In biblical theology the departed-body tradition is often linked with its return in Christ's second coming when believers will also be resurrected in their glorified bodies, whether for an 'other-worldly' heaven or for a transformed earth that can, itself, be considered as being 'resurrected'. Belief that Christ would soon return may have meant that some early Christians expected not 'to die' at all but to be instantaneously transformed in greeting him,[22] a belief reflected in the Rapture Theology favoured by some in America as the twenty-first century begins.[23]

Why afterlife: happy families or justice for all?

For many, a key issue concerns their personal future, raising the crucial theological, existential and pastorally incisive question of the purpose of any afterlife: a potential focus for funeral or memorial sermons. Basic to any answer is the theme of human identity, that sense of being self-grounded in our bodies and in relation with other persons and, indeed, with God. Some theologians press resurrection precisely on the assumption that to be real selves in any future existence we will need to exist as bodies, albeit with sin removed and our marred and fractured selves transformed by divine grace, and with forgiveness allowing a fuller knowledge of God and of each other.[24] Some stress the ultimate worship of God as the goal of eternal existence, something we might call our doxological destiny: the fact that others think of that as potentially boring is itself an intriguing issue. In much popular belief, however, that day will see us meet our loved ones again and, through renewed relationships, find us growing further as persons within a divine community. Theologically important is the belief in heaven as the site of ultimate justice, when judgement will be passed on evil and life's wrongs righted, when the vale of tears passes into rejoicing in the paradise city of God.

Not everyone will find such images easy to accept, for reasons grounded in changing views of the world and the cosmos. Changing times affect belief, with scholars often portraying the Enlightenment, modernity and postmodernity as a scene where individuals no longer accept tradition, whether religious or not, and whose natural attitude to life neither accepts miracles nor images of a personal God guiding a particular nation or Church. Such individuals 'know', in an emphatic and pragmatic way, that corpses remain dead, including that of Jesus, with any accounts to the contrary being explained by some psychological or literary theory. Despite that, many define themselves as spiritual, are concerned for others and for the world, and wish to live in and through the biblical accounts of Jesus, using them as stories filled with power to inspire life, especially when part of a community seeking to live that same way.[25] For them the Eucharist, for example, may speak of their contemporary experience of Jesus' death and resurrection for their sake and a frequent sense of newness of life, opportunity and hope as, daily, they die and rise with Christ. Using biblical ideas, especially Johannine ones perhaps, they may wish to speak of possessing a quality of eternal living within the normality of mundane life.

Living with difference

Given these differences, one challenge for contemporary Christians is for traditional believers to try to understand how others can also be inspired to live by faith even though their understanding of 'resurrection' may differ from their own. Non-traditional Christians, too, need to understand that they may seem to others to be selling the truth of the gospel message of resurrection. There is no hiding the problems involved here but, equally, I hope this chapter may persuade readers not to assume that only one approach exists. Ethically it is worth recalling that Crossan concluded his debate with Wright not simply by stating that the issue of whether the resurrection ought to be accepted as literal or metaphorical had been 'argued to impasse', but by exhorting Christians to see the resurrection – however understood – as motivating them to 'take back the world from the thugs'. His emphasis fell upon the unwieldy but focused 'eschatological life of justice-as-the-body-of-love-as-the-soul-of-justice'.[26]

Resurrection challenge

For many, traditional notions of resurrection are hard to accept precisely because of widespread ideas of the soul. Quite different from the natural attitude which 'knows' that corpses do not live again is the intuitive sense that we possess a life that does not end with bodily death. Seeing the corpse of a relative, many sense – in the popular misreading of the Henry Scott Holland sermon[27] extract – that 'they are not there', an experience that can foster belief in an inner force that enlivens the body and departs at death. Historically, many traditions have asserted that the dead survive as ancestral spirits and have paid them appropriate ritual service after their death. Today, for example, a significant minority of about a third of Britons reckon to have had some experience of their dead after bereavement. Indeed, a similar number of English Anglicans have also reported that their attendance at the Eucharist allows them some form of being with their dead.[28] And such things influence patterns of belief. Indeed, sensing the dead has been posited as the origin of religion as ancestors rose in dignity to evolve into gods.[29] The worlds of India, of the ancient Near East, Egypt, and of classical Greek and Roman cultures, all possessed versions of soul belief, often with notions of the soul's judgement after death, its relocation in a paradise or its transmigration through spiritual domains and reincarnating in new bodies while journeying to an ultimate release.[30] Today, a small but significant presence of pagan groups gives fresh voice to similar beliefs.

Against this mixed background, Christian thinkers have faced the problem of how to relate the challenging narratives of Jesus, his empty tomb and resurrection on the one hand to the widespread, 'easy' and not so challenging ideas of belief in souls on the other. If we all possess souls that go to God after death, what is the point of resurrection? For Christian leaders this was and remains a problematic point concerning the very nature of salvation, one demanding specific consideration. What emerged in beliefs on the resurrection – for one cannot speak of any single 'doctrine' of the resurrection – became fundamental for a theological understanding of the incarnation with its goal of salvation of humanity and, ultimately, for the theology of the Holy Trinity. Tradition says that God became man in order to save humanity from its sin and give it hope for a life triumphant over death that was the outcome of sin. The resurrection demonstrated God's conquest of death in a theological vision of a divinely created physical world in which the Jews were a chosen people. Jesus, as God's specially appointed one, a second Adam, triumphed just as the first Adam of Jewish scriptures had failed. Built into this outlook is a sense of the reality of material things, of the world God created at the outset and which, through Jesus as a sacrifice for sin, is now redeemed and will be transformed. The resurrection demonstrates a vindication of God's will for humanity that bursts out of Israel to all the world as the resurrection triggers a new, Holy Spirit-generated community of the faithful of all nations. The Acts of the Apostles comes to advance the book of Genesis. The theological conviction underlying this sacramental form of theology is that a soul is inadequate for the job of saving a material world. A material saviour must save a material world and that is why early debates insisted on Jesus being a real and body-full man and not some spiritual manifestation only appearing to be physical.

Few ordinary Christians will ponder how these doctrinal ideas hold together, though they may well consider topics of resurrection and soul when pondering loss and possibly meeting loved ones again. For Christian leaders, however, doctrinal issues of resurrection and soul may constitute a point of tension. Gregory of Nyssa[31] and John Calvin[32] in their respective eras, for example, commented on the way people easily accept the appealing idea of possessing souls while ignoring or giving little place to pondering the resurrection. Does traditional Christian belief then mean that someone must reject a natural belief in a soul in order to accept belief in the resurrection of Jesus?

These issues of pastoral theology and church teaching circle around the universal human problem of pondering how life and death impinge upon individuals. Christianity's traditional Trinitarian formulation offers a direct theological approach to this by personalizing life and death in the figure of Jesus and also by reference to the dynamism of the Holy Spirit, especially in association with the faith's prime rites of baptism and the Eucharist. Together, these ritual media introduce and sustain the believer within the community of faith, with the bipolar dynamism of death and life playing a major part in each of them. Theologically, baptism and Eucharist are driven by the centrality of Jesus as the Christ and by the activity of the Holy Spirit. These speak of ordinary life being transformed and are powerful reminders that the place of the Holy Spirit in Christian death and new life must not be ignored. [33]

Alternative models

Changing times introduce new topics to life–death discussion. This is evident in the growing personalizing of funeral ritual with the use of non-scriptural readings, popular music as well as memorial events with eulogies from family and friends, as Brian Parsons' chapter shows below. For people without an embedded baptismal–eucharistic identity it makes sense to create a ritual discourse conveying life-values reflecting family, and friendship and work relationships. In an increasingly therapeutic[34] yet non-narcissistic[35] society without afterlife belief it is understandable that the needs of the bereaved will predominate over those of the dead. Afterlife beliefs are replaced by life-focused, family and community concerns including ecological values that link life and death and add value to each. Here, perhaps, we should speak of 'secular depth' to refer to the concern of agnostics, atheists and others over life's meaning and the relationships underlying personal identity, death, bereavement and funerals. Ecological issues, embedded in Peter Jones' chapter below, certainly raise timely questions concerning the ongoing life of the world, as evident in the innovation of woodland burial, 'green' or 'ecological burial'. Psychological factors of near-death and out-of-the-body experiences also contribute to a sense of the depth of life while also adding to it a certainty about an afterlife highly reminiscent of religious conversion and drawing on notions of soul. That is quite unlike the clinging to life reflected in cryogenic freezing of the dead until their terminal illness can be cured and they can be re-animated.

Cybernetic immortality

Different again are the possibilities emerging from artificial intelligence. Ideas of transferring human, embodied knowledge to computers for an apparently unlimited future led Herzfeld[36] to oppose the computerizing of personal information as a means of establishing a kind of life after death. To equate a person's body to the hardware of a computer and the 'self' with its information leads to seeing the 'uploading' of the brain as paralleling the 'resurrection of the body'. Recent studies in neuroscience and human behaviour also provide valuable means of evaluating relationships between fear, hope and death. All these emotions are involved in the human proclivity to attribute causal agency to events perceived as possessing a clear outcome, suggesting that resurrection and soul beliefs help assuage fear and prompt hope – experiences intimately linked in the human emotional constitution and which may even be reflected in ancient Jewish laments as fusing 'mourning and rejoicing behaviours'.[37] Since fear and hope are basic to both secular and religious life, and enter into the 'Tragedy of Cognition' – as Atran speaks of human self-awareness in the face of death[38] – it is unlikely that humanity will cease to speak 'words against death'.[39] Contemporary Christian pastoral concern lies with the appropriateness of those words to express human hopes and fears, and of the capacity of the broad community of the faithful to address them.

Conclusion

Clergy can benefit themselves and their churches if they discuss mortality more often. For the taxing, potentially invisible nature of funeral ministry can be appreciated and supported by congregations, with many benefiting from airing their doubts and hidden anxieties. Because the reality of biblical and theological differences is often matched in the pew, street, crematorium and cemetery,[40] the exploration of doctrinal, mythical and scientific ideas relating death and life could add enormously to popular theological awareness. Is the afterlife wishful thinking? Is there a hell for the wicked, a heaven to right wrongs, to unite happy families, to complete a divine plan through unimagined transformations of the cosmos? So to ponder is to live an examined life.

Notes

1 I introduce this term to describe parents of a neo-natal or infant death who appear childless to society while possessing a deep sense of once having a child.

2 E. D. Chapple and C. S. Coon, *Principles of Anthropology*, London: Cape, 1940.

3 Douglas Davies and Alastair Shaw, *Reusing Old Graves: A Report of Popular British Attitudes*, Crayford: Shaw and Sons, 1995. This survey was based on 1,600 home interviews.

4 Paul Sheppy, *Death, Liturgy and Ritual*, Vol. 1, Aldershot: Ashgate, 2003.

5 Peters discusses Arthur Peacocke's science-based emphasis upon complete recreation. Ted Peters, 'Resurrection: The Conceptual Challenge' in Ted Peters, Robert John Russell and Michael Welker (eds), *Resurrection*, Grand Rapids: Eerdmans, 2002, pp. 297–321, 313.

6 Evers develops the theme of God's memory in relation to Augustine on divine memory. Dirk Evers, 'Memory in the Flow of Time and the Concept of Resurrection' in Peters et al., *Resurrection*, pp. 239–54.

7 John Polkinghorne, *Science and Christian Belief*, London: SPCK, 1994, p. 163.

8 Ted Peters, 'Resurrection: the Conceptual Challenge', in Ted Peters et al., *Resurrection*, pp. 308–11.

9 1 Thessalonians 4.15–17; 1 Corinthians 15.42–54.

10 1 Peter 3.18–19.

11 Christopher Carlile, *A Discourse Concerning Two Divine Positions*, London: Roger Ward, 1582; Richard Parkes, *A Brief Answer to Certain Objections and Reasons against the Decension of Christ into Hell*, Oxford: Joseph Barnes, 1604.

12 Tom Wright, *The Resurrection of the Son of God*, London: SPCK, 2003, pp. 468–9, 477.

13 Assuming souls are immortal either because they are created to be, henceforth, immortal or else, as uncreated entities, have always been so as, for example, in Mormonism.

14 Anne Taves, *Fits, Dreams and Visions*, Princeton: Princeton University Press, 1999.

15 William Temple, *Nature, Man and God*, London: Macmillan, 1935, p. 472.

16 David Kraemer, *The Meanings of Death in Rabbinic Judaism*, London: Routledge, 2000, pp. 123, 145.

17 Michael Goulder, 'The Baseless Fabric of a Vision' in Gavin D'Costa (ed.), *Resurrection Reconsidered*, Oxford: One World, 1996, pp. 48–61; Jack A. Kent, *The Psychological Origins of the Resurrection Myth*, London: Open Gate Press, 1999.

18 John Barclay, *The Resurrection in Contemporary New Testament Scholarship* in D'Costa, *Resurrection Reconsidered*, pp. 13–30.

19 Jaime Clark-Soles, *Death and the Afterlife in the New Testament*, London: T&T Clark, 2006, p. 1.

20 1 Corinthians 15.12, 29.

21 Rowan Williams, 'Between the Cherubim: The Empty Tomb and the Empty Throne' in D'Costa, *Resurrection Reconsidered*, pp. 87–101.

22 1 Thessalonians 4.15–17.

23 Gary DeMar, *End Times Fiction: A Biblical Consideration of the Left Behind Theology*, Nashville: Thomas Nelson Publishers, 2001.

24 David Brown, 'The Christian Hope' in Dan Cohn-Sherbok and Christopher Lewis (eds), *Beyond Death*, London: Macmillan, 1995, pp. 42–53.

25 Gerard Loughlin, 'Living in Christ: Story, Resurrection and Salvation' in D'Costa (ed.), *Resurrection Reconsidered*, pp. 118–34.

26 John Dominic Crossan, 'Appendix: Bodily-Resurrection Faith' in Robert B. Stewart (ed.), *The Resurrection of Jesus*, London: SPCK, 2006, pp. 185–6.

27 H. S. Holland, 'The King of Terrors' in H. S. Holland, *Facts of Faith*, London: Longmans, 1919.

28 Davies and Shaw, *Reusing Old Graves*, p. 96. Approximately 35 per cent of the population experienced their dead in some way.

29 E. B. Tylor, *Primitive Culture*, London, 1871.

30 Jon Davies, *Death, Burial and Rebirth in the Religions of Antiquity*, London: Routledge, 1999.

31 Peters describes Gregory not wanting people to see resurrection as an absurdity. Peters, 'Resurrection: The Conceptual Challenge', p. 309.

32 John Calvin, *Institutes of the Christian Religion*, London: Tegg & Son, 1838, Sections I, XV, VI.

33 Gunther Thomas, 'Resurrection to New Life: Pneumatological Implications of the Eschatological Transition' in Peters et al., *Resurrection*, pp. 255–69.

34 Philip Rieff, *The Triumph of the Therapeutic*, Harmondsworth: Penguin, 1968.

35 Christopher Lasch, *The Culture of Narcissism*, London: Abacus, 1980.

36 Noreen Herzfeld, 'Cybernetic Immortality versus Christian Resurrection' in Peters et al., *Resurrection*, pp. 192–201.

37 Samuel M. Olyan, *Biblical Mourning*, Oxford: Oxford University Press, 2004, p. 131.

38 Scott Atran, *In Gods We Trust*, Oxford: Oxford University Press, 2002, pp. 62–79.

39 Douglas Davies, *Death, Ritual and Belief*, London: Continuum, 2002, p. 7.

40 As revealed in the 1995 survey in Davies and Shaw, *Reusing Old Graves*.

9

Concepts of Heaven and Hell in the Modern Era

PAUL BADHAM

Heaven and hell in traditional thought

There is probably no area of Christian theology where the gulf between contemporary and traditional belief is so great as in beliefs about heaven and hell. For the Christian Fathers, heaven was in the sky, indeed it *was* the sky, because the Greek word '*ouranos*' means both sky and heaven, and for any person in the ancient world the two meanings would have been indistinguishable.[1]

This is very clear if one reads the chapters in St Augustine's *City of God* in which he responds to objections that resurrected bodies, being heavier than air, could not stay up in the sky but would inevitably fall to earth. Augustine responds to such objections by pointing out that, although iron is heavier than water, human skill can shape iron ships that stay afloat, so God's skill can shape us for life in the sky. Alternatively, we might be given powerful feathers like birds, or perhaps God would 'enable the perfect spirits of the blessed' to carry the weight of a human body into the sky just as immaterial angels are enabled to carry weights. Augustine also argues that since the whole earth hangs in space without support, so too could our resurrected bodies.[2] Rufinus in his early *Commentary on the Apostles' Creed* argues on the basis of 1 Thessalonians 4.17 that we will be taken up to heaven on clouds.[3]

Not all the Fathers were troubled by such considerations, for in ancient Hebrew thought the floor of the sky was thought to be as solid as anything could be,[4] so the problem of not falling to earth did not arise. Others thought, not of a three-decker universe, but of an earth surrounded by the heavenly spheres. In such cases Christians like Origen placed the 'the good land' or the ultimate 'abiding place' of the blessed above the 'spheres which surround the earth'.[5] But whatever view they took, almost all the early Christian writers were confident that heaven was a literal place. Of the writers included in the Ante-Nicene Library and the Nicene and Post-Nicene Fathers the only exception I could find to this was St Gregory of Nyssa who talked of 'hades' as a state of being rather than a place, and who affirmed that God is our locality.[6] For all the rest, heaven had a clear location in the sky.

Hell also had a clear location. It was the lake of fire in the centre of earth which could be observed if one looked down into the craters of Etna and Vesuvius and saw how the fire and brimstone within those 'vent-holes of hell' appeared to burn continuously without being consumed. This would provide precisely the means for the endless torture of the damned who would end up in the fiery lake below us.[7]

The cosmological discoveries of the seventeenth century have so completely changed our understanding that it is hard for us to believe now that for most of the Christian centuries heaven was thought of as a place in the sky. However, to recognize this should help us to understand why Christian leaders saw the discoveries of Copernicus and Galileo as a threat to their Christianity, and why Pascal was terrified by the realization that the music of the heavenly spheres had been replaced by 'the eternal silence of those infinite spaces'.[8] It is surprising how unselfconsciously Christians continue to sing Easter and Ascension Day hymns which locate heaven in the sky, and that as late as 1951 the bodily Assumption of Mary was made *de fide* for the Roman Catholic Christian. Since the seventeenth century, educated Christians have found it hard to integrate their hope for heaven within their overall understanding of reality. However, in the twentieth century at least four ways of tackling this problem were made. These are the focus of this chapter.

A theocentric heaven

In their *Heaven: A History*[9] McDannell and Lang show that one way the Reformers responded to the Copernican revolution in astronomy was to place the whole emphasis of thinking about heaven into life in God. If there was no longer any place for a literal heaven 'above the bright blue sky', God himself would be our place. In the twentieth century this way of thinking was pushed to its limit by scholars who stressed the importance of the view expressed in 1 Timothy that 'God alone has immortality.'[10] Karl Barth and Karl Rahner, arguably the most influential Protestant and Catholic thinkers of the twentieth century, adopted this course. Barth is insistent that we have only one life, which begins at birth and ends at death. This is our 'real and only life'; there can be 'no question of a continuation into an indefinite future of a somewhat altered life'. Rahner is equally clear, 'with death it's all over. Life is past, and it won't come again.' However, neither sees his respective position as incompatible with belief in eternal life. For Barth, 'death will make our lives complete in God', while for Rahner 'our emptiness will be filled in timeless eternity with the light of the divine spirit'.[11] A theocentric heaven in which God will be all in all can also be seen as a development of the Orthodox concept of deification; the idea that we will live in God as 'partakers of the divine nature'. It also takes more seriously than does much traditional thought the persistent emphasis of the Requiem Mass that heaven is an eternal rest. As St Augustine put it, 'We shall rest in the Sabbath of eternal life . . . in the repose which comes when time ceases.'[12]

A clear exposition of how this could be understood can be seen in the writing of the process philosopher Charles Hartshorne. He argues that after death we will

> live on in the complete and infallible memory of God. He to whom all hearts are open remains ever more open to any heart that was once apparent to him. What we once were to him, less than that we can never be, for otherwise he himself as knowing us would lose something of his own reality. Hence, if we can never be less than we have been to God, we can in reality never be less than we have been. Death cannot be the destruction or even the fading of the book of one's life; it can only be the fixing of the concluding page. Death writes 'The End' but nothing further happens to the book either by addition or subtraction.[13]

This view is echoed by David Edwards: 'God's memory of us will be more powerful and altogether better than our own memories', and because God remembers us 'we will share in God's life and God's glory'.[14] According to Unamuno, to be remembered by God is 'to have my consciousness sustained by the Supreme consciousness'.[15]

Many theologians, particularly those with historical interests, find this an attractive picture which makes sense of the concept of heaven in ways that do not conflict with a full recognition of our own mortality. However, as John Hick points out, *the* argument presupposes that 'the state of being remembered constitutes as full and real existence as the state of being alive. But this is manifestly false.'[16] There is actually all the difference in the world between continuing to live on and simply being remembered, even by God. In a secular parallel the internet offers the possibility of a kind of immortality if in the end it contains every surviving book, film or tape within itself. But neither to be recorded in God's 'book of life' nor even to be immortalized on the pages of the internet is in any way comparable to a 'real' life after death.

An eschatological heaven

A major theme of New Testament scholarship since the time of Schweitzer and Weiss has been a recovery of the apocalyptic emphasis which is believed to characterize the earliest Christianity. This has been taken up into systematic theology by Pannenberg and Moltmann. Pannenberg insists that 'the basis on which the understanding of Jesus rests is always linked to the apocalyptic framework of Jesus' earthly life . . . if this framework is removed then the fundamental basis of faith is lost'.[17] For Moltmann, eschatology is 'the key to the whole of Christian faith'.[18] He looks forward to the transformation of the whole world and the whole future. For such writers, belief in the empty tomb and bodily resurrection of Jesus is central to faith because what happened to Jesus then will happen to us all at the universal resurrection of the dead at the end of time. This theme is central to N. T. Wright's influential work *The Resurrection of the Son of God* and it is spelt out particularly clearly in Andrew Chester's chapter on 'Eschatology' in *The Blackwell Companion to Modern Theology*. Chester sees the key advantage of this way of thinking in that it does full justice to the biblical stress on the psychosomatic unity of the whole person, and on our place within the created order. The popularity of this view is that it enables one to dispense with the 'Greek' concept of the soul and accept as an absolute the 'Hebrew' understanding of the importance of embodiment to our personal identity. For Chester, the true Christian hope entails 'the recognition that the whole future and all time are set within God's control'.[19] This way of thinking takes absolutely seriously St Paul's thought that 'the creation itself is to be set free from its bondage to decay and will obtain the freedom of the glory of the children of God'.[20]

Nancey Murphy believes that it is vital that Christians today accept the physicalist position that we are simply bodies. There is no additional metaphysical element such as a mind or soul or spirit. This doesn't in any way affect the fact that we can be intelligent, moral and spiritual, but simply insists that these characteristics are part of our embodied being. She stresses that this does not in any way affect the Christian hope for a future life because, like the other writers we are discussing, she locates that hope in the expectation of the resurrection of the dead and the transformation of the world at the end of time.[21] In this eschatological perspective heaven is not a place or state of being *other* than this world. Heaven *is* this world transformed at the end of time.

The virtue of this way of thinking is that it places the resurrection of Jesus at the centre of Christian thinking and that it takes with the utmost seriousness a theme which is undoubtedly present in the earliest structures of Christianity. The difficulty with it is that the apocalyptic imagination of the first century is the only basis for such an expectation, and key elements in that understanding of reality are utterly different from our own. The most obvious is that St Paul initially expected that this would happen within his lifetime.[22] But an even greater difference is that for St Paul a recently created three-decker universe comprised the whole of reality and it was therefore not at all implausible to imagine that God would bring the existing structures to an end and create a new world for us. However, we now know that the universe is at least 12,000 million years old and vast beyond our imagining. According to Sir Bernard Lovell, there may well be 1,000 million galaxies, each containing perhaps a 100,000 million stars.[23] It is of course possible that millions of years hence the present universe may come to an end through some 'big crunch' analogous to the initial 'big bang'. But to imagine that God will then collect together the molecules of all human beings who have ever lived, together with 'long extinct animals'[24] and even 'every blade of grass'[25] and resurrect every creature bodily into this new creation is to present a picture that is utterly implausible the moment one tries seriously to imagine it.

Heaven in another space

A more promising approach takes modern physics utterly seriously and recognizes that it accepts the logical possibility of a plurality of spatial systems in no relationship whatever with each other. Austin Farrar claims that 'According to Einstein's unanswerable reasoning, space is not an infinite pre-existent field . . . Space is a web of interactions between material energies . . . so heaven can be as dimensional as it likes without ever getting pulled into our spatial field.'[26] In other words, a spatial heaven could exist in another space or another dimension. One huge advantage of this schema is that it is actually preachable as a way of thinking about a future life. In Austin Farrer's writing this was part of a sermon and, given the importance of the Christian hope to Christian faith, it is important that while we are in good health we should be advised of the credibility of this key Christian belief. John Hick argues that if at the moment of our death God were to create a 'replica' of each of us possessing sufficient correspondence of characteristics with our present bodies and sufficient continuity of memory with our present consciousness, then we could validly claim that belief in a resurrection life in a spatial heaven is once more possible.[27]

The difficulty with this whole schema is of course that philosophical speculation about a bare logical possibility does not take us very far. On the other hand, if we believe in an all-powerful God to whom each individual truly matters, and if embodiment in a spatial heaven is essential for any genuinely personal human life, then the picture sketched by Farrer and developed further by Hick and myself[28] is one way in which heaven could at least be thought of. However, one condition for plural spaces is that they must each be subject to different physical laws. Hence continuity between this life and the next must depend on the continuity of consciousness rather than that of matter. Hence the theory will only be intelligible if we can also imagine that the bridging stage of existence is a mind-dependent world.

Heaven as a mind-dependent world

The most important contribution of John Hick to discussion of heaven is his idea that at death our consciousness temporarily enters a mind-dependent world, somewhat as described in the *Tibetan Book of the Dead* or in the writings of Hick's former supervisor at Oxford, Professor H. H. Price. This world would be a kind of dream environment built out of our memories and desires and thereby revealing to us their true nature. This would provide an opportunity for life-review, self-revelation and self-assessment. It would also provide opportunity for 'meeting' through telepathic rapport with deceased relatives and friends and perhaps an enhanced awareness of the divine. After a period in this *bardo* world the person would be reborn into another embodied existence not on earth but in another space. Hick believes that a succession of such lives with intervals for reflection in between would provide the most suitable means for the human pilgrimage towards ultimate reality.

When Hick sketched out this idea of consciousness leaving the body and temporarily entering a mind-dependent state to enable life-review and telepathic meeting, he was engaged in pure speculation. He was asking the question of what an immediate post-mortem existence might conceivably be like. Neither Hick nor I had at that point heard of near-death experiences (NDEs) even though both of us had been researching beliefs about a future life for the previous decade. What is extra-ordinary, however, is the way in which reports from people resuscitated from apparent death provide empirical support for Hick's speculation. They consistently claim that when their hearts stopped beating and their lungs stopped breathing 'they' went out of their bodies. They describe looking down and remembering the resuscitation procedures, and they talk of life-review, telepathic meetings and enhanced religious aware-ness. Hence what was initially put forward as pure theory might in fact turn out to be the way things are. That certainly is the view of the vast majority who have the experience.

It will be fascinating to see whether or not further research strengthens or weakens this possibility! The research of Dr Penny Sartori is impor-tant here. She did what many others have done and showed that people who have out-of-the-body experiences correctly describe how they were resuscitated. But what she also did was to ask people who had been resuscitated without an NDE to say how they thought they had been resuscitated.[29] This second group had not the remotest idea how they were resuscitated and their proposed reconstructions were wildly in-accurate. This suggests that those who had an NDE and who claimed to observe their resuscitation may actually have done just that, since their observations were correct while in all other respects their situation was identical to the control group.[30]

The classic doctrine of hell

We have already seen that hell was initially thought of in spatial terms, and hence locating hell faces the same kind of difficulties as we noted in the case of heaven. However, hell faces a further question; namely is it a post-mortem existence that one might rationally expect an all-powerful and all-loving God to hold in being? It is important to note that the classic understanding of hell is that it constitutes a state of endless torture. According to the Catechism of the Council of Trent, hell will provide an accumulation of every possible punishment.[31] One charac-teristic of mainstream Christianity in the past 250 years is that the Christian conscience has rebelled against such a picture either by explic-itly repudiating hell, or redefining it as extinction or as no more than a state of separation from God. However, this movement of thought is by no means universal. In 1981 the University and Colleges Christian Fellowship which formerly had made no explicit mention of hell introduced an affirmation concerning hell into its doctrinal basis. I do not know why this happened unless it was the case that they had come to suspect that some of their members were being tempted to the 'more merciful' alternative position of 'conditional immortality' under which those not saved by Christ simply cease to exist, and that they wished to block off this belief. Certainly, since 1995 all officers of University Christian Unions are required to affirm belief that 'the Lord Jesus will return in person, to judge everyone, to execute God's just condemnation on those who have not repented and to receive the redeemed into eternal glory'. In the year 2000 a report of the Evangelical Alliance rejected both universalism and 'mere annihilation at death' and reaffirmed the reality of hell. According to the Evangelical Alliance, 'As well as separation from God, hell involves severe punishment . . . both physical and psychological' and will be 'conscious experience of rejection and torment'.[32]

The nineteenth-century critique of hell[33]

In 1830 F. D. E. Schleiermacher argued that the existence of hell would make heaven impossible. The more truly Christlike a person became, the more concerned one would be about the suffering of others. Consequently no truly saintly person could be perfectly happy in heaven while being aware that others were suffering in hell.[34] This argument turns on its head the appalling medieval idea that one of the greatest joys of heaven would be to watch the damned being tortured, and represents a major moral advance.[35]

The moral case against hell was taken further by F. D. Maurice, who argued that the belief was 'in direct contradiction to the primal and quite decisive Christian doctrine of the love of God. If we start from belief that "God is actually love", we shall dread any representation of him which is at variance with this [and] will shrink from attributing to him acts which would be unlovely in man.'[36] Maurice believed that the doctrine of hell made a mockery of Jesus' picture of the loving fatherhood of God. For if it were indeed the case that all humanity is damned except those who accept Christ as their personal saviour it would condemn 'most of the American slaves, besides the whole body of Turks, Hindus, Hottentots, Jews . . . to hopeless destruction'. Such a conclusion would negate belief in the infinite love of our heavenly Father and utterly destroy the credibility of the Christian gospel.[37]

In 1860 H. B. Wilson in his contribution to *Essays and Reviews* challenged belief in hell on the grounds that people do not come in two clear-cut categories. He argued for an intermediate state.[38] He was brought to trial for heresy but acquitted because originally 42 Articles of Religion had been drafted for the Church of England but only 39 were promulgated. Since one of those dropped had affirmed hell, the Lord Chancellor ruled in 1864 (on behalf of the Judicial Committee of the Privy Council) that no Anglican has ever been required to believe in everlasting torment. The two archbishops issued a dissenting note accepting the judicial verdict but affirming that in their view Anglicans ought to believe in hell. Shortly afterwards approximately half the clergy signed a petition to say that they did believe in everlasting torment, but it was noted that almost all the leading thinkers of the Church had refused to sign, and since that time belief in hell has gone into steep decline. Wilson's alternative of an intermediate state has been seen as a more Christian alternative, and sometimes this has been related to the Roman Catholic doctrine of purgatory. Both belief in an intermediate state and belief in purgatory allow for the possibility of development after death so as to become 'fitted for heaven'.

Hell in Anglican and Catholic thought today

Within the Church of England the doctrine of hell was finally repudiated by the Doctrine Commission as incompatible with belief in the love of God in their report on *The Mystery of Salvation* in 1995. In reality I think this is also true of much Roman Catholic thought today, though that Church finds it particularly hard explicitly to repudiate ideas which have once been accepted. Consequently sporadic references to hell are occasionally made by church leaders, notably by Pope Benedict XVI who on 27 March 2007 was reported as teaching that 'the fires of hell are real and eternal'. However, a subsequent Vatican 'clarification' of the Pope's 'language' said that he had intended to 'reinforce' what the Catechism affirmed about hell as a 'state of eternal separation from God' to be understood 'symbolically rather than physically'.[39] The Catechism itself is illuminating. It begins by asserting unequivocally 'the sad and lamentable reality of eternal death also called hell'. However, this assertion is then qualified by the statement that 'it is also true that God desires all men to be saved' and 'for God all things are possible'. Finally, the Catechism concludes: 'At the end of time the Kingdom of God will come in its fullness . . . and God will be all in all.'[40] A similar situation occurs in Archbishop Carey's *Letters to the Future*. He also speaks of hell but immediately follows this with talk of the wideness of God's mercy which will embrace all humanity, so that in the end God will be all in all.[41] The clearest statement of the universality of the Christian hope appears to have been made by Pope John Paul II, who unequivocally affirmed in his first Encyclical Letter that 'Every human being without any exception whatever has been redeemed by Christ because Christ is in a way united to the human person – every person without exception even if the individual may not realize this fact.'[42]

Notes

1 Paul Badham, *Christian Beliefs about Life after Death*, London: Macmillan, 1976, p. 59.

2 Augustine, *City of God*, 13.18; 22.4; 22.11.

3 Rufinus, *The Apostles' Creed*, para. 46.

4 W. Eichrodt, *Theology of the Old Testament Vol. 2*, London: SCM Press, 1967, p. 93.

5 Origen, *First Principles*, 2.11; 6–7.

6 Gregory of Nyssa, *On the Soul and the Resurrection*, 443, 452.

7 Augustine, *City of God*, 22.11; Minucius Felix, *Octavius*, ch. 35; Basil, *Letter* 8; Lactantius, *Divine Institutes*, 7.21; Justin, *First Apology*, 8; Hippolytus, *Treatise of Christ and Anti-Christ*, ch. 65

8 Blaise Pascal, *Pensees*, section 2, no. 206.

9 Collen McDannell and Bernhard Lang, *Heaven: A History*, New York: Vintage, 1990.

10 1 Timothy 6.16.

11 Quoted in McDannell and Lang, *Heaven: A History*, pp. 342–3.

12 St Augustine, *Confessions*, 13.36–7, Harmondsworth: Penguin, 1961, p. 346.

13 Cited in John Hick, *Death and Eternal Life*, London: Collins, 1976, p. 218.

14 David Edwards, *The Last Things Now*, London: SCM Press, 1969, p. 89.

15 M. de Unamuno, *The Tragic Sense of Life* [1912], London: Fontana, 1967, p. 154.

16 Hick, *Death and Eternal Life*, p. 219.

17 Cited in C. F. D. Moule, *The Significance of the Message of the Resurrection of Jesus Christ*, London: SCM Press, 1968, p. 130; cf. W. Pannenberg, *Jesus – God and Man*, London: SCM Press, 1970, pp. 63–73.

18 A. Chester, 'Eschatology' in G. Jones, *The Blackwell Companion to Modern Theology*, Oxford: Blackwell, 2004, p. 251, summarizing Moltmann's *Theology of Hope*.

19 Chester, 'Eschatology', p. 256.

20 Romans 8.21.

21 Nancey Murphy, *Bodies and Souls, or Spirited Bodies*, Cambridge: Cambridge University Press, 2006.

22 1 Thessalonians 4.15.

23 Sir Bernard Lovell, 'Creation' in *Theology*, September 1980, p. 362.

24 John Macquarrie, *The Christian Hope*, London: Mowbrays, 1978, p. 128.

25 N. Berdyaev, *The Destiny of Man*, London: Bles, 1955, p. 294.

26 Austin Farrer, *Saving Belief*, London: Hodder, 1964, p. 145.

27 Hick, *Death and Eternal Life*, pp. 278–90.

28 Badham, *Christian Beliefs about Life after Death*, pp. 65–94.

29 Penny Sartori, *Near-death Experiences in a Hospital Context*, University of Wales Lampeter, PhD thesis, 2005 (Edwin Mellen Press, forthcoming).

30 For further data on NDEs, see Mark Fox, *Religion, Spirituality and the Near-death Experience*, London: Routledge, 2003; Paul Badham, *Religious and Near-Death Experience in Relation to Belief in a Future Life*, second series of occasional papers no. 13, Lampeter: RERC (Religious Experience Research Centre), 1997.

31 Percy Dearmer, *The Legend of Hell*, London: Cassell, 1929, p. 25.

32 The Evangelical Alliance Commission on Unity and Truth among Evangelicals, *The Nature of Hell*, London: Acute, 2000, p. 132.

33 For full documentation of this, see Geoffrey Rowell, *Hell and the Victorians: A Study of the Nineteenth-Century Theological Controversies Concerning Eternal Punishment and the Future Life*, Oxford: Oxford University Press, 1974.

34 F. D. E. Schleiermacher, *The Christian Faith* [1830], Edinburgh: T&T Clark, 1960, pp. 709ff.

35 St Thomas Aquinas, *Summa Theologia*, Pt III Supp. 94, art. 1.

36 F. D. Maurice, *Theological Essays* [1853], Macmillan, 1871, p. 14.

37 Cited in F. Higham, *Frederick Denision Maurice*, London: SCM Press, 1947, p. 93.

38 B. Jowett, *Essays and Reviews*, London: Parker, 1960.

39 *The Times*, 27 March 2007.

40 *Catechism of the Catholic Church*, London: Chapman, 1994, pp. 240–1.

41 G. Carey, *Canterbury Letters*, London: Kingsway, pp. 220–33.

42 Pope John Paul II, Encyclical Letter, *Redemptor Hominis*, 1979, para. 14.

10

The Past, Present and Future of Burial

LEONIE KELLAHER

Introduction

Thirty per cent of people in the UK are buried when they die, representing a significant minority choice about which many hold strong views, sometimes religious but more frequently having other rationales, especially around bodily decay and coping with loss and grief.[1] Temporalities enter into this, the 'finality' of cremation being contrasted with longer time-scales of burial. While this research-based chapter[2] focuses on past and present forms and meanings of burial, it is difficult to put aside the cremation alternative since burial preferences tend to be explained in opposition to cremation rather than for intrinsic meaning. Accelerating secularity may account for this, as for infrequent references to eternity and afterlife by research participants.

Two linked themes, arising from several centuries of change, underpin the argument put forward here to account for contemporary dispositions towards burial with which clergy must now engage. The first is equality in death and the way earlier theological meanings are now located in individuals and families rather than in communities. In parallel runs a second theme: the body and how possession and control of corporeal remains can influence disposal choices and commemorative style. Thus, as the fate of the body comes to the fore, traditional frameworks, which speak of eternity with God through the body of Christ, fragment.[3]

Full body burial in earth as the Christian norm gave ecclesiastic authorities millennia of control over proceedings – absolving, comforting and preparing the faithful for death with absolution, last rites and burial in the local churchyard.[4] Influential until the twentieth century, the Churches standardized ritual styles and forms for inhumation as entry to eternity. It is true that distinctions operated in parish churchyards, with prime positions and impressive monuments overshadowing inconspicuous, modest, common and pauper graves[5] but equality in death was the theological rule and publicly accepted sentiment. Although the egalitarian signal carried by local burial weakened with urbanization and secular advances, traces of Christian burial customs persist even now as cremation dominates[6] and place-associations remain significant for choice of ash destinations. In the face of accelerating mobility, burial becomes even more strongly associated with fixedness,[7] though family and generational implications may have shifted, especially with enthusiasm for the release from grave-tending and cemetery attendance that 'green burial' can offer. Furthermore, despite recent developments on the reuse of grave space, perpetuity as a concomitant of burial has yet to unravel.[8]

Burial's long association with non-disturbance of human remains – earlier made manifest by the body-snatching scandals and by the revelations of George Alfred Walker from 1839[9] – is revealed in contemporary hesitation about grave reuse, and is as likely to reflect issues around possession of the body as pollution, corpses and decomposition.[10] Although churchyards were once central to rural communities, with the dead kept close by, burial rituals set them symbolically apart from the living. Physical, social and spiritual perils associated with the corpse may have receded, and the place now occupied by the dead — structurally, sentimentally and locationally — seems set to change burial style and meaning.[11] The trajectory that has shaped and carried these transformed views of equality and bodies extends back at least to the eighteenth century and is the subject of the next section, to be followed by observations on what this means for the next decade in terms of Christian ministry.

Equality embodied in death

Many accounts show how medieval and post-Reformation burial grounds, notably in London and Paris, were overwhelmed by a volume of corpses for which they were unfitted.[12] These scandals, arising as population densities accelerated, led to the establishment of cemeteries at the, then, peripheries of the new metropolitan and urban centres.[13] In the face of public health concerns, emergent local authorities, joint stock companies or churches, concerned for their members' religious and socio-ethnic sensibilities, established new forms of burial ground: cemeteries.[14] Jewish, Roman Catholic, Orthodox and Nonconformist communities were just some groups to acquire cemetery land. These could be bounded acres or consecrated sections of larger cemeteries; either way, the living and the dead were protected with a membrane that separated but also connected, until deconsecration removed its safeguarding symbolism. Nineteenth-century administrative municipality, commerce and religion thus established some kind of balance for dealing with the dead, even as the Anglican authorities were deemed unable to manage the scale of urban mortality. Furthermore, as religious frames were overtaken by scientific enlightenment, confidence in -- and possibly within -- the Churches declined.[15]

Burial was part of all this, as its displacement from churchyard to cemetery following upon the nineteenth-century Burial Acts,[16] also led to diminished burial income for churches. With the 1857 Act, buried remains were protected from the disinterment that had scandalized society a few decades earlier. Codified and legislatively secured, individual identity was privileged over common cause, an irresistible invitation to the middle classes for monumental display in a new cemetery terrain.[17] Equality in death as a generalized sentiment undoubtedly became increasingly problematic as social divisions were exposed – materially and politically.[18]

Also to be taken into account in tracing how disposal and mourning ideals evolved towards the practices that now attach to burial, whether we are considering full inhumation or ash burials, is that of dispossession. That a segment of nineteenth-century society other than the wealthy exerted the powerful but silently negative influence of pauperized dispossession is argued by Strange.[19] The formal record of Victorian and Edwardian death, mute on grief as experienced by the poorest with the highest mortality, generated assumptions that they were so accustomed to death they did not bother to mourn. Strange effectively demolishes this with an explanation that can be invoked here to explain contemporary burial and disposal.

Dispossession of the body and ignorance as to its burial place is the crucial key. Without a body in an *identifiable* grave, conduits to expression became blocked and grief appeared to be, but was not, argues Strange, absent. Only with World War One, when all families with war dead were similarly dispossessed of bodies to bury and of burial places in which to fix restorative memory, did the silence and restraint forced upon paupers become the twentieth-century norm and 'equality in death' assume secular meaning. The design for war graves signified this explicitly and was adopted in the inter-war years with some enthusiasm as cemeteries opened up reserve land and established uniform lawn grave sections, now viewed as hallmarks of municipality.[20] The simple gravestone and grid layout exposed and expressed a universality of loss and equal distribution of death so urgently as to eclipse the Last Judgement of religious tradition. This wartime-wrought form for dealing with death became the model for a post-war civil society that had to frame new paradigms for equality, individuals, collectivities, the body and eternity.

Pared-down burial practices often gave poorer people a first property acquisition – a grave plot. This group, much enlarged by the time of our interviews with grave owners in the late 1990s, spoke with satisfaction at having an identifiable grave.[21] The Beveridge reforms were partly responsible but egalitarian trends had already been set in train. The associated 'anonymity' has since been reinterpreted and rejected, often in favour of cremation so that ashes may be placed somewhere safer, warmer and, emotionally if not geographically, closer to home.[22]

So, the significance of equality in death underwent a first transformation during the Victorian and Edwardian periods with a shift from theological to patriotically secular significance. The collective sacrifice to defend country that engendered that change may still be held sacred in public memory, but as a symbol it appears to have become less potent. The idea of public place has changed and the cemetery is often not seen as fitting for expressing sentiments that are now centred upon the individuality of the deceased. Concern for the dead body that, arguably, directed the transformation of the 'equality in death' ideal and was closely associated with burial seems to have taken a new turn. Possibly because sight has been lost of any overarching belief system – religious or patriotic – the 'unit' of concern appears to be the individual person and, where disposal is at issue, the individual body unrelated to any notions of sacred community.

Burial in the twenty-first century

The body certainly preoccupies twenty-first-century British society[23] and a shift during inter-war years now appears to have reached new levels, partly attributable to the medicalization of life and death,[24] as well as to concerns with the health and appearance of the body through which the world reads individual status, if not worth.[25] Such currents shaping everyday life are relevant in considering the future of burial, for, even as death is an extraordinary event in the life of a family, its catastrophic nature draws people to seek reassurance in habitual patterns. Consumer choice, for example, purchase of artifacts, comparison and competition now come into play rather than prayer or reflections on morality and mortality.[26]

Insofar as the term 'soul' is now invoked less frequently than spirit, non-corporeal aspects of personhood continue to be acknowledged by bereaved people, who invariably hope for, and report, experience of a supernatural realm.[27] Limbo and purgatory, along with heaven and hell, have generally ceased to register as stopping-off places for the soul-spirit: Limbo has been disposed of,[28] and Purgatory[29] mostly abandoned at the Reformation, though the notion of a purgatorial interval following death has not entirely gone away[30] and continues to occupy secular interstices. For instance, the year following burial is generally thought of as an unsettled time for all concerned. Recollections of agitation about this time of bereavement – often triggered at the raw, unfinished appearance of the grave – were common among research participants.[31] Cemetery rules, however, often allow leeway for 12 months after burial and do not constrain the mourner as much as in later years, when the grave's boundaries are policed more sternly. 'Purgatorial' states of unease were mirrored in expressions of concern as to the 'well-being' of the deceased and questioning as to where they now were, along with worries sometimes being voiced about the corpse. The relief often expressed after the first anniversary is palpable, particularly when the grave is finished, usually with an inscribed stone.[32]

We are accustomed to dichotomize disposal modes as burial or cremation, but the reality is that families and individuals engage in a wider range of post-mortem choices than this suggests.[33] Certainly, people and families make self-identifying statements about burial or cremation that often appear to be set, but these descriptors cover a considerable range of options. Moreover, labels often obscure ideas and actions that follow more complex and even contradictory lines. We only have to note the tenacity in public parlance of the 'stages' model of grief to see how discontinuous are statements about letting go and actions that spell out a different determination to remain bonded with the deceased.[34] Populations in the UK may now choose to cremate and then put aside the whole business or, at the other extreme, may retrieve the ashes for private disposal at several locations.[35] The range of grave and memorial options introduced since the early 1990s by many cemeteries has also expanded the possibilities for inhumation, from simple lawn headstones to vaults and monuments that encompass the whole grave. Minority ethnic families (for example, Chinese, Greek or other Orthodox) may well choose these larger edifices. Most burial grounds have also identified a section where a version of green or natural burial is offered. Such developments follow from revisions of the public–private sector interface that set out to increase choice in local service.[36] Although cemeteries and crematoria were probably the last areas of local government to respond to these developments, the consequences for burial have been welcomed by bereaved families. *The Dead Citizens Charter* in 1998 was part of an ongoing movement to take people's experiences into account, as was the ICCM's *Charter for the Bereaved*.[37]

The landscapes of many cemeteries are, consequently, somewhat altered, the expensive exuberance evident at some graves resonating with the previous flourishing of Victorian monumental style. While nineteenth-century expansions in choice did not foreclose on religious meanings around death, monumental extravagance seeming to reflect the dominant Christian culture, contemporary versions, tending to follow the celebration of life more than mourning, can be a source of tension between professionals – including clergy and managers – and bereaved people. The body, formerly seen as the vessel containing the immortal soul and now as a material manifestation of personality,[38] has been – and continues to be – a contested area between the individual and the range of institutions that frame the ways in which we live, die and inhabit our post-mortem states. A divergence from, if not resistance to, a particular burial authority's rules is seen, for example, where disputes about grave design and the formal or colloquial style of inscriptions arise.[39] At the root of these there may be an unwillingness or inability on the part of some families to see their deceased and the resting place as part of any public or collective entity. Their dead have not really 'gone before': they are still around and have to be protected from outsiders. For others, a particular grave is all they acknowledge, the cemetery being only a backdrop. A majority, nonetheless, seem content to accept the cemetery as guardian of the dead. Having said this, their terms are likely to be personally held ideas as to who 'owns' or has possession of the 'embodied' dead and should therefore control the site of burial. Equality in death remains a frequently intoned truism, but without much conviction.

The future of burial and Christian ministry

Decline in burial is reported to have levelled out, partly because it is now the choice of many migrants from rural, so-called traditional communities. The religious style of many of these groups – Orthodox, Caribbean, Chinese and Muslim for example – tends to be more inclusive than that of Anglican or longer-settled Roman Catholics, in the sense of involving extended family and community. This could reinvigorate burial and cemetery attendance as a public, religiously structured, rather than an individual, event.[40] At the same time, it is difficult to envisage current trends being reversed, though enthusiasm for woodland, natural or ecological burial may represent a gesture towards less individualistic disposals. Thinking about the implications of all this for Christian ministry, several points might be drawn.

A first observation is on how the voice of bereaved people has become amplified over the last century and even more so over the last decade. This corresponds to legislative and societal changes that have acknowledged and protected the identity of the deceased. Families, as Rugg notes,[41] can claim control over grave space in a way that was formerly only possible for wealthy and high status groups. Possession of the body – once denied to those in extreme poverty – remains crucial, though is now manifest in challenges to official appropriation of the corpse, as already noted, at the grave, and more sensationally where aspects of post-mortems (for example, children, babies at Alder Hey, young people in the *Marchioness* disaster) are disputed. And yet, with burial declining among home-grown populations, possession of an 'intact' body appears a questionable matter – until account is taken of the possibilities for possession and control increasingly enacted with ashes.

This suggests new and different paradigms of departure and the shape of post-mortem identity, especially when burial is widely understood to be less 'final' than cremation. Attempts to adjust to the death of someone who had been close in life take time – time that burial has been seen as allowing.[42] Family retention of ashes[43] is now reclaiming that time from the haste of cremation, as secondary disposal practices are improvised by families, without much awareness and less involvement on the part of the Churches. The body, vulnerable to end-of-life medical intervention and to post-mortem discontents as to ownership and control, is released as ash to the custodianship of those who knew the deceased and often continue the practical habits of caring.[44]

Second, pastoral lapses in the aftermath of the funeral are often acknowledged by clergy, usually as a consequence of workloads. Nonetheless, the popularity of commemorative events that funeral directors now arrange and are sometimes part of cemetery open days indicate bereaved people's needs to acknowledge the dead in a public arena. A kindred sense of support, between bereaved people and sometimes with cemetery staff, often develops for those who have chosen burial and make an economic and emotional investment in the grave, especially if they visit regularly. But alongside this more individually centred activity, there are culturally special days when large numbers gather at cemeteries in displays of public, socio-religious or community solidarity. For example, Christmas, Easter, Mothers' and Fathers' Days feature largely for all groups and many denominations – even Jewish and Muslim mourners with quite distinct ritual calendars and special days. November is a time when Roman Catholics and Orthodox families visit, though Anglicans less so. Orthodox mourners[45] will visit in November and sometimes on name days, for which others may substitute birthdays. Anniversaries of the death are significant for many mourners, whether at the grave or in domestic settings.

Inter-faith gatherings on annual open days, when clergy said Mass or officiated at commemorative services in cemetery chapels, were well attended and appreciated. This strongly suggests how bereaved people grasp opportunities for *association* as much as institutional recognition of the deceased and as part of the renegotiation and revalidation of changed identities. In this post-funeral vacuum individuals and families are left somewhat adrift and resorting to their own devices. Even those who claim some connection with organized Christianity have started to improvise alternative ways of managing the questioning and searching which death brings in its wake. The Roman Catholic practice of naming the dead at anniversaries or offering Mass for particular deceased parishioners represents a public acknowledgement that the dead remain, somehow, connected. The Orthodox liturgy marks different intervals with a formality familiar to older generations, though the more secularized young may admit to its strangeness.[46] In this they represent the many for whom church involvement is not habitual, or even occasional, but who are not necessarily hostile and who appear to need and value a frame for continuing lifetime bonds.[47]

Third, increasing trends to celebrate life rather than to acknowledge death emphasize, as Davies notes,[48] retrospection rather than a future in which the personal purgatories of bereaved people can have a legitimate place. This is not to say that Christian ministry can solve the difficulties or answer the questions, rather that more publicly framed rituals for commemoration and association might be offered. New demographics of burying communities may already mean that some Churches are already so engaged; the Pentecostal churches are important for many black communities in conferring such public recognition.[49] New Eastern European Catholics and, as already noted, established Orthodox communities, regenerate rituals – including requiem – that have become dormant for longer-settled populations. It would be foolish to suggest that these intensities would be widely acceptable for those accustomed to restraint and who might now find the ritual strange, but some of the traditional ritual threads may resonate for and on behalf of the bereaved.

Finally, cemetery managers and perhaps some clergy may think that the public has too loud a voice, particularly where grave and cemetery customs become exuberantly out of control. These individual expressions to acknowledge that the dead still matter could be restrained and tempered, non-confrontationally, if there were more collective and public opportunities for bereaved families to 'perform' their mourning. Many see themselves as having transcended the catastrophe of death. They may well have taken central roles during the illness, at the moment of death, through its immediate consequences and the awfulness of the funeral. This stays with them as they attend to the grave and regard it as a sort of stage, with the cemetery as a backdrop to a public or 'audience' that comments, remarks, copies and may criticize if 'performance' falls short of local expectation.

This account suggests that though secularity, with its emphasis on the present and the material, now dominates, supernatural – even spiritualistic – inclinations persist in the dispositions of bereaved people to their dead. The need to attend to such impulses to 'continue bonding' with the dead is one with which Churches and other professionals have had difficulties, not least because of workloads. The suggestions that arise from the foregoing discussion build on less labour-intensive strategies that acknowledge how mourners favour occasions for coming together in the cemetery and at other places seen as significant. The value of denominational and inter-faith services has been mentioned. Additionally, more information to those who bury ash remains – and ultimately many ashes are placed in earth[50] – that clergy may be able to perform a committal ceremony could resolve the puzzlement that some speak of, once they have the ashes at home and are faced with action in the absence of any established custom. Might an annual blessing of the consecrated areas, to which people are invited, be possible? And how far might local organizations for supporting bereaved people be involved? The paradigm of departure that now seems to shape dispositions and actions is one where death is experienced as final but where people try to sort out ways of constructing it as 'not so final'. Any theological clues as to how to do this that they may once have glimpsed seem to have evaporated, and yet nearly all go on hoping against hope to understand and find some light. The Churches surely have a place in this.

Notes

1 Douglas Davies and Alistair Shaw, *Reusing Old Graves: A Report on Popular British Attitudes*, Crayford: Shaw and Sons, 1995.

2 a) The Secret Cemetery: this ESRC-funded research project entailed ethnographic study in six ethnically diverse London cemeteries. The aim was to research the meaning of the contemporary cemetery. Between 1996 and 2000 approximately 1,500 individuals, some in family groups, talked to us. Some 300 recounted at length details of their experiences and reflections, mainly of burial. The book was published in 2005, preceded by several journal articles.

b) Environments of Memory: this research, also funded by ESRC, focused on cremation and the destinations of those ashes removed in increasing numbers from crematoria for individual disposal. Four regional sites were selected and a total of 30 professionals, including clergy, gave information and views. A total of 60 bereaved people who had been responsible for arranging a cremation were at the centre of this research which used in-depth methods to explore a range of issues around death, beliefs, ritual and practices in relation to ash remains.

3 Tony Walter, *The Eclipse of Eternity: A Sociology of the Afterlife*, Basingstoke: Macmillan Press, 1996; Colleen McDannell and Bernhard Lang, *Heaven: A History*, 2nd edn, New Haven and London: Yale, Nota Bene, 2001.

4 Christopher Daniell, *Death and Burial in Medieval England 1066–1550*, London: Routledge, 1997; Peter Jupp, *From Dust to Ashes: Cremation and the British Way of Death*, Basingstoke: Palgrave Macmillan, 2006.

5 Vanessa Harding, *The Dead and the Living in Paris and London, 1500–1670*, Cambridge: Cambridge University Press, 2002.

6 Harding, *Dead and the Living in Paris and London*. Leonie Kellaher, David Prendergast and Jenny Hockey, 'In the Shadow of the Traditional Grave', *Mortality*, Vol. 10, No. 4, 2005, pp. 237-50.

7 Kellaher, Prendergast and Hockey, 'In the Shadow of the Traditional Grave'. Peter Jupp, 'Cremation or Burial? Contemporary Choice in City and Village' in D. Clark (ed.), *The Sociology of Death: Theory, Culture, Practice*, Oxford: Blackwell/The Sociological Review, 1993, pp. 169-97.

8 Still to find a recent reference – any suggestions Peter?

9 Ruth Richardson, *Death, Dissection and the Destitute*, London: Routledge and Kegan Paul, 1987; Jupp, *From Dust to Ashes*. George Alfred Walker's book *Gatherings from Graveyards*, London, 1839, caused a sensation on publication and contributed enormously to the reform of burial grounds in the 1840s and 1850s.

10 Mary Douglas, *Purity and Danger: An Analysis of Concepts of Pollution and Taboo*, London: Routledge and Kegan Paul, 1978; Richard Huntingdon and Peter Metcalf, *Celebrations of Death: The Anthropology of Mortuary Ritual*, Cambridge: Cambridge University Press, 1979.

11 Ian Hussein and Julie Rugg, 'Managing London's Dead: A Case of Strategic Policy Failure', *Mortality*, Vol. 8, No. 2, 2003, pp. 209-21.

12 For example, Harding, *The Dead and the Living*.

13 J. S. Curl, 'The Architecture and Planning of Nineteenth-Century Cemeteries', *Garden History*, Vol. 4, No. 3, 1975, pp. 223-54.

14 Julie Rugg, 'Defining the Place of Burial: What Makes a Cemetery a

Cemetery?', *Mortality*, Vol. 5, No. 3, 2000, pp. 259–76.

15 Jupp, *From Dust to Ashes*.

16 Between 1852 and 1906 15 Burial Acts were passed. The 1857 Burial Act was a landmark Act and shaped cemetery development up until the 1972 Local Government Act which gave us the cemetery regimes we now witness.

17 Ronnie Scott, *Death by Design: The True Story of the Glasgow Necropolis*, Edinburgh: Black and White Publishing, 2005.

18 Ken Worpole, *Last Landscapes: The Architecture of the Cemetery in the West*, London: Reaktion Books, 2003.

19 Julie-Marie Strange, *Death, Grief and Poverty in Britain 1870–1914*, Cambridge: Cambridge University Press, 2006.

20 Julie Rugg, 'A Few Remarks on Modern Sepulture: Current Trends and New Directions in Cemetery Research, *Mortality*, Vol. 3, No. 2, 1998, pp. 111–28.

21 Doris Francis, Leonie Kellaher and Georgina Neophytou, *The Secret Cemetery*, Oxford: Berg, 2005.

22 See Grainger, this volume.

23 Mike Featherstone, Mike Hepworth and Bryan Turner, *The Body: Social Process and Cultural Theory*, London: Sage, 1990.

24 Clive Seale, *Constructing Death: The Sociology of Dying and Bereavement*, Cambridge: Cambridge University Press, 1998.

25 Zygmunt Bauman, *Mortality, Immortality and Other Life Strategies*, Cambridge: Polity Press, 1992.

26 See Jupp, this volume, chapter 2.

27 Gillian Bennett and Kate Bennett, 'The Presence of the Dead: An Empirical Study', *Mortality*, Vol. 5, No. 2, 2000, pp. 13–57.

28 See Rogers, this volume.

29 See Jupp, this volume, chapter 7.

30 Jon Davies, 'Vile Bodies and Mass Media Chantries' in G. Howarth and P. C. Jupp, *Contemporary Issues in the Sociology of Death, Dying and Disposal*, Basingstoke: Macmillan Press, 1996, pp. 47–59; Geoffrey Rowell, 'Changing Patterns: Christian Beliefs about Death and the Future of Life' in P. C. Jupp and T. Rogers, *Interpreting Death: Christian Theology and Pastoral Practice*, London and Washington: Cassell, 1997, pp. 17–29, 21.

31 Francis et al., *The Secret Cemetery*, pp. 67ff.

32 This is as true for bereaved people of all denominations as well as for Jewish mourners, for whom the stone-setting represents a rather more formal point of departure for the living and the dead.

33 Contrast Jones, this volume.

34 See Valentine, this volume.

35 David Prendergast, Jenny Hockey and Leonie Kellaher, 'Blowing in the Wind: Identity, Materiality and the Destinations of Human Ashes', *Journal of the Royal Anthropological Institute* (N.S.) No. 12, 2006, pp. 881–98.

36 Under the Best Value initiative, which was introduced in the late 1980s by the Thatcher administration, local authorities were expected to become brokers of services rather than direct providers and to take serious account of user views and preferences across all local authority services. One consequence was the introduction of competition into services, and while cemeteries have generally remained

within the public sector (apart from very recent private sector initiatives in natu-ral/green burial sites), a range of choices has emerged for mourners.

37 *The Dead Citizens Charter*, 2nd edn, Bristol: The National Funerals College, 1998; *Charter for the Bereaved*, 2nd and rev. edn, London: The Institute of Burial and Cremation Administration, 1998.

38 See Davies, this volume.

39 For example, the Freckleton case: see Diocese of Blackburn, Judgement in the Consistory Court, 16 July 1994.

40 Philip Bachelor, *Sorrow and Solace: The Social World of the Cemetery*, Amityville, New York: Baywood Publishing Company Inc., 2004.

41 Julie Rugg, 'Introduction: Cemeteries', *Mortality*, Vol. 8, No. 2, 2003, pp. 107–12.

42 Robert Hertz, 'A Contribution to the Study of Collective Representation of Death' in *Death and the Right Hand*, trans R. and C. Needham, London: Cohen and West, 1960 (*Annee Sociologique* 10:48–137, 1907).

43 Ash retention increased rapidly, as *Pharos International* periodically reports. Between the 1970s and 2000, the proportion of ashes removed from crematoria increased from around 12 per cent to over 50 per cent. In some regions and areas, the figure reaches 80 per cent.

44 Jenny Hockey, Leonie Kellaher and David Prendergast, 'Of Grief and Well-being: Competing Concepts of Restorative Ritual', *Anthropology and Medicine*, Vol. 14, No. 1, April 2007, pp. 1–14.

45 See Nankivell, this volume.

46 See Nankivell, this volume.

47 See Valentine, this volume.

48 Douglas J. Davies, *Death, Ritual and Belief*, 2nd edn, London: Continuum, 2002.

49 See Hilborn, this volume.

50 Jupp, 'Cremation or Burial?'

II

Overcoming 'An Architecture of Reluctance':

British Crematoria, Past, Present and Future

HILARY J. GRAINGER

Introduction

Until the 1990s, little had been written about the history of cremation and crematoria in Britain, other than groundbreaking work by the architectural historian James Stevens Curl (1972). Thereafter Peter C. Jupp (1990), Douglas J. Davies (1990, 1995, 1997), Tony Walter (1990, 1995 and 1997) and Kate Berridge (2001) brought their respective disciplines of religious history, theology, social anthropology, sociology and journalism to bear on the subject.[1] The recent publication of three full-length studies (Parsons, 2005; Jupp, 2006; and Davies, 2006) represents a burgeoning interest.[2]

The fact that the architecture of British crematoria had hitherto escaped detailed study is all the more remarkable particularly because crematoria represent the outward physical and symbolical expression of a movement that sought to provide a radical alternative to burial. However, a fourth detailed study now provides the first architectural history of crematoria, placed in the context of social, liturgical and religious changes.[3]

It seems timely therefore to revisit some of the issues surrounding the oft-vexed relationship between the crematorium and Christian ministry[4] by exploring the development of cremation and crematoria through the lens of architectural history. This chapter seeks to facilitate a more effective Christian ministry in crematoria, first by explaining the historical constellation of determinants shaping their design, in order to promote a better understanding of the problems that these buildings pose and, second, by offering resources and insights to inform the ways in which clergy might work within the existing physical parameters in order to enrich the emotional experiences of all those involved in crematorium services.

Crematoria: a paradigm of modernity

Given that over 70 per cent of deaths in the UK are followed by cremation, Britain's 253[5] crematoria emerge as a significant element within contemporary life, offering an architectural form that reflects the values and social life of a modern, urban and increasingly socially and geographically mobile society. Crematoria offer a paradigm of modernity. A new building type, firmly located in the twentieth century, without architectural precedent, reliant on innovative and complex technology, their location, planning and design predicated to a considerable degree on motor transport – crematoria were expressive of a new social order. By rejecting the aesthetic of the overcrowded and sentimentalized Victorian cemetery they created a new landscape for collective mourning.

And yet crematoria are rarely iconic buildings. They are invariably consigned to the physical and psychological periphery, shrouded by a veil of anonymity that has rendered them the invisible buildings of the twentieth century. Nevertheless they play an undeniably important role in the life of towns and cities and in the renegotiated landscape of death.[6]

Increasingly, secularization renders the crematorium a highly significant public building, largely replacing the church as the main focus for the important function of saying farewell to people we love, and yet the 'secular' crematorium and its Gardens of Remembrance can be invested with 'sacredness' by repeated visits.[7] Thirty years ago the crematorium was a place for cremation and built to accommodate a brief committal ceremony, with the assumption that the main service would continue to be taken at the local church. Increasingly, however, the ritual, the function and the remembrance are centred on the crematorium and its landscape setting – an onerous responsibility for buildings over three-fifths of which were designed between 1950 and 1970 and which are owned for the most part by local authorities. Paradoxically, despite the increasing popularity of cremation, both mourners and clergy often find crematoria unsatisfactory, their design uninspiring, banal and inconsequential.

The redesigning of disposal

Cremation was revived in the late nineteenth century as an alternative to burial but did not claim widespread support until the second half of the twentieth century.[8] Its history in Britain reveals a long and sustained struggle against religious prejudice and conservatism. Historically secular and informed by concerns over hygiene, overcrowded burial grounds and cemeteries, the revival was supported by advances in technology. Christian influences throughout Europe had, for very nearly 2,000 years, fostered burial as the traditional form of funeral. A belief in the doctrine of the resurrection of the body further reinforced the importance and symbolism of burial. It is therefore remarkable that cremation should have so rapidly attained cultural normality, indeed ritual dominance, by the late twentieth century.[9]

In contrast to the Indian tradition of cremation, the practice in Britain was developed from the outset as an indoor disposal activity and, as such, one that called for a new building type. The necessity for dedicated buildings stems in part from the practical concern raised by the celebrated landmark Price trial of 1884 in Cardiff, at which Judge Stephen concluded that no criminal act was committed by burning a dead body provided that it did not 'amount to a public nuisance at common law'.[10]

Complexity, ambiguity and evasion

As cremation slowly gained acceptance in Britain, this progress was reflected in its architectural expression, and each crematorium can therefore be seen as 'a symbol of social change'.[11] The crematorium, however, presents a series of challenges to the architect. The lack of a shared expectation of what is required has given rise to the cultural ambivalence lying at the heart of many designs, and so, not surprisingly, architectural responses have often been ambiguous and evasive. There has been no consensus on style and, just as surprisingly, no espousal of European modernism. Instead, contemporary interpretations of traditional architectural vocabularies were explored.

Not the least difficulty facing architects was the necessary chimney. This did not sit happily either with Greek temples, Renaissance domes or Gothic chapels. In the majority of cases it was clear that it had been concealed within a bell-tower – Headingley, Leeds (1904) being a good example: 'The louvres that should have emitted joyful peals often belched smoke.'[12] The Neo-Renaissance design for Northampton

(1939) hid the chimney in the dome, while at Honor Oak, London (1939), it was concealed in a tower modelled on the Campanile in Piazza San Marco, Venice.[13] This was the architecture of deception.

At once religious and secular, crematoria are fraught with complexity. Two very distinct spaces are required: the functional and the symbolic, linked by a transitional space through which the coffin passes from the chapel or meeting hall to the cremator. This space acts both as a barrier between and a threshold over the 'death' and 'life' sections of the building. While the utilitarian purpose – that of reducing a dead body at high temperature to vapour and ashes – has remained unequivocal, the search for symbolic architectural forms has proved highly problematical from the outset. Indeed, as recently as 2000 a panel from the Royal Institute of British Architects described the crematorium as 'a meeting point for complex human and cultural issues whose resolution into a successful building is potentially very difficult'.[14]

Cost and planning permission represent perennial constraints. Crematoria have to conform to the 1902 Cremation Act – they must therefore be 200 yards from the nearest dwelling, and 50 yards from any public highway. This 'radius clause', based on the Cemetery Clauses Act of 1847, restricted crematorium planning in the first half of the twentieth century, Edinburgh (1929) being a fine example of the delay caused to crematorium planners by an urban environment. Furthermore, crematoria cannot be built in a consecrated part of the burial ground of any burial authority, a consequence of the Anglican Church's decision to eschew cremation. As a result, they require a disproportionately large site, which partly explains their often being consigned to the margins of towns and cities, assisted by the dual carriageways necessitated by an age of mass car ownership. Their location is reminiscent of Ebenezer Howard's proposals for garden cities (1898), in which the less savoury public buildings such as hospitals and asylums were placed in the outer rim of his concentric plan, and suggests an element of social engineering.

But it is the challenge of accommodating both the religious and the secular that confounds the design process. The crematorium must provide a stage for the ritual of all denominations and none. For those individuals for whom cremation remains a religious act, the principle determining the arrangement needs to be the physical expression of a religious rite, whether for example Christian or Hindu. The premise must therefore be the embodiment of ritualistic purpose in a coherent and recognizable architectural form. For those not belonging to the dominant religious groups, their spiritual and emotional needs must also be provided for in a meaningful way.

The earliest crematoria were designed deliberately to look like churches, often lamely Gothic in style, but clearly intended to offer reassurance to the sceptical, and respectability to cremation through a visual connection with the Church and its tradition of burial as at Woking (1889), Liverpool (1896) and Bradford (1905).[15] This associative value of style was somewhat ironic, since the Church, in choosing to distance itself from the cremation movement, effectively relinquished any sway over issues of design and planning. In denying the theological issues surrounding cremation, the Church has undoubtedly contributed to the absence of liturgy and the resulting anomalies surrounding the committal and the disposal of ashes.[16] If it is stripped of any ritual and ceremony, any depth of spiritual meaning, cremation becomes merely a modern method of burning the dead – an impersonal, unimpassioned and emotionally detached 'process', undertaken in a 'facility' separate from the ritual hall or chapel.[17]

Uncertainty of purpose is most clearly felt in crematorium chapels. The word 'chapel' is applied gingerly, especially in light of the changing patterns of religious belief and unbelief which unfolded during the twentieth century. For Rowell 'the character of crematoria, both architecturally and symbolically' has been determined outside a Christian frame of reference. These are 'churches which are not churches, often having altars which are never used as Christian altars'.[18] It comes as a surprise to many, however, that crematoria are not consecrated buildings, partly as a result of Anglican reluctance and partly local authority preference. This lack of religious certainty is often revealed in the decoration, which can only hint at denomination. This continues to be the subject of heated debate, witnessed most recently in Torquay, where in June 2005 council officials removed a fixed cross and renamed the 'chapel' a 'ceremony hall'.

But most telling is the indecision surrounding the positioning of the catafalque in relation to the altar, if indeed an altar has been provided. Some architects chose to position the catafalque[19] centrally, raised and lit from above or from the side, in order to establish it as the centre of attention in accordance with traditional funeral services. Others place it 'off-centre' in a recess or projecting from either the side-wall or the facing wall beside the altar, emphasizing the distinction between cremation and burial.

The means by which the coffin moves at the point of committal has varied from the outset.[20] There are three main options. First, the coffin resting on the catafalque is passed mechanically and slowly through an aperture in the wall to the committal chamber. Second, the coffin, resting on the catafalque, slowly descends to a lower level, or the coffin, resting on the 'paving' of the 'chancel', descends similarly. Third, the coffin resting on the catafalque or draped trolley is placed in a recess, and either a curtain or gates are slowly drawn across at the point of committal, the coffin being removed after the mourners have left. Alternatively, the coffin remains in situ until mourners leave the chapel.

Although the third and fourth options are the most common,[21] some interesting regional patterns emerge. In Scotland and Wales, where the progress of cremation was slower than in England, the majority of coffins descend, seemingly an endorsement of local deep-rooted imagery associated with burial.

But the point of committal, which ought to be the emotional climax, the moment of departure and final separation, is often one at which the greatest uncertainty arises. Mourners watch from a distance as the coffin is removed and remain passive observers rather than active participants. While there may be something theatrical about the event, there is more disturbingly something mechanical and sometimes even comical about it. The curtains are often closed by remote control. It is at this point that the lack of ceremony becomes most marked and mourners are likely to become distressed, as characterized in Blake Morrison's account of his father's funeral.[22]

The search for emotional and spiritual fulfilment

Fragmentation, disassociation and depersonalization compound to leave many mourners feeling emotionally cheated, dissatisfied and uncertain at the point of committal. Moreover, there is evasion. While mourners acknowledge tacitly the departure of the coffin for cremation, there still remains a great deal of ignorance, perhaps calculated, about the ensuing process. The most certain way of facing finality is to witness the cremation. Although it is a legal right to view the event, and despite exhortations from the architect Peter Bond in 1967 who subscribed to Geoffrey Gorer's view[23] that those who have participated in some form of ritual are better equipped to cope with their loss after the funeral, very few choose to do so, other than for religious reasons, perhaps as a result of historical associations attached to burning of the dead.[24]

The ultimate point of separation, the entry of the coffin into the cremator, is distanced both physically and emotionally from those assembled in a space where they would normally expect some participatory ending to a funeral.[25] This would be signalled traditionally by the carrying out of the coffin, followed by the procession of mourners leaving the church by the same door through which they entered, in accordance with the important social and religious rituals of baptisms, weddings and ordinary church services.[26] But in the vast majority of newly designed crematoria, mourners enter through one door and leave by another, a circulation route first introduced by Ernest George at Golders Green Crematorium in 1902, where mourners entered through one door and left by another into the gardens, as if to indicate the crossing of an emotional threshold, a change of state – something which clergy might want to exploit.[27] The benefits of George's plan were not to be fully appreciated until the 1930s when the number of cremations increased, making it necessary to keep groups of mourners apart. When this new ritual was combined with a 20-minute slot, it magnified the impression of a 'production line'. The important act of mourning is impeded therefore by abruptness, peremptoriness and banality.

An appropriate architectural language

Ruskin's contention that 'architecture proposes an effect on the human mind, not merely a service to the human frame' is particularly apposite in the case of the crematorium where, arguably, the emotionally evocative qualities of the building ought to contrive to create a relationship between spatial arrangement and inner condition, and in so doing exceed the functional aspects of architectural design. It was perhaps with this in mind that the architects of the award-winning Llwydcoed Crematorium Aberdare, Mid-Glamorgan (1970) argued that 'a crematorium is almost pure architecture, even more so than a church'.[28] But as architectural historian Alan Crawford points out:

> Christian burial is a hard act to follow. And in a sense it makes the design of a successful crematorium impossible. How, without a framework of belief and shared meanings, can the design of a building reach out to the hearts of mourners, the people who have lost someone in death? It is hard enough for a person to do this, but a building? It is as if modern secularism and relativism ties the hand of the crematorium architect, makes her work only with the quietest, blankest, and sometimes blandest, of forms. If there is an emptiness in an atmosphere of some crematoria, it is because we live in a society which cannot frame the passage from life to death.[29]

In order to understand Crawford's perspective fully, some insight into architectural developments is instructive.

Stylistic pluralism persisted and was employed somewhat tentatively in crematorium design with the result that, for the most part, the potential power of architectural language was underexploited. Conversions from cemetery chapels were favoured, particularly during the 1950s, since they kept costs down at a time of material and labour shortages, and required little in the way of landscaping and facilitated planning permission. But many were highly insensitive and the cause of much criticism. The Cinderellas of local authority provision, crematoria were almost invariably denied the architectural embellishment reserved for prestigious civic buildings. By the early 1960s death professionals were joined alarmingly by the architectural profession in finding little to recommend. However, not all architects took the undemonstrative path. The award-winning local authority-owned Blackley, Manchester (1957) took a lead by adopting a bolder architectural statement about the modernity of cremation. Margam, Mid-Glamorgan (1969), quite unprecedented in its frank expression of modernist forms, is arguably the most dramatic crematorium design in Britain – its chimney, conceived as the focal point, emphasized its function in a refreshingly uncompromising way.

Some crematoria succeed in their difficult task, the difficulty making them all the more remarkable. They provide a benchmark for the future. Basil Spence's Edinburgh, Mortonhall (1967), with its 'calmly expressionist forms' recalls the best traditions of European modernism. At Coychurch Crematorium, Bridgend (1969–1970) architect Maxwell Fry maintained that a procession or ritual passage of mourners through the grounds could assume some spiritual significance. This he expressed architecturally by privileging two elements – time and distance – with the intention of enriching the ceremony 'so that both it and our own lives thereby become significant' and endorsing the notion of 'sacredness'.[30]

Many crematoria, in their own ways, create a sense of place, and whether by association with nature or with history, or by means of their landscaping or their use of materials, provide a feeling of continuity and sureness, which transcends the choice of architectural style. In these instances the singular function of the crematorium is outweighed by the spiritual and symbolic language of its architecture and landscape setting.

The search for a meaningful ministry

Author and playwright Alan Bennett reflected with humane insightful-ness in *Untold Stories* that the municipal crematorium is 'decorum-led architecture which does not draw attention even to its merits . . . This is the architecture of reluctance, the furnishings of the functionally ill at ease, décor for a place you do not want to be.'[31] Such criticisms lend weight to contemporary perceptions that the Church has lost its hold on the great ceremony of death, which has been replaced by diminished rites and the sentimental functions of the commonplace crematorium. This perception represents a real challenge for clergy conducting funerals for those holding religious beliefs. The present crematoria are likely to remain, and the likelihood of a clear conceptual basis emerging in the light of an increasingly multi-faith, secular and individual society is tendentious. We remain a society seemingly incapable of framing with certainty or consensus the passage from life to death.

Architecture cannot be held solely accountable for the emotional emptiness felt by some. Other factors come into play: inadequate ser-vices forced into 20-minute slots, poor music, even poor weather. But there are ways in which the Church might prepare mourners. By dis-cussing with their congregation first what to expect at the crematorium, given that uncertainty arises from lack of familiarity, clergy could obvi-ate a great deal of stress and apprehension. Options regarding whether or not the coffin leaves the mourners or mourners leave the coffin[32] ought to be made clear. Whether mourners might derive comfort from either their or the celebrant's touching the coffin at the point of com-mittal ought to be explored fully before the funeral, as might the vexed issue of curtains. The potential 'sacredness' of both the building and its surroundings[33] ought to be better explained, and clergy could endorse this further by more conspicuous presence at memorial services organ-ized by crematorium managers. Furthermore, clergy in the first instance, rather than funeral directors, ought to discuss with families the issue of what will happen to the ashes. Fry's emphasis on the spiritual signifi-cance and importance of ritual procession, for those both of faith and of no faith, might be further exploited in the approach both to the crema-torium and the catafalque. Clergy training could address the challenge that, unlike wedding preparations, funerals are almost never rehearsed.

But perhaps the greatest challenge to clergy would be that of holding the committal first and then a service of thanksgiving and commemora-tion either the next day, or some time later. This would allow families and friends to regroup, re-gather and reconcile themselves to their loss without the problems wrought by time, distance and transport.[34]

The crematorium buildings and surroundings cannot carry the burden of relieving pain or giving meaning: it is the mourners who invest a funeral with meaning.[35] The challenge for Christian ministry remains that of finding ways in which to prepare mourners with the means by which they can make such an investment.

Notes

1 James Stevens Curl, *The Victorian Celebration of Death*, Newton Abbot: David & Charles, 1972; James Stevens Curl, *Death and Architecture: An Introduction to Funerary and Commemorative Buildings in the Western European Tradition, with Some Consideration of Their Settings*, London: Constable & Co., 1980, rev. edn, Stroud: Sutton, 2002; Peter C. Jupp, 'From Dust to Ashes: The Replacement of Burial by Cremation in England 1840–1967', *The Congregational Lecture 1990*, London: The Congregational Memorial Hall Trust (1978) Ltd, 1990; Douglas J Davies, *Cremation Today and Tomorrow*, Nottingham: Grove Books, 1990; *British Crematoria in Public Profile*, Maidstone: The Cremation Society, 1995; and *Death, Ritual and Belief: The Rhetoric of Funerary Rites*, London: Routledge, 1997. Tony Walter, *Funerals and How to Improve Them*, London: Hodder & Stoughton, 1990; *The Revival of Death*, London and New York: Routledge, 1995; and 'Committal in the Crematorium: Theology, Death and Architecture' in Peter C. Jupp and Tony Rogers (eds), *Interpreting Death: Christian Theology and Pastoral Practice*, London: Cassell, 1997, pp. 203–14. Kate Berridge, *Vigor Mortis: The End of the Death Taboo*, London: Profile Books, 2001.

2 Brian Parsons, *Committed to the Cleansing Flame: The Development of Cremation in Nineteenth-Century England*, Reading: Spire, 2005: Peter C. Jupp, *From Dust to Ashes: Cremation and the British Way of Death*, Basingstoke: Palgrave Macmillan, 2006; Douglas J. Davies with Lewis Mates, *The Encyclopedia of Cremation*, Aldershot: Ashgate, 2006.

3 Hilary J. Grainger, *Death Redesigned: British Crematoria, History, Architecture and Landscape*, Reading: Spire, 2005.

4 An issue first raised by Davies, 'British Crematoria', and Walter, 'Commital in the Crematorium'.

5 Numbers as of December 2007.

6 See Cobb, this volume.

7 Douglas J. Davies, 'The Sacred Crematorium', *Mortality*, Vol. 1, No. 1, March 1996, pp. 83–94.

8 Jupp, *From Dust to Ashes*.

9 Davies, *British Crematoria*.

10 Stephen R. G. White, 'A Burial Ahead of Its Time? The Crookenden Burial Case and the Sanctioning of Cremation in England and Wales', *Mortality*, Vol. 7, No. 2, 2002, pp. 171–90.

11 Davies, *British Crematoria*.

12 Curl, *Death and Architecture*, p. 310.

13 For illustrations, see Grainger, *Death Redesigned*.

14 S. Hardingham, *Guide to England: A Recent Architecture*, London: Ellipsis, 2001.

15 For illustrations, see Grainger, *Death Redesigned*.

16 See Lampard, this volume.

17 Berridge, *Vigor Mortis*.

18 Geoffrey Rowell, *The Liturgy of Christian Burial*, London: SPCK, 1977, p. 113.

19 Catafalque has a specific meaning in the context of crematoria, being not only the structure upon which the coffin rests but also often the means by which it is removed.

20 Davies, *British Crematoria*, pp. 20–3.

21 Grainger, *Death Redesigned*.

22 Blake Morrison, *And When Did You Last See Your Father?*, London: Granta Books, 1993. But see Sheppy's critique of Morrison's account: 'a specific instance of ritual disorder', Paul P. J. Sheppy, *Death Liturgy and Ritual Vol. 1: A Pastoral and Liturgical Theology*, Aldershot: Ashgate, 2003, pp. 16–17.

23 Geoffrey Gorer, *Death, Grief and Mourning in Contemporary Britain*, London: Cresset Press, 1965, was quoted by Peter Bond (p. 88) in 'Architecture for Mourning' in G. Cope (ed.), *Death, Dying and Disposal*, London: SPCK, 1970, pp. 85–98.

24 See Lampard, this volume.

25 See Berridge, *Vigor Mortis*.

26 Davies, *British Crematoria*, pp. 35–8.

27 For a full account of Golders Green Crematorium see Grainger, *Death Redesigned*; and Grainger, 'Golders Green Crematorium and the Architectural Expression of Cremation', *Mortality*, Vol. 5, No. 1, 2000, pp. 53–73.

28 'Building Study, Crematorium, H. M. R. Burgess & Partners, Architects' Account and Appraisal by Alan Lipman', *Architects' Journal Information Library*, Vol. 153, No. 20, 1971, pp. 1133–46.

29 Alan Crawford in 'Foreword' in Grainger, *Death Redesigned*, pp. 11–12, 12.

30 E. Maxwell Fry, 'The Design of Crematoria', The Alfred Bossom Lectures, *The Journal of the Royal Society of Arts*, 117, 1968–9, p. 262.

31 Alan Bennett, *Untold Stories*, London: Faber and Faber, 2005, p. 121.

32 Walter, 'Committal in the Crematorium'.

33 Davies, 'The Sacred Crematorium'.

34 Outlined by Walter, 'Committal in the Crematorium'.

35 Crawford, 'Foreword', p. 12.

12

Ashes to Ashes, Dust to Dust:
A Theology for Burial

KEVIN MCGINNELL

Introduction

Genesis tells us that the human being was formed from the dust of the earth: 'The LORD God formed man from the dust of the ground, and breathed into his nostrils the breath of life; and the man became a living being' (Genesis 2.7). Death emerges later as a consequence of human sin: '. . . you return to the ground, for out of it you were taken; you are dust, and to dust you shall return' (Genesis 3.19b).

While today's believer will not necessarily take those texts literally, they founded the Judaeo-Christian burial tradition. Burial reflects this natural cycle compared to other methods of disposal, which are all, to differing degrees, artificial. From that starting point we move as Christians to the burial of Jesus, the Saviour: 'Joseph took the body . . . and laid it in his own new tomb, which he had hewn from the rock. He then rolled a great stone to the door of the tomb' (Matthew 27.59). It is from this tomb that Jesus is raised to life in his human body. He proves he is not a ghost but real in the flesh by his various resurrection appearances. In imitation of him, then, the Christian is buried with Christ in baptism so as to rise with him to a new life: '. . . we have been buried with him by baptism into death, so that, just as Christ was raised from the dead by the glory of the Father, so we too might walk in newness of life' (Romans 6.4). We live this baptismal life in the hope that we too will not be overpowered by death but rise with him: 'For if we have been united with him in a death like his, we will certainly be united with him in a resurrection like his' (Romans 6.5).

Thus burial, as the Christian tradition for disposal, expresses the hope of the historical Christian creeds for eternal life and for the resurrection of the body. Burial grounds, be they catacombs, churchyards or cemeteries, are important and valuable foci for communities in many

different ways. The historical Christian choice for burial is rooted theologically while also having valuable spiritual and pastoral, and even
political, dimensions. We do not have the time here to explore that
history; rather, against the above synopsis[1] I propose to develop a theology of burial for our present time.

Baptized into Christ's death and resurrection[2]

The Christian faith is centred in the person of Jesus Christ, truly God
and fully human. Throughout its history the preaching has proclaimed
his birth and death, his being buried for three days and his bodily resurrection. A stronger emphasis on incarnational theology in the twentieth
century only serves to reinforce this point. Theology and spirituality
have expressed a more developed understanding of what it means for
God to have fully assumed human flesh in the person of Jesus as the Son
of God. That total integration of human and divine emphasizes the
value of our own humanity as children of God.[3] For his resurrection to
be real, we have to affirm his death and the burial of his body. 'When
they had carried out everything that was written about him, they took
him down from the tree and laid him in a tomb. But God raised him
from the dead' (Acts 13.29–30). This teaching is affirmed by typology
drawn from the Jewish testament referring to Christ, such as Jonah
being buried in the belly of the whale for three days.

The Christian, someone who follows Christ, is initiated into the
Christian mystery by being buried with Christ in baptism. Before entering the waters of baptism, candidates have to affirm their belief in 'the
resurrection of the body and life everlasting', so that the water bath
becomes a clear sacramental expression of entering into this mystery of
Christ's death and resurrection.[4] 'May all who are buried with Christ in
the death of baptism rise also with him to newness of life.'[5] The developing practice of immersion in more churches symbolizes this truth ever
more clearly.[6]

Week by week the Christian proclaims in the Creed, 'I believe in the
resurrection of the body and the life everlasting.' What we proclaim we
need to live out, walking the way of Christ himself through life to death.
In our death we seek to be buried with him, so as to rise with him. Burial
expresses that unity with him directly.

Living like Christ is also an affirmation of the value of being truly
human. Christ shared our human flesh, and the people who loved him
cared for his body in death. Our incarnational faith establishes such

dignity for the human body that any mode of committal should truly and fully celebrate the value of the body that was once shared by Jesus as the Son of God, and is still so shared in heaven. Paul develops this for us: '. . . do you not know that your body is a temple of the Holy Spirit within you, which you have from God, and that you are not your own?' (1 Corinthians 6.19, cf. Romans 12.1). Thus the human body as the temple of the Holy Spirit is at the heart of sacramental liturgy. It is washed in the waters of baptism, anointed with the oils of strength and healing, fed at the table of the Eucharist, united in marriage to the body of another. In this way the Christian faith exalts the human body. How we then dispose of this temple of God's Spirit at death is very important, theologically and personally, both for the individual Christian and for the family, the community and the Church.

Celebrating burial

Most cultures and religions have great care for the disposal of the dead person. The book of Tobit[7] tells how God rewards a pious Jew for his devotion to the burial of the dead. Christian traditional belief in Jesus' resurrection and the dignity of the human body as a temple of the Holy Spirit demands the same care. Jesus' followers were very concerned to honour his body, which had to be buried so hastily.

> Joseph of Arimathea . . . asked Pilate to let him take away the body of Jesus . . . Nicodemus . . . also came, bringing a mixture of myrrh and aloes, weighing about a hundred pounds. They took the body of Jesus and wrapped it with the spices in linen cloths, according to the burial custom of the Jews . . . And so, because it was the Jewish day of Preparation, and the tomb was nearby, they laid Jesus there. (John 19.38–42)[8]

All Gospel narratives point out the care his people wanted to give to the body of Jesus. Christian burial is not, therefore, just about dealing respectfully with a human body. It is about how we relate to this person in his or her death. 'They laid *Jesus* there', says the Gospel. They bury a person, an individual they knew and loved, not just a physical body. Any funeral rite needs to express this aspect of the Christian story, in a balanced and reflective way which burial does more clearly than cremation. Those close to the dead person can be involved at the graveside, even to digging the grave and filling it afterwards. Visiting the grave later continues to express this care.[9]

More and more, Christian funeral liturgies are celebrated at several stages, marking the journey of the person from this life to God. The Roman Catholic tradition, like others, offers prayers and rites for the dying, for the moment of death, after death, for a vigil at home, in the church. These precede the funeral rites (now often within the Eucharist) and the committal rites. Through them all we speak of an individual human being who is going to meet his or her God. The image is of a physical, bodily journey, as the prayers say:

> Go forth, Christian soul, from this world in the name of God the almighty Father, who created you . . . May you live in peace this day, may your home be with God in Zion . . .[10]

and

> I commend you, my dear brother/sister, to almighty God, and entrust you to your creator. May you return to him who formed you from the dust of the earth . . . May you see your Redeemer face to face and enjoy the vision of God for ever.[11]

Burial then comes as the committal moment in this person's journey to God, and it needs to reflect the belief we proclaim in the resurrection of this body.[12]

Here we enter the rich world of liturgical signs and symbols. Our contemporary world is often the poorer for not valuing them properly. We need to be very careful not to forget that the power of liturgy and worship often lies in the unspoken, even what cannot be spoken. In an interior way people grasp meaning from what we do in celebration that can even change understanding and belief. Burial, I hold, has a much richer symbolic power than cremation, and losing that means a loss spiritually, theologically and pastorally.[13] It is expressed in the prayer over the place of committal, prior to burial:

> Lord Jesus Christ, by your own three days in the tomb, you hallowed the graves of all who believe in you and so made the grave a sign of hope that promises resurrection even as it claims our mortal bodies.
>
> Grant that our brother/sister may sleep here in peace until you awaken him/her to glory, for you are the resurrection and the life.[14]

The words express directly the relationship between the human body, the grave, and our belief in resurrection for that person. When people are asked about the resurrection of the body, survey data[15] suggest a low level of belief, even among practising Christians. Yet addresses at funerals, Christian or not, often reflect an unspoken belief of meeting again. This is a fact we experience in pastoral care, and anecdotal evidence would suggest a deeper level of belief in the actual resurrection of the body, as well as eternal life. Words used at the moment of burial express this too:

> We commit his/her body to the earth, for we are dust and unto dust we shall return. But the Lord Jesus Christ will change our mortal bodies to be like his in glory, for he is risen, the firstborn from the dead. So let us commend our brother/sister to the Lord, that the Lord may embrace him/her in peace and raise up his/her body on the last day[16]

Our liturgies from the time of dying to that of burial consistently and quite explicitly express this belief in the resurrection of the body.[17]

Cremation has emerged over the past century to become the dominant mode of disposal of bodies in British society. Some will see it as clearly complementary to burial, some as necessary and practical, while others will find it difficult for different reasons. It has only been permitted in the Roman Catholic tradition since May 1963. The Code of Canon Law of 1917 opposed cremation because it could be used to deny the resurrection of the dead (n.1203). The 1983 Code continues to express preference for burial:

> The Church earnestly recommends that the pious custom of burying the bodies of the deceased be observed; nevertheless the Church does not prohibit cremation unless it was chosen for reasons contrary to Christian doctrine. (Canon 1176, para. 3)

Consistent with this preference for burial is the statement that 'cremated remains should not normally be scattered above ground but reverently returned to the earth'.[18] Even ashes (cremains) need to be returned to the dust from which the body originally came if we are to be consistent in our thinking here about images of the resurrection of the body.[19]

Waiting for the resurrection – valuing the grave

How does a theology of burial also sustain the living? Their prayer and care for the grave is an important expression of the faith in the resurrection of the body too. *Lex orandi, lex credendi* (In our prayer we express our heartfelt belief). Here theological statement has to yield to deep-seated emotions and feelings that vary according to age, culture and experience. Instinctive and natural responses need to be valued as the real reaction of an individual to the death of someone who matters to them.

Burial thus enables greater participation by the community of faith than at cremation. People can throw earth and flowers or sprinkle holy water onto a coffin several feet beneath them. The soil is sharing in the burial, while the holy water reminds us of the life-giving waters of baptism promising the resurrection of the body. Burying permits people to spend time at a committal, to gather around, compared with a crematorium chapel.

Then the grave becomes a focus for prayer for the mourner. Any tradition that encourages prayer for the dead often provides prayers at the grave. People make private visits to pray for the repose of the soul. In different ways Christians mark the feasts of All Saints and All Souls (1 and 2 November) by visiting, cleaning, decorating, even feasting at, graves. Crowds come for Cemetery Sundays (often in November) to pray for the dead buried in one place. Nationally, Remembrance Sunday, the Cenotaph, the grave of the Unknown Soldier[20] express a similar care. The secular world has found the same when trying to mark death, especially of someone in the public eye. The consequent emotional outpouring finds expression in flowers, teddy bears, lights, wayside pseudo-shrines, and the like.[21] The burial ground has provided this historically, offering a locus for grief and sentiment, and the expression of hope – for the Christian, of eternal life and the resurrection of the body.

Burial, not cremation

People often make a choice between burial and cremation because they are following their religious or cultural tradition. Thus Muslim and Jew share a decision for burial with many Christians, especially Roman Catholics. In many Catholic countries, as elsewhere, because of such a decision there are so few crematoria. Here the choice is that, just as the body expresses the temple of the Holy Spirit, so the body is honoured in death by burial. Such respect for the created human body means that some people question whether it is right to burn a body.[22] Burial is seen as being both more respectful and also celebrating that return to the earth from which God created the human person.[23]

For those who mourn, burial and its associated rites become their way of celebrating the life and death of someone who matters to them. It would still be customary in some Catholic countries for people to dig the grave for a family member or neighbour. They, too, may wait after the burial and fill the grave as last acts of respect for the dead. It is honoured as familial and religious duty. These actions are devout responses to the death of someone in the community and signs of support for those who grieve. While these pious acts may not often be normal nowadays in a society such as ours, some cemeteries try to accommodate some of these rituals because they are so important to cultures like that of the Afro-Caribbean and Italian communities.[24]

This patterns for them what happens to the person of Christ. The actors in the burial narrative, especially Joseph of Arimathea, show charity at work even in death. There is personal involvement in taking the body, and in committing it to the tomb. This becomes a service for Christ. The Judaeo-Christian understanding of burying the dead as a work of charity is clearly associated with this and continues in the burial guilds and societies that still exist.

Burial and society

Churchyards, and even cemeteries, provide distinct burial grounds for different communities. Burial in specific places marked the identity of the dead.[25] Their religious faith, their dying and their resting formed a coherent whole. While this may not necessarily have encouraged community cohesion, it offered support to the grieving. For our society there is much to be said for reinvigorating the practice of Christian burial, especially where the burial ground is local, part of a churchyard. Many churchyards lie at the heart of rural communities in villages, and in some urban settings can be central foci for an area. Their historical roots as gathering places should not be forgotten. As more communities try to open up church buildings for increased local use, so too the value of churchyards needs to be explored. More recently the Victorian vision of urban cemeteries as public open spaces has been rediscovered.[26] For Christians, these burial places are a constant reminder of faith in eternal life, of the communion of the saints. In many cemeteries especially they are places where we override denominational differences as Christians, where we bury side by side with people of other faiths and none. What pastoral opportunities they offer remain to be seen.

The present discussion about the reuse of graves will have come as a surprise to some in these islands.[27] This practice is ancient and, in other parts of the world is both normal and widespread. Family graves and tombs were often the norm, and were used again and again. Sensitivity will be essential as we return to this practice and change the habit of nearly two centuries. To be buried with others, especially where people share family ties or faith, expresses a community of persons that once again talks to us of the resurrection of the body, of returning to God with others, of the image of Christ calling his people home.[28]

Our society needs to face the reality of death, rather than to be duped by a certain sanitization of mortality that has overtaken us.[29] Death so often occurs in a clinical context of hospital, nursing home or hospice. People are unaccustomed to seeing, let alone touching, a dead person, and 'waking' the dead at home is now very rare. The resurrection of the body is a tenet of Christian faith that can only be proclaimed when death is understood in a very real way.

Even our Christian practice is being diluted. In some places the coffin is committed into the hearse at the church and the committal takes place perhaps without the priest, or even anyone, present. Memorial services are now much more frequent, spoken of as funerals without a coffin, to which people are invited after a private funeral.[30] This hints at the societal attitude of avoiding death. Burial insists very forcibly on the reality of death, and the grave becomes a continual reminder of our fragility, our dependence on God, that our fulfilment lies outside this world, actually in the resurrection of the dead.

People speak of a post-Christian society, as if the Church has become irrelevant. Yet what we describe as Christian hope and faith is often paralleled in the hope and vision of many people who say they have no faith. Any dialogue is difficult because society has lost both language and symbols to express the hope it struggles to articulate. While people may not have an articulated faith in God, so many seem to believe that somehow life continues after death. Graves embody the deeper reality of the life and death of a human person. Even when ashes are buried, the size of space has not the same power to challenge. Christian graves are places of proclamation, proclaiming our faith in eternal life, and thus the resurrection of the dead. Christian memorialization needs to be ever more clear – expressing faith in the resurrection of the body.[31]

Conclusion

Burial expresses in different ways many of the fundamental hopes and aspirations of the Christian and the Church. It honours the individual as created by God in God's own image, destined to return to that same God. The body as the temple of God's Holy Spirit is honoured in burial as in life. The grave reflects our fundamental Christian belief that in baptism we die and rise with Christ, so as to live here in this world to share glory with him after death.

Christian liturgies of dying, death and burial reflect this thinking, and proudly celebrate this hope for the resurrection of the body. That belief draws many Christians to pray for the dead and also for even more to honour their burial places. In remembering our own dead we recall who have died and so proclaim the communion of saints to be a reality for the Church. In a world that seems to keep death at arm's length the Christian grave (and that of many other believers) becomes not just a place of memory and prayer, but of proclamation and belief, that cremation just cannot achieve. The challenge to the Churches today is to proclaim Christ risen from the dead to a world that does not like the thought of death – and the grave is at the heart of this.

Notes

1 For example, the Catholic prohibition on cremation from 1886 until 1963 was much influenced by the way in which cremation was proposed as a denial of belief in life after death, or seen to be supported by Protestant and Masonic groups.

2 For a broader survey of the issues involved, see D. Davies, 'Theologies of Disposal' in P. C. Jupp and T. Rogers (eds), *Interpreting Death: Christian Theology and Pastoral Practice*, London: Cassell, 1997, pp. 67–84.

3 See K. Rahner, 'Jesus Christ' in *Encyclopedia of Theology*, London: Burns and Oates, 1975, pp. 751–72; W. Pannenberg, *Jesus, God and Man*, London: SCM Press, 1970; and many others.

4 Cf. *Rite of Christian Initiation of Adults* (Roman Catholic) (henceforth *RCIA*), London: Geoffrey Chapman, 1987, n. 219; *Methodist Worship Book*, Peterborough: Methodist Publishing House, 1999, p. 80; *Common Worship: Christian Initiation* (Church of England), London: Church House Publishing, 2006, p. 115; *Book of Common Prayer* (Church of Ireland), Dublin: The Columba Press, 2004, p. 365.

5 *RCIA*, n. 215.

6 'The washing with water should take on its full importance as the sign of that mystical sharing in Christ's death and resurrection, through which those who

believe in his name die to sin and rise to eternal life.' *RCIA*, n. 206.

7 Tobit 2 (The Apocrypha).

8 Cf. Matthew 27.57ff., 28.1ff., Mark 15.42ff., 16.1ff., Luke 23.50ff., 24.1ff.

9 I want to suggest that burial permits this and many other aspects of faith with greater ease and more directly than cremation. This is developed in my article, 'Why Catholics Prefer Burial', *Pharos International*, Vol. 72, No. 2, Summer 2006, pp. 3–4.

10 *Pastoral Care of the Sick*, London: Geoffrey Chapman, 1983, pp. 178, 9 (cf. *Common Worship: Pastoral Services*, London: Church House Publishing, 2000, p. 229. *Methodist Worship Book*, p. 431). See J. Lampard, *Go Forth, Christian Soul: The Biography of a Prayer*, Peterborough: Epworth, 2005.

11 Lampard, *Go Forth*.

12 For example,'The liturgical symbols and liturgy as a whole stand in the closest relationship to faith and theology. In the liturgy the content of faith and theology, the mystery of salvation that runs through the whole of human history, is again and again made present and effective under sacred signs. Therefore, the liturgical actions themselves are symbols of the faith of the community. This relationship between liturgy, faith and theology has important consequences for theology itself and for the liturgical symbols.' K. Richter, *The Meaning of Sacramental Symbols*, Collegeville: LTP, 1990, p. 26.

13 Richter, *The Meaning*. Cf. N. Mitchell, 'Sign, Symbol' in Paul Bradshaw (ed.), *New SCM Dictionary of Liturgy and Worship*, London: SCM Press, 2002.

14 *Order of Christian Funerals*, Chapman, 1990 (henceforth *OCF*), p. 131.

15 For example, Douglas Davies and Alastair Shaw, *Reusing Old Graves: A Report on Popular British Attitudes*, Crayford: Shaw & Sons, 1995, where only 18 per cent of Roman Catholics expressed belief in the resurrection of the body, and were the largest percentage in any of the five major UK denominations included in the survey.

16 *OCF*, p. 133. See the text used by the Church of England in *Common Worship: Pastoral Services*, p. 314: We commit his/her body to the ground: earth to earth, ashes to ashes, dust to dust: in the sure and certain hope of the resurrection to eternal life through our Lord Jesus Christ, who will transform our frail bodies that they may be conformed to his glorious body, who died, was buried, and rose again for us.'

17 For a much fuller discussion of the Roman Catholic liturgical texts, see H. R. Rutherford (with T. Barry), *The Death of a Christian*, Collegeville: LTP, rev. edn, 1990. For *Common Worship*, see P. Bradshaw (ed.), *A Companion to Common Worship Vol. 2*, London: SPCK/Alcuin, 2006, pp. 194–218.

18 *OCF*, n. 239.

19 For a much fuller discussion of this, see H. Richard Rutherford, *Honoring the Dead: Catholics and Cremation Today*, Collegeville: LTP, 2001. Cf. *The Book of Common Prayer for use in the Church of Wales*, Vol II, p. 797 – an example of another Church which permits only the burial of ashes (see Denison, this volume).

20 Whereas Westminster Abbey in 1910 had insisted on only cremated remains being buried within the Abbey, an exception was made for the burial of the Unknown Warrior in 1920. I would suggest that this reflects the symbolic value of the burial of a person as such in popular understanding.

21 See, for example, A. Rowbottom, 'A Bridge of Flowers' in T. Walter (ed.), *The Mourning for Diana*, Oxford: Berg, 1999, pp. 157–72 and other chapters in that volume.

22 Cf. P. Benn, 'Cremation as Violence', *Pharos International*, Vol. 72, No. 1, Spring 2006, pp. 8–9, which discusses how a body 'sustains a personal life' and the consequences of such thinking.

23 We also need to advert to human reaction to the thought of one's body being burned (see Davies and Shaw, *Reusing Old Graves*). This is balanced by the similar reactions to being buried alive, eaten by worms, etc.

24 See Hilborn, this volume.

25 See Kellaher, this volume.

26 See the ongoing work of the Commission for Architecture and the Built Environment, *Cemeteries, Churchyards and Burial Grounds*, 5 November 2007.

27 Bishop Christopher Hill, 'A Note on the Theology of Burial in Relation to Some Contemporary Questions', *Ecclesiastical Law Journal*, Vol. 7, July 2004, pp. 447ff. For the debate leading to the reintroduction of reuse, see Environment, Transport and Regional Affairs Committee Eighth Report (ETRAC), *Cemeteries Vols I and II*, London: The Stationery Office, 2001.

28 1 Thessalonians 4.16–17.

29 See the quotation from Alan Crawford in Grainger, this volume, p. 122.

30 See D. Gray, *Memorial Services*, London: SPCK/Alcuin, 2002.

31 'I was struck by the vigour of the introduction to the Church Regulations in one northern diocese. Under the heading of "Remembrance" it says, "Christian burial is the act by which the mortal remains of a person are laid to rest until the Day of Resurrection. A memorial stone is by no means essential. Burials in church-yards are always recorded in church registers. The best form of remembrance is in prayers, sacrament and witness, or by a gift to the church which can be a useful and worthy memorial" Powerful language.' S. Cameron in 'Churchyards: Burial Spaces and Memorial for the Future', unpublished seminar paper, London: The National Funerals College/The Memorial Advisory Bureau, 1995.

13

Theology in Ashes:
How the Churches Have Gone Wrong
Over Cremation

JOHN LAMPARD

Introduction

The standard question asked by a funeral director after a death is, 'Will it be a burial or a cremation?' My thesis is that this is not an appropriate question, because burial and cremation are not equal choices. Of course it is possible to answer one or the other, as almost everyone does, but they are not alternative methods of disposal, because the outcome of the two routes is not the same.

This false choice is the result of the Church's failure to think theologically about cremation, or of its production of 'bad' or inadequate theology. If there is a burial, the whole body enters the earth, there is no remainder above ground, and the traditional Christian pastoral act has been carried out: if there is a cremation, there is a remainder, and the Christian disposal of that remainder, two kilos or so of ash and bone, should be a matter of equal Christian concern. Our honouring of the dead, our handing down of a 2,000-year-old tradition of Christian burial and, difficult as it is, retention of the imagery of resurrection, is diminished if we do not treat the ashes in a Christian way.

The Church's failure to respond in a Christian way to the modern introduction of cremation is symbolized by the unfortunate mistake which happened in 1874 when one of the very first cremations took place in Germany. The body was lying ready by the brand-new Siemens cremator, the mourners were assembled, Herr Siemens himself had his finger on the button to start the fire. All were ready to begin, but the clergyman designated to take the service failed to turn up. Siemens was forced to ask those assembled to bow their heads and say a private prayer.[1] One might say that the Church got cremation wrong then, and has continued to do so ever since.

How we got where we are

It is not widely realized that, until the Christian era, burning was widely used as a method for the disposal of a dead body in much of Western Europe. One of the major factors that swung European societies away from cremation to burial was the influence of the Christian Church and its emphasis on the resurrection of the body.[2] In its simplest form the argument went that a Christian should try to follow the way of Christ both in life and in death, leaving the body in the best possible position for resurrection. A second, and equally powerful, impetus away from cremation came in the Middle Ages, when burning became the ultimate means of punishment for people who were to be obliterated, like witches or heretics. The ashes could then be scattered so that the person's place was known no more; they were a non-person, not worthy of remembrance, memorial or memory. Behind this practice of diminishment lay a general belief that in some way the integrity of the body was necessary for the final judgement. Of course it was recognized that some people died in unfortunate circumstances and left little or no bodily remains. Early theologians such as St Augustine recognized that God had the power to re-create a body; but a cremated body, which had had this punishment visited upon it, had symbolically lost the power that body and soul might be reunited.[3]

This first 'negative' theology of cremation has been the traditional Christian viewpoint, expressed with varieties of intensity, that cremation is wrong. It is a theological statement that the primary and 'only way' of disposing of the dead is by way of burial of the corpse.

The fact that for 2,000 years burial and not cremation had been the accepted Christian way only emphasizes how powerful were the social forces which in the UK have virtually swept burial away in only 100 years. In four generations the proportion of people cremated in this country moved from nothing to over 70 per cent today. Even more remarkable still is that this social phenomenon has until recently been a silent revolution, hardly commented on, even less explained.

We owe to Peter Jupp a clear understanding of the combined influences that brought about this change. There is only space to headline what these were before looking at the theological issues. Jupp points to the slow but steady lobbying and influence of the Cremation Society; the invention of indoor cremators in which bodies could be placed; the sense of pressure for land usage after the two World Wars; the low cost of cremation compared with burial; the support of the medical profession who favoured a clean and hygienic method of disposal; the support of funeral directors who could organize more funerals in one day; the funeral which could be conducted without fuss; and finally the lack of opposition from the Churches (apart from the Roman Catholic Church).[4]

The Church in the twentieth century did not significantly reiterate the traditional theological objections to cremation, neither did it come up with any sound theological reflection. I want to look at the poor theological reflection of the Church of England (other Churches in England, apart from the Roman Catholic, were largely silent once cremation had been legally established by the Cremation Act 1902),[5] and then look at new attempts at a theology.

This second 'theology of cremation' was a denial by the Church of England that cremation was a theological issue at all. This position came about in the years during World War Two when there was a series of debates in the Convocation of Canterbury about cremation. These have been well covered by Jupp in his book *From Dust to Ashes*, and I draw from his fascinating account of the debates.[6] They are important because they raised over a period of years a number of important issues, many of which unfortunately became lost from view in the decisions of later years.

Very importantly, the question was asked, how could the Church demonstrate that cremation was not an alternative to burial? This view was stated against those who said that cremation should be regarded as an acceptable alternative to burial in the ground, just as a burial at sea was a justified alternative. What this view failed to recognize was that the body was disposed of when buried at sea, but that there was a remainder after cremation. This issue was subsumed into the minority view that cremation was acceptable only as preparation for burial (and in consecrated ground).

A point raised in the debates concerned the shape of the funeral liturgy when cremation took place. If a funeral was to include services in both church and crematorium, when did the service end? Was it at the moment the coffin began its journey into the cremator, or was the scattering or burial of the ashes to be included as part of the liturgy? Until quite recently the general attitude has been the former. Most services which included cremation ended at the cremator, and the Christian disposal of the ashes was of no theological significance (except in Wales).[7]

Several Convocation speakers raised pertinent points about the ashes, points which have been sadly neglected in theological and liturgical thinking in the last 60 years. One speaker made the obvious, but much overlooked, point that cremation was the end of the body as an organism, but it was not the end of the body as mortal remains, as the ashes were still left. The two Houses were divided in their views. The bishops in the Upper House took the view that cremation was a form of burial itself, while the clergy of the Lower House took the view that it was a preliminary to burial. Not for the first time the clergy proved to be better theologians than the bishops. An attempt to defend the position that cremation should only be viewed as preparation and (crucially) that the final disposal should be by burial in consecrated ground (the traditional Christian view) failed in a vote.

The Church of England finally abdicated all theological responsibility or sense (in spite of the words of warning offered) when the bishops stated that 'we attach no theological significance to the practice [of cremation]'.[8] In fairness, they were trying to defend a wholly permissible view that cremation in no way affected the Church's belief in the doctrine of the resurrection of the body, but their 'hands-off' approach encouraged a laxness in liturgical practice, a 'bad' theological understanding of cremation, and an encouragement for Christians and non-Christians to engage in practices which have had no parallel in 2,000 years of Christianity.

The Church of England has begun to claw back a theologically appropriate position from the errors of the 1940s in its two prayer books of 1980 and 2000.[9] Its first liturgical response to the increase in the number of cremations came in the *Alternative Service Book*, when cremation was acknowledged in the funeral service. At the Committal the minister says, 'We now commit *his* body to the ground (*or* to be cremated)'.[10] This is in line with the statement that cremation is a form of burial. There is also a brief 'Form which may be used at the Interment of Ashes', which includes the words 'We now commit *his* ashes to the ground'.[11]

Liturgical thought developed, and in the year 2000 *Common Worship* (CW) was published. Here there are alternative words of Committal: if there is to be a later Burial of the Ashes, the minister says, 'and now, in preparation for burial, we give *his/her* body to be cremated'. The *Companion to Common Worship, Volume 2*, rightly comments that the word 'give' 'acknowledges the functional, practical business of cremation, and accommodates the handing back of ashes for later interment. In this context, the sentiments of "ashes to ashes" are delayed, because this is not the final Committal, but rather the first part of a two-stage process.'[12] The Committal then takes place when the ashes are buried, and a double Committal is avoided. The authors of CW are to be commended for adopting the position that cremation should be seen as a preparation for burial, but obviously if there is not to be a burial, which

Christian tradition upholds, these words cannot be said at the time of Committal.

The *Companion to Common Worship* continues to amend the errors of the bishops 60 years ago by commenting, 'The burial of ashes is to be preferred over scattering, as it makes the Christian hope in bodily resurrection more coherent if the remains lie in a grave.'[13] Furthermore, in CW the Burial of the Ashes is contained in a separate section, 'After the Funeral'. It would perhaps have sent out a stronger message of wholeness if it could have been included more noticeably as a part of the funeral, as is the burial of the body, even though it may be separated by a space of time.

Is there a positive theology of cremation?

The increasing use of crematoria has led to an opportunity for a 'creative' development of new rituals. If the ashes are to be disposed of in a Christian context, most Churches have developed a new funeral liturgy for burial or scattering of ashes (one of only two new funeral liturgies developed by the Church in the last thousand years). But this liturgy has not caught on and has not been positively advocated. Davies puts well the reasons for this:

> A great deal of confusion came to exist in the mid- and later twentieth century . . . when priests were involved in the actual cremation service connected with the body and coffin but not with the cremated remains. In symbolic terms the crematorium service was directly equated with the burial service and the question of ashes left very much open and uncertain. This became increasingly the case when family members took the ashes and engaged in the private placing of them.[14]

Looked at this way it is possible to ask the question, what are Christians doing in crematoria at all? If we had heard or accepted the arguments of the 1940s, that cremation was a method of preparing the body for burial, why have we ever got into the position of holding our services there? At a funeral director's offices other acts are carried out to prepare the body for burial, laying out, various types of embalming, dressing the body etc., but we do not feel the need to attend to watch this, or start again the ancient practice of saying prayers and Psalms as the body is washed. It is because we have collided burial and cremation in our minds, and live with the fiction that cremation and burial are the same thing, that we have got into the mess we are in today.

If, when the earliest crematoria were built, the Churches had said, 'We accept this new process as an acceptable way of treating or preparing a body for burial and will be pleased to accept the ashes for burial as generations of corpses have been buried before', the whole field of the disposal of the dead would have been very different today.[15] The Churches were reacting to the new evangelical zeal of the cremationists, whose espousal of their cause made it seem to be an alternative to burial. In fairness to the early cremationists, they did intend the ashes which resulted from their new process to be buried.

Until a few years ago the majority of ashes remained at the crematorium and were scattered by the staff in one of a number of flower beds. In some crematoria the flower beds are given monthly titles, so the ashes can be scattered either in the month of a person's death or of their birthday, etc. This final disposal has been an act of the crematorium operatives, and until recently clergy have rarely been involved. Ministers have recounted how crematorium staff have devised their own 'liturgy' of prayers and hymns as they have scattered the ashes.

What is remarkable, in this sad story of theological neglect, is that the Churches and their Christian members have been so willing to allow this ritual to be left to crematorium staff.[16] Its significance never registered on their spiritual radar. No doubt the reason for this neglect was that clergy swallowed the fiction promulgated by the bishops that burial and cremation were equal routes.

Some theologians and liturgists have argued that there should be a distinctive theology of cremation and have latched on to some of the imagery of cremation, in particular that of 'fire', and attempted to develop a distinctive cremation liturgy. The problem with the imagery of fire is that it is, like fire itself, a double-edged weapon. I have already mentioned the practice of setting fire to people, particularly in the Middle Ages, to obliterate them. Fire has a dangerous destructive face, particularly when associated with hell-fire.

Of course there are many images of fire which could be used in a cremation liturgy, and more than one liturgist has tried his hand at this. As we know, fire purges and refines. The third-century theologian Origen spoke of fire as healing, and Catherine of Genoa spoke of God's fiery love. The presence of the Holy Spirit is symbolized by tongues of fire. Our hymn books are full of positive fire images.

The most sustained, and sophisticated, theology of cremation has been offered by Douglas J. Davies in his book *Cremation Today and*

Tomorrow (1990). He argues that there is a fundamental distinction between burial and cremation. 'Where cremation has occurred in other cultures it has not had to play the role of preparing the dead for resurrection.'[17] Davies argues here, as he has elsewhere, that our 'success culture', with its emphasis on this life, has meant that funerals now are retrospective rather than prospective, and this has major repercussions for cremation.[18]

Davies outlines the different theological perspectives of the resurrection of the body and the immortality of the soul. The former is better suited for burial and the latter for cremation, as cremation has 'violently' destroyed the body. The relationship between the two images is complex, and Davies argues that 'it may well be that the time is right for a more open consideration of these basic yet hard issues in the contemporary church where implicit and half formed ideas rule the day'.[19]

I want to both agree and disagree with Davies' next point:

> The ashes of cremation symbolise the fact of bodily dissolution rather than the perpetuation of the deceased until some future day. In other words the ashes of cremation carry the opposite message from the remains of burial. The speed of the operation and the explicit technology involved make this evident to many people.[20]

I think it is easy to posit a view that everyone up to the age of modern cremation happily went along with the resurrection of the body, and that once cremation came in, this assumption disappeared and bodily dissolution was the order of the day.[21] Certainly cremation may have increased the difficulty of a belief in some form of resurrection, but it need not destroy it, as Augustine and others pointed out. It may prove that the rapid introduction of cremation in the period 1945–85, with scattering of ashes the assumed final method of disposal, hastened a change in worldview which the recent re-claiming of ashes is countering. The disappearance of the deceased in an anonymous Garden of Remembrance has left too deep a 'hollow', a too dramatic separation of the living and the dead. The current practice of re-claiming the ashes for traditional Christian burial, albeit with altered perspectives, as Davies indicates, means that the living have a measure of control over the 'rate of departing' but is also a way of affirming that the body is significant, echoing something of a doctrine of the resurrection of the body.[22]

What should the Christian Church do?

I want in this final section to propose some actions which might be followed by the Church in order to address the conclusions I have reached.

First, I hope that we can raise awareness of the issues surrounding burial and cremation. I am aware that this is hardly the most popular or appealing of topics. A few years ago I was asked to speak about funeral liturgies at a Guild meeting, being assured that there were always 20 to 30 people present. I spent a pleasant evening with the Guild secretary who had invited me, the only person who turned up! If we are able to encourage people to think about the significance of burial and cremation, it is more likely that they will think through what a Christian funeral should be.

Second, I would like to see all the Churches moving towards insisting that cremated remains must be buried.[23] The theological conviction, which underlies that discipline, is the traditional understanding that the body has an integrity about it, which is not diminished either in death or by cremation.[24] In this we can hear an echo of the doctrine of the resurrection of the body, which is symbolized by the return to the earth, from which we came, of all human remains.

Third, I would like to see one order of service which would be held in church. The liturgy would move from the church service to burial of the ashes. Cremation could either take place beforehand, as it now often does, or between the service and burial. If cremation is understood to be what it really is, a preparation of the body for burial, there would be no need or requirement for anyone to attend the crematorium.[25]

One possible model for crematoria of the future is that of a number of new crematoria built in South Africa. These crematoria have no public facilities at all. They are purely functional, with one or more cremators, and there is no place for worship or meeting, and no gardens or grounds for burying ashes. This means that any religious ritual will take place before and after cremation, but that the act of cremation is seen for what it is: a processing of the body which has no religious or theological significance in itself. Such a solution also avoids all the problematic aspects of the function and design of a crematorium discussed earlier.

Lastly, for those who wish to express their discipleship in death as Christian, there should be a distinctive Christian way of departure, as there is of entry into the Church. Christians are buried with Christ, either in full bodily form, or in reduced bodily form as ashes after cremation. This seems to me to be an authentic theology of burial and cremation. The way the body is prepared for that moment is not relevant. What I am arguing for is a distinctive Christian style of disposal, more in keeping with the way of Christ and Christian tradition, even though belief in the doctrine of the resurrection of the body is declining.[26] It is part of a distinctive Christian life-and-death style that we are buried and our remains are committed to God by being placed in the earth. They are not to be the object of continual handling, entertainment or endless temporary abodes. I am aware that what I am proposing is counter-cultural, but much of what remains of Christianity today is counter-cultural.

Notes

1 See J. M. H. Keizer, 'Siemens, Friedrich' in D. J. Davies and L. H. Mates (eds), *Encyclopedia of Cremation*, Aldershot: Ashgate, 2006, p. 376.

2 See chapters by Badham, Jupp and Davies, this volume.

3 Augustine, *Retractions*, Book ii, Chapter 64.

4 Peter C. Jupp, *From Dust to Ashes: Cremation and the British Way of Death*, Basingstoke: Palgrave Macmillan, 2006, pp. 125–55. See also McGinnell, this volume.

5 For an example of Scottish opposition to cremation, see Murray, this volume.

6 Jupp, *From Dust to Ashes*, pp. 135–41.

7 See Denison, this volume.

8 *Chronicle*, Lower House of the Convocation of Canterbury, 13 October 1943, p. 234.

9 See Lloyd, this volume.

10 *Alternative Service Book*, Clowes: SPCK/Cambridge University Press, 1980, p. 316; *Common Worship: Pastoral Service*, London: Church House Publishing, 2000.

11 *Alternative Services Book*, p. 324.

12 P. Bradshaw (ed.), *Companion to Common Worship, Volume 2*, London: SPCK, 2006, p. 211.

13 Bradshaw, *Companion*, pp. 215–16.

14 D. J. Davies, 'Rites of Passage' in Davies and Mates (eds), *Encyclopedia*, pp. 359–62, 361.

15 For a general discussion on this issue, see H. J. Grainger, *Death Redesigned: British Crematoria: History, Architecture and Landscape*, Reading: Spire, 2005. On the prevention of the original intention to bury ashes, the refusal in 1875 of the Bishop of Rochester, Dr T. L. Claughton, to sanction the use of New Southgate Cemetery as a site for the first crematorium, was the decisive factor here; see Brian Parsons, *Committed to the Cleansing Flame*, Reading: Spire, 2005, p. 46.

16 For the delegation of funeral music choice to crematorium staff, see Parsons, this volume.

17 D. J. Davies, *Cremation Today and Tomorrow*, Nottingham: Grove/Alcuin, 1990, p. 30.

18 See D. J. Davies, 'Theologies of Disposal' in P. C. Jupp and T. Rogers (eds), *Interpreting Death: Christian Theology and Pastoral Practice*, London: Cassell, 1997, pp. 67–84.

19 Davies, *Cremation Today and Tomorrow*, p. 31.

20 Davies, *Cremation Today and Tomorrow*, p. 33.

21 But see P. C. Jupp, 'From Bishop Wordsworth to Dr Major: Cremation and Resurrection, 1874–1922', *Resurgam*, Vol. 49, No. 1, March 2006, pp. 32–6, which takes a different view.

22 See Kellaher, this volume.

23 For the Church in Wales' insistence that ashes must be buried (in consecrated ground), see Keith Denison (this volume) and K. Denison, 'The Theology and Liturgy of Funerals: A View from the Church in Wales', *Mortality*, Vol. 4, No. 1, March 1999, pp. 63–74, 71–2.

24 See also McGinnell, this volume.

25 This point is expanded in my paper, 'Cremation: How the Churches Got it Wrong', given to the International Cremation and Burial Conference and Exhibition, Newcastle/Gateshead, 14 November 2007, to be published in *Pharos International*.

26 See the discussion in Jones, this volume.

The Challenge of Green Burial

PETER OWEN JONES

The necessity of death

Death is needed to create space for new life, for new shapes, for new dreams, new imaginings, new combinations. Can there be anything new without the death of the old, especially as we humans are concerned? In that sense the process of death in old age is familiar to all of us, a slowing down, a gradual loss of vigour, a fading, an inability to embrace the new, an atrophy of the physical and the sensory: these are signs of approaching death. This is what the Christian Church in the West feels like: its ideas, its current theological constructs, its self-image, its alliances, its allegiances are hardening and eroding.[1] The Church as we have known it is dying, it has been dying for some time; yes, death is our future, it is necessary and needed. The Christianity that will emerge from this death, as woodland burial perhaps hints, is likely to assume a new form and character.

The threat of climate change

As the population is wearying of the Christian message as currently presented, the consequences of humanity's actions in relation to the environment are becoming more and more apparent. Unfortunately, whichever way we add it up, there can be no doubt that this planet is heading for some very testing times. Whether or not we subscribe to the theory, it appears that the planet may be warming. This might be part of a natural cycle, but the evidence suggests otherwise. The human population is set to expand at a greater speed and at a greater rate than ever before. This will place huge pressures on human beings and our environment, promising a range of extinctions and a further loss of biodiversity. The voices that started to raise this alarm in the 1960s for the most part did so from outside the Christian tradition, and continue to do so. In fact many of the members of the largest groups campaigning for understanding and change are at best indifferent to the Christian perspective or otherwise openly scathing of the position of the Christian Church in the West and its relationship with the environment. Why?

Why environmentalists are indifferent to the Church

First, by aligning itself with earthly power structures, the Church has ended up beholden to them. Power structures are notoriously self-serving; they are dependent on adherence and acquiescence. Power structures are very good at maintaining vested interests, and many of those who rely on the *status quo* will invest heavily in the power structure that supports it. The vested interests at work regarding the current legislation surrounding burial and cremation are no exception. The Church of England has inherited the legal authority to bury people within its churchyards; that is, within the bounds of its own ring-fenced and consecrated property. By and large these systems for disposing of the dead work, as long as there is enough space. As long as people believe they have a reasonable chance of going to heaven and as long as there are enough priests to reassure them of that, theological or belief 'systems' may be said to work – for those claiming some level of denominational affiliation at least. It is just that the Churches' current participation in burial and cremation practices is based on a view of the world and sustainability that was, and seemingly still is, operating as if our relationship with the environment doesn't matter. Some might think that the Churches – along with very many other institutional forces – are not always giving the sustainability message much space apart from its new ventures into green burial. This chapter argues that green burial is one of the ways in which the Church should put environmental concern into practice.

Environmental concerns and the spiritual imperative

I have long argued with some of my firm environmental friends that the environmental difficulties and challenges we face are rooted in our understanding of what is sacred. I would claim that the environmental problem is spiritual, not only biological. Climate change is a spiritual problem as is deforestation and loss of biodiversity. It needs spiritual determination to underpin action. Whether we are Christian, Muslim, Hindu, Buddhist or atheist, our relationship with the earth is constructed and informed by our understanding of what is sacred and what is not, by what is precious and what is not – particularly in a generational sense. The religions emanating from the Judaeo-Christian tradition see this beautiful planet as having been created, with life being given breath, by God. How we as humans relate to the earth is entirely in relation to our understanding of God's hand in creating both it and ourselves. How we treat the earth is down to our interpretation of dominion, often based on Genesis 1.28–30. Verse 28 reads, 'God said to them, "Be fruitful and multiply, and fill the earth and subdue it; and have dominion over the fish of the sea and over the birds of the air and over every living thing that moves upon the earth".' That verse has been the traditional yardstick by which our relationship with our environment has been measured. Going back through time, we have always looked to God or gods as the masters of creation, regardless of who those gods happened to be. Our understanding of what is sacred is at the heart of the debates over matters relating to creation: these debates include genetic modification and abortion. The problem – and it is a massive problem – is that dominion has been interpreted in the Christian West as domination.

Domination denounces love

Domination denounces love. It is not therefore concurrent with a state of grace for any Christian Church or any religion to become, or to align itself with, a dominating power. That is to say, a system that promotes and practises domination compromises completely any claims it may have on love. Domination always leads to some level of enslavement of the dominated and the moral and spiritual corruption of the dominator, who in time will devise all sorts of justifications as to why subjugation, cruelty, mistreatment and murder are perfectly acceptable when they are carried out in the interests of the dominating power. This dreadful state of affairs perfectly describes our current relationship with our environment, as it perfectly describes the actions and *modus operandi* of any dictatorship.

The natural world – God's creation – is characterized by balance

Looking at nature as the creation of God, we see no one species dominating another. The mightiest lion does not dominate the ant. Nature exists in harmony with itself. Creation is essentially symbiotic. Chameleons cannot exist without flies, and flies cannot exist without the gift of a dead chameleon every now and again. Likewise, human beings cannot exist without nature, God's creation. 'God saw everything that he had made, and indeed, it was very good' (Genesis 1.31). At the heart of creation is the victory of life, desire, colour, yearning, joy and praise over non-existence, the state of permanent death, the death of everything. So what is our place in creation? However much we dress it up, presume or hypothesize, the Christian tradition does not apparently contain any substantial body of workable instructions regarding the land, the treatment of animals, and animals' treatment of us. There is no manual, no Torah. The spiritual consequences of this have been devastating for all of us. What has emerged, with a few exceptions, is a myopic anthropocentric spirituality based on 'my relationship with Christ' or 'my propensity for sin' which is centred on my treatment of other human beings and the promise of 'my own salvation'. The environmental challenges we face, the climate change, the extinction, have largely therefore been generated by an anthropocentric monotheism that sees salvation solely in human terms and has not recognized the connectedness of all that is 'good'.

Romans 8.20–21

'The creation itself will be set free from its bondage to decay and will obtain the freedom of the glory of the children of God' (Romans 8.21). Christians need to start to see creation as 'good'. Until I can do that, I give myself permission to destroy what is apparently subjected to futility and barren, and I will continue not to notice or care or mind how much of it is treated in this manner. I have to understand that I am one of billions of creations, all of whom are loved by God, and that I am taking part in creation, something beautiful, something 'good'. Does God really love the swallow less than me? And does God draw distinctions between a swallow nesting in a consecrated building and a swallow nesting in a garage? As the Churches of all traditions have made their property more holy than the land around them, have they not effectively condemned the land that is not consecrated as somehow being less holy, less loved by God? The consequences of this are far too apparent, and while I appreciate that consecration in particular is to safeguard the position of churches and churchyards in law, the spiritual legacy of this has been far from healthy. Really, is a garden, a river, a woodland less holy than a burial ground? And, to a certain extent, this question lies at the heart of the emerging practice of woodland burial.

Woodland burial: an introduction

The woodland burial concept was first promoted in the early 1990s, promoted by John Bradfield with the Natural Death Centre.[2] The concept was first introduced by a local authority at Carlisle, Cumbria, as the initiative of Ken West, then Head of Bereavement Service.[3] There are now over 220 sites in England and Wales, with 12 in Scotland. While there is no one organization that oversees these sites, many of them have links with the Natural Death Centre in London, which actively promotes and encourages woodland, or green burial as it also known. The number of woodland burial sites is set to double over the next three years, so something significant is happening. The woodland burial site I helped set up seven years ago just outside Cambridge – the Arbory Trust – is now the second busiest woodland burial ground in the county.

From small acorns

I think it is fair to say that all of us who are involved with woodland burial have been surprised at just how quickly this very new idea has taken root. In the first year that the Arbory Trust was opened for burials, our projections were for two burials and four reservations. What actually took place were 40 burials and over 60 reservations. Clearly, woodland burial was striking a very deep chord. Woodland burial sites are non-denominational, so Christians are buried alongside Buddhists, and atheists next to Muslims. I think it is fair to say that this religiously inclusive approach is part of the reason why more and more people are choosing woodland burial. In a world and at a time when religion is a dividing line – and in some cases, sadly, a justification for violence – this inclusive approach represents a very real eschatology for families choosing woodland burial. It represents a very real choice for peace in a world increasingly fracturing along religious lines.

Since the 1960s the spectacular rise of environmental groups such as Greenpeace, Friends of the Earth and many more local wildlife trusts and special interest groups has had a huge impact not only upon the way we live our lives but also upon environmental consciousness. This has taken hold of the future in a much more powerful and persuasive manner than traditional Christian eschatology. Perhaps, with the rise of multiculturalism, British people no longer believe in the basic Christian story of original creation and the New Jerusalem – what postmodernists call 'the overarching meta-narrative' – but in a plurality of worldviews.

In this sense the salvation of self became disconnected from the salvation of society and the salvation of the natural world. The idea of the Christ returning to save the just and the pure – which usually in the Christian mind means Christians – looks increasingly ludicrous in light of Christianity's associations with the behaviour and mannerisms of the dominating power structures. Seen through the eyes of a tiger, it might appear that Christ is arriving to save it from us. Let's look at the semantics here. We still 'kill' tigers; we don't apparently murder them. If you were a tiger, whom would you bet on to save you from extinction, a Christian or an environmentalist? The long and the short of it is, we have mostly all been persuaded that the planet is in real trouble. As things stand, is Christianity going to save us, or environmentalism?

Why environmental issues have captured the imagination more persuasively than eschatology

First, Christianity in the West has remained by and large silent and predominantly disengaged from the accelerating level of debate and changes in attitudes and behaviour generated by a deep well of environmental concern. Second, because of its links to the dominating power structures which up until recently have been licensing the wholesale destruction and poisoning of the environment, the Christian Church is not the natural home of those who are emotionally and spiritually connected to the environment. Third, many people may feel understandably uneasy about a traditional religious burial if they have not adhered to those religious traditions in a meaningful manner during their lives. Fourth, with the collapse of the rigid social structures that took place in the 1960s, a woodland burial is viewed as much more in keeping with the lifestyle choices made by subsequent generations not mesmerized by the need to mimic the establishment. Perhaps also woodland with open glades, which is managed for the benefit of wildlife and human beings, is seen as a little closer to our imaginings of heaven (as a restored Eden?) than a graveyard or a municipal cemetery. Graveyards, cemeteries and crematoria can be busy places, since many are located near centres of population and access is relatively easy; woodland burial sites which may be rurally located still offer space, privacy and peace.[4] Fifth, crematoria are generally experienced by the mourners who use them as emotionally and aesthetically insubstantial.[5]

The redefining of dignity

Another important factor in the rapidly increasing popularity of woodland burial sites has been a steady change in what is understood to be dignity. The rituals of a traditional funeral, whether within a church, chapel or crematorium, may be viewed by many as either 'cold' or 'stuffy' and not capable of reflecting the identity of the deceased. Even during the short time that I have been a clergyman, it has become quite apparent that much music now chosen for cremation services comes straight out of the popular music charts, not straight out of a hymn book.[6] So a religious format does not necessarily resonate with or define what is popularly considered 'dignified' behaviour. This increasing blend of the religious and the secular may suggest why woodland burial is rapidly gaining in popularity. What is interesting is that those who are choosing woodland burial are doing so because, while they see the funeral element as somehow more secular, they also see the environmental element as resonating with their view of the sacred. Seen from the perspective of environmental consciousness, the anthropocentric view of salvation offered by Christianity is losing ground. This suggests that in the long term, unless Christian communities are prepared to address this issue rather than indulge in window dressing, traditional Christian burial, in churchyards or cemeteries, is set on the path of further slow decline.

The case for woodland burial

There are very sound environmental reasons why woodland burial is being chosen above burial in the traditional churchyard or in municipal cemeteries or above cremation. Let's look at cremation first of all. Just over 70 per cent of the UK population are cremated. That's a huge proportion; it is also a huge amount of fuel, a huge amount of (coffin) wood and a huge amount of heat and carbon being released into the atmosphere. Some of the gardens around crematoria are delightful, but with the best will in the world they are not natural environments. Many local authority cemeteries are setting aside smallish areas for a form of woodland burial. So I would imagine that the numbers of people being cremated will begin to decline over the next 30 years, partly because of the availability of woodland sites, but also because of increased cremation costs.[7]

Municipal cemeteries, especially in urban areas, are filling up rapidly. The reuse of grave space seems to be the solution. While this means that new burial ground does not have to be opened and that existing memorials can be adapted, should we really carry on supporting a system of memorialization that from an environmental perspective can be damaging to the environment? Most woodland burial sites don't use headstones at all, allowing the setting or a tree to be the focus for remembering and grieving. There is a general acceptance that to mine the stone (and most of the stone used as headstones comes from abroad), to transport it here and then deposit it in a graveyard is, environmentally speaking, akin to madness. Sadly, most contemporary graveyards are laid out for the convenience of a lawnmower, with their long ranks of stone, almost as a car park for the dead. Fly over any city and you will soon see just how much space is taken up with these seas of stones. I am not in favour of the reuse of graves. We should let our urban graveyards be adapted to provide the much-needed natural open spaces within our urban environments – as memorial parks, with Gardens of Remembrance within them.

What we are witnessing with the arrival of woodland burial is a genuine change in pattern, a definite change of emphasis. It is really a new choice in an issue that had limited choice. But the reasons for that choice and the effects of making it will either define a generation or act as a marker for a change in consciousness – a fundamental shift, a shift in which human beings see their place in the natural world. With this change of approach driven by the apparent scientific consensus that we are facing some difficult times ahead unless we change our relationship with the environment, it is hard to see from this perspective other alternatives such as promession[8] or resomation,[9] despite their ecological credentials, gaining ground. Our relationship with the environment is set to inform and redefine our actions and behaviour on every level, and I have little doubt this will affect every aspect of human being, practical and spiritual. Also, I feel there is much more change to come, including the disposal of ashes in space, the stars as memorials, wilderness burials, memorial areas inside football grounds. The future of how we deal with death and celebrate the lives of the departed is going to look and feel very different from how it does today.

The most interesting aspect of this is that this change of emphasis is being driven by those from outside the funeral industry and outside the influence of the Christian and religious communities in this country. It is essentially the public who are driving green burial forward, and initially at least the funeral service industries were not convinced. The religious communities see themselves almost as akin to undertakers in relation to death and dying: they see their role primarily as providing a service at a time of need. If the link between anthropocentric monotheism and environmental decline is better understood, there will be fewer and fewer individuals prepared to engage the services of those institutions that, in their mind at least, have appeared largely indifferent to the plight of the natural world. Obviously with the decline of the Christian element in funerals, this leaves a huge space for others to step in.[10]

The new black

On a back street in Lewes in Sussex is a certain shop front. The glass is opaque and it is not possible to see inside. The shop is called 'The Ceremony Shop', and in big blue letters it spells out that it can organize 'Naming ceremonies. Weddings and funerals'. Really, it is selling a 'rites of passage' service and I have little doubt that, as the party planners took hold in the 1970s and 1980s and as the wedding planners arrived in the 1990s, funeral planners are riding in over the horizon as we speak. This is confirmation, if anyone really needed it, that the days of undertakers and the religious communities having a monopoly over funerals are coming to an end. In this brave new world I have no doubt that green burial will continue to thrive, because it resonates with a new sense of the sacred and will be viewed as the responsible dignified choice. In the place of priests will be various configurations of modern-day shaman and women tailor-making the ceremony to suit the needs of the bereaved family. Once funerals are conducted outside of religious buildings, religious traditions will not be able to impose as strongly their vision of the sacred. And, yes, while there are some very sound environmental reasons why woodland burial is resonating with the raised levels of environmental consciousness, I think the popularity of woodland burial is emerging from a renewed sense of the sacred located within the natural world. This renewed sense of the sacred will develop its own distinctive rituals and behaviour so, in place of wooden coffins, people will increasingly choose recycled cardboard. In place of headstones there will be trees and wildflowers. In place of one liturgy there will be many different forms of ceremony developed around the persona of the deceased and the character of those attending the funeral. I am quite sure the undertaking profession will adapt to these new ways. It remains to be seen whether or not the established religious traditions are able to adapt to the energy of the rising levels of environmental consciousness and the relocation of the sense of sacred.

Notes

1 See, for example, Callum G. Brown, *The Death of Christian Britain: Understanding Secularisation 1800–2000*, London: Routledge, 2001; and 'The Secularisation Decade: What the 1960s Have Done to the Study of Religious History' in H. McLeod and W. Ustorf (eds), *The Decline of Christendom in Western Europe, 1750–2000*, Cambridge: Cambridge University Press, 2003, pp. 29–46.

2 See John Bradfield for the Natural Death Centre, *Green Burial: The D-I-Y Guide to Law and Practice*, 2nd edn, London: The Natural Death Centre, 1994.

3 For a recent exposition of contemporary issues regarding the ecology of disposal of the dead, see K. West, untitled paper in *MAB Bulletin*, No. 96, June 2007. This is the text of an address given in the House of Commons organized by MAB (the Memorial Advisory Bureau). See also Ken West, 'How Green Is My Funeral?', *Funeral Service Journal*, Vol. 123, No. 1, 2008, pp. 104–8.

4 By contrast, see D. Francis, L. Kellaher and G. Nyophytou, *The Secret Cemetery*, Oxford: Berg, 2005, pp. 41, 110, for mourners' experience of cemeteries as places for peace and comfort. Cemeteries can also provide the support and conviviality of other grave visitors.

5 See, for example, H. J. Grainger, this volume and *Death Redesigned: British Crematoria – History, Architecture and Landscape*, Reading: Spire, 2006, pp. 25–6.

6 See Parsons, this volume.

7 For an exposition of the contemporary issues about cremation and the environment, see K. West, 'Ecology' in D. J. Davies with L. Mates, *Encyclopedia of Cremation*, Aldershot: Ashgate, 2005, pp. 172–4.

8 For an account of the promession process, see S. Wiigh-Mäsak, 'Promession', *Pharos International*, Vol. 72, No. 1, Spring 2006, pp. 3–4. The dead body is frozen in liquid nitrogen and then gently vibrated to turn into a powder. The remains, buried in a biodegradable box in a shallow grave, will be converted by the action of the soil into compost.

9 For an account of the resomation process, see S. Sullivan, '"Water Resolution" – a Mercury Free Alternative to Cremation', *Pharos International*, Vol. 72, No. 4, Winter 2006, pp. 14–17; S. Sullivan and D. Fisher, 'Resolution TM User', *Pharos International*, Vol. 74, No. 1, Spring 2008, pp. 3–18. The dead body is placed in water with added alkali at 170°C. This alkaline hydrolysis process turns the body into liquid and calcium dust. This powder can be given back to the relatives as in cremation. It is a non-burn, water-based process that returns the body to its natural elements.

10 For example from the increasing numbers of secular celebrants, trained and promoted by such organizations as the Institute of Civil Funerals and the British Humanist Association.

15

The Church of England's *Common Worship* Funeral Services

TREVOR LLOYD

Introduction

In 1997 the Church of England Liturgical Commission circulated the core text of a new draft Funeral Service to 800 parishes licensed to use the service 'experimentally'. With it went an introductory paper[1] indicating some of the major changes in the background and approach to the new rite since the Church's last major discussion of (significantly) 'The Burial of the Dead' in 1964. Referring to the list of answers then to the question 'What ought we to be doing at a burial service?'[2] the Commission said:

> The major change since 1964 has been the beginning of a new open-ness in talking about death, of which the growths of the hospice movement and of bereavement counselling are both symptoms and causes. We would probably not want to say as they did in 1964 'It would, perhaps, be natural to add a sixth point, namely the consolation of the mourners; but the Commission believes that this object should be attained by means of the objects already included in its answer.' We would want to see the funeral playing its part, not as the only way the church offers comfort to the bereaved, but as a focus or tool in a much longer process of helping the bereaved, not just to cope or overcome but to grow as people and to grow in faith. A short liturgical rite cannot do much in the way of caring, but it can open doors, lay foundations and avoid creating problems for the future.[3]

The 1997 draft was the result of four years' work by the Commission. In the Church of England there had been growing dissatisfaction with the Funeral Service in the *Alternative Service Book 1980* (*ASB*),[4] and as part of the preparations for revising the *ASB* the Liturgical Commission began discussing the Funeral Service in 1993, setting up a small group to work on proposals. After a brainstorming exercise and the circulation of theological background papers, the main principles were becoming clear, and by early 1995 the Commission was discussing the outline and basic text of the new rite, together with a vast amount of resource material. Some of this had come in as a result of letters in the church press[5] from the chairman of the Funerals Group, Trevor Lloyd, saying what the Commission was doing and inviting suggestions. This was a change in style from a way of working in secret behind locked doors producing texts which are revealed only when finely polished, making it very difficult for people who want things changed to do so without being adversarial and throwing the whole thing out. The Commission decided that, if there was to be any hope of getting behind the 'political consensus' of 1979–80, especially over prayer and the departed, the discussion had to be as wide and open as possible. So there were discussions with diocesan liturgical representatives, whose annual meeting gave an opportunity both for leaking the texts to a wider audience and for debating the principles. Bodies such as Cruse, the National Association of Funeral Directors (NAFD), the Society of Allied and Independent Funeral Directors (SAIF), the National Association of Bereavement Services, the ecumenical Churches' Funeral Group and the Church's ecumenical partners were consulted, and there were symposia on prayer and the departed in two successive years in York with members of General Synod, selected to represent differing theological and cultural outlooks.[6] The culmination of this was the massive consultation exercise in 1997, resulting in an enormous volume of responses from the 800 parishes – the longest was 42 pages! The overwhelming response was in favour of what the Commission was doing, with many suggestions for change and improvement being incorporated. Part of the report[7] on the responses included verbatim quotes:

- A very helpful improvement giving a powerful structure to the service.
- There is a clear acknowledgement of the process of the grief and it is possible to trace the sequence of denial, chaos and eventual reintegration, especially in the prayers.
- After 11 years of ministry I at last felt that I was officiating at a real act of worship instead of 'just a funeral'.
- I find the proportion of those saying 'Lovely service Vicar' much higher with this service.

The result of the consultative approach was twofold: a set of services which had been subjected to rigorous testing and criticism and which were more polished as a result, and an unexpectedly smooth passage through the Synod, with not one vote against.

The external structure

In seeking to get back beyond 1980, the Commission had reached back beyond the Middle Ages, as it noted in the background paper already quoted:[8]

> Perhaps the most significant thing about the 1964 Introduction is that it starts from the Reformation and the debates at that time. So it sees 'the chief theological question involved' as prayer for the dead. The current work of the Liturgical Commission both starts much further back and is wider in its theology, putting prayer about the departed into this wider context. The pattern of the Roman secular, early Roman Christian rites (for example in the Rheinau Sacramentary of 800) and in 13th Century and later monastic liturgy, sees the funeral rite as a continuum, broken by movements from place to place, from home to church, to the place of burial and back to the home, a pattern which was severely truncated by the actions of the Reformers.

The theme of movement and journeying from one place to another, reflecting the pilgrimage of the whole of the Christian's life, was one of the key planks in the formation of the new rites, picked out again in the Introduction to the 2000 *Common Worship: Pastoral Services*, which begins:

> We are all on a journey through life. One of the presuppositions on which the Church of England's Pastoral Services are based is that we do not travel alone. Where is God in relation to that journey? He is both the starting point and the ending point, the Alpha and the Omega.[9]

and says of the Funeral Service:

> The Funeral Service is both the end of the human journey in this world and a whole series of journeys in itself. The funeral rite from the eighth century or earlier was a continuum . . . Today's pastoral

needs suggest a return to it. As grieving is a process marked by different stages, we believe that one helpful contribution the church can make pastorally is to have a series of services and resources where some of these different stages can be seen, spoken of in advance or recapitulated.[10]

So the external structure of this collection of funeral rites begins at that point where the laying on of hands in the hope of healing, in the 'Ministry to the Sick',[11] turns to the laying on of hands in the comfort and hope of death, in 'Ministry at the Time of Death'.[12] Though many of the ancillary rites will not be regularly used, especially by those who are not church members, it is important that they are there, providing both a context in which the main funeral service is set and an opportunity for lay ministry, including ministry by other members of the family. In keeping with the rest of the new rites, 'Ministry at the Time of Death' has enough flexibility to meet most of the situations that arise as people die in the twenty-first century, providing both for one-to-one ministry in reconciliation and preparing for death, and also for a time when friends and family might be present. The last Communion may be individual, or shared, and happen more than once if necessary. It is in this context, often with the dying person still alive, that the use of prayers of commendation such as 'Go forth from this world . . .' and 'Acknowledge, we pray, a sheep of your own fold . . .' are perfectly acceptable to all shades of theological stance, and it is their use here which opens the door to their optional use later on, in the Funeral Service.

After the death, five further rites are provided in a section entitled 'Before the Funeral'. 'At Home before the Funeral'[13] might be part of a minister's visit to the family before the funeral, or part of a family's response on hearing news of a death. 'For those Unable to be Present at the Funeral',[14] deliberately based on the Funeral Service and, again, capable of adaptation, aims to meet the needs of those who cannot be present at the funeral. 'Receiving the Coffin at Church'[15] may happen at the start of the service or on the day before the funeral, in which case it might be followed by 'A Funeral Vigil'.[16] For this, a number of different themes are provided, each with readings, psalms and prayers. 'On the Morning of the Funeral' puts into print the kind of informal prayer and reading that might be led by the minister or a family member before setting off for the funeral. 'At Home after the Funeral' provides some prayers at home after the funeral, including one which might be used as a grace if there is food after the funeral. There is also provision for the Burial of Ashes, for a later memorial service, and for annual memorials.

'So the Funeral Service is part of a longer continuum, though it stands perfectly well on its own if necessary . . . The bereaved will need to be able to say different things to God and to one another at each of these different stages.'[17]

The internal structure

Just as the journey provides the structure for the process of which the Funeral Service proper is the central part, so within the Funeral Service there is a clear movement from one place to another. The Introduction in *Common Worship: Pastoral Services* puts it like this:

> The structure within the Funeral Service itself moves from the human to the divine, from earth to heaven. It begins with an acknowledgement of the different groups of people who come to mourn, for some of whom the early part of the service will be a recapitulation of those stages since the death in which they have not been able fully to participate. The service provides an opportunity for the celebration of the life of a person who has died, and moves from this into the reading of scripture and prayer, before reaching its climax in the commendation and the committal.[18]

In a curious way, the service is both less and more overtly Christian than its predecessor, the 1980 *ASB* service. It does not begin with sentences of scripture, followed by a prayer proclaiming faith in the resurrection to be said by all. The sentences are still there, but not mandatory, though there are nearly three pages of them at the request of those with long churchyards. The service begins with an introduction which indicates the reasons why people have come – to remember, to give thanks, to commend and commit, and to comfort: it is all focused on the human level – of recognizing one another and the needs of those who are there. The opening prayer, said by the minister, is about recognizing grief:

> God of all consolation,
> your Son Jesus Christ was moved to tears
> at the grave of Lazarus his friend.[19]

So the way the service starts acknowledges where people are, and attempts the very difficult job of drawing people with very different relationships with the dead person into one worshipping congregation.

Starting by focusing on our common humanity is one way of doing this; another is to move almost immediately into the one thing that does unite us: the shared memories of the one being mourned. So it is at this point that the tribute comes, defined in Note 4:

> Remembering and honouring the life of the person who has died, and the evidence of God's grace and work in them should be done in the earlier part of the service, after the opening prayer, though if occasion demands it may be woven into the sermon or come immediately before the Commendation. It may be done in conjunction with the placing of symbols, and may be spoken by a family member or friend or by the minister using information provided by the family. It is preferable not to interrupt the flow of the Reading(s) and Sermon with a tribute of this kind.[20]

If the service starts in a way that is less overtly Christian than the *ASB* service, it is soon apparent that the structure of the service is more overtly Christian. The movement from the human to the divine, from earth to heaven, from word to action seems familiar, and it is. Why? The next paragraph offers an explanation of the Commission's thinking.

One of the issues about any funeral service is, 'Who is it for?' Is it for the departed – to honour them, to lay them to rest decently, to send them on their way into eternity, to pray for them? Is it for the mourners – to comfort and challenge, to help them remember, celebrate and be put in mind of their own impending death? Is it for the benefit of society at large – to mark the passing of a member of the community, to remind us that death is around the corner for all of us? And within each of these options, are we making provision for Christians or non-Christians, for those with faith or those without? Both the Commission and the Synod discussed how far we should be providing funeral services for those clearly outside the faith, and whether there should be two different services, one for church members and one which would enable the Church to fulfil its duty to provide funerals for everyone without forcing either minister or congregation to commit perjury.

The answer can be seen in a note from the Commission to the House of Bishops in 1997, which also shows why the structure is familiar:

> The basic rite is a Christian rite for Christians. We believe that it should be possible to have the same basic rite for all, and not one service for church members and one for others. Hence, the basic structure is eucharistic, but that does not mean that every service will

include the Holy Communion. This is clearly a change from past practice, but we would encourage it because:

(i) It is the characteristic Christian thing for Christian families to do, a familiar way for them to pray at a time of stress.

(ii) It ensures the focus is on Christ and not on the corpse.

(iii) It involves using familiar texts.

(iv) It provides a context in which confession and absolution are there not because there are good psychological reasons for them, but because they are part of the rite.

(v) It emphasises the nature of the church as a community which is providing support for the bereaved.

(vi) It ensures that the action on one level is set in eternity.

The Commission hopes that by emphasising the eternal time-scale, and by acknowledging that there are some ways of speaking about the departed which can be used at the time of death which some would consider inappropriate later, but which might be used as part of the recapitulation of the earlier stages of grieving during the funeral service, it may be possible to use a slightly richer language about the departed than was possible in the ASB.[21]

To judge from the voting in Synod and the subsequent approving comments from those using the service, it would seem that the Commission's hope has been fulfilled, and that the possibility of a service with much richer and more heaven-centred language has become a reality. That this has been done without causing gratuitous and un-Gospel-like offence to those on the fringe of or outside the Church is due both to the measure of flexibility provided and to the vast amount of resource material to meet most needs. The flexibility is partly achieved by authorizing an 'Outline Order for Funerals',[22] a kind of 'skeleton' rite (though that term is studiously avoided) on the pattern of the earlier 'Service of the Word' indicating what the essential structure is and where authorized texts must be used. This provides the basis on which many funerals of children and babies are now planned, with much less rigidity, using the resources in the *Pastoral Services* volume.

In *Common Worship* the Church of England Funeral Service structure has undergone a fundamental change. In 1552 Cranmer grudgingly constructed a minimalist service from the old funeral office, with no Communion and no need even to go into church.[23] The 'office' has now gone, its opening sentences give way to greeting and welcome; penitence and the ministry of the word have their natural place; and the service becomes empty-tomb and heavenly banquet-centred rather than coffin-centred. It moves in a 'normal' way to a eucharistic climax and, at that moment, conscious of the open door between heaven and earth, we move to the Commendation and Farewell, followed by the Committal. Now, clearly, there are all sorts of practical problems like: how you do all this where the crematorium only offers 20 minutes; how do you end the first part of the service when not many will be present at the Committal; and how do you retain the heavenward movement when there is no Communion? But all these are dealt with in the copious notes and stage directions in the services,[24] and do not diminish the fact that a significant change has taken place.

Humanity, celebration and grieving

Both the personalization of funerals and the acknowledgement of grief are recent innovations in Anglican funerals.[25] It was only in 1965 that 'N' for inserting the person's name first appeared in an official service, and now it would be thought unusual not to take advantage of some of the other ways of personalizing the service, involving the mourners, and making it a genuine celebration of an earthly life that has ended – placing suitable symbols of the person's life and faith on or near the coffin and perhaps saying a brief sentence about them, sharing in placing a pall over the coffin, taking part in the tribute or providing information to the minister about what to say at that point.[26]

In common with many post-1980 funeral rites across the Anglican Communion, there is a clearer acknowledgement of the part the funeral rite can play in helping people to grieve. As people work their way through a whole complex variety of stages, emotions and activities, it is tempting to see the funeral liturgy as in some way reflecting a pattern of grieving, almost as if people could pass through or even recapitulate all the stages of grieving in the course of one service.[27] The *Common Worship* service does not attempt to do this, but does provide echoes of the different aspects of grieving, to go with some rituals and signs and symbols which might help not only those mourning this death, but those mourning other losses who need a gentle reminder and acknowledgement of where they are on that other journey.

So we have:

- Encouragements to tell the story, both of the death and of the person, to focus on what they have done and to place it in the past, e.g.,

'Those present may be encouraged briefly to share their memories of the one who has died.'[28]

- Actions to locate the death in the past: the very fact of receiving the coffin and holding a vigil points in this direction, and that the service ends with 'the mourners may come near and touch the coffin or gather around it and pray'.[29] Involving the mourners in having physical things to do such as the placing of symbols is helpful.
- Words which recognize the reality of shock and numbness, e.g., 'O God, who brought us to birth and in whose arms we die, In our grief and shock contain and comfort us'[30] or 'God of hope, we come to you in shock and grief and confusion of heart.'[31]
- Words echoing anger, yearning and searching. Anger is explicitly acknowledged in some of the prayers, e.g., 'We are hurt by our parting from N whom we loved; when we are angry at the loss we have sustained . . .'[32]
- Other prayers echo the feeling of emptiness and yearning, e.g., 'Father, the death of N brings an emptiness into our lives. We are separated from *him/her* and feel broken and disturbed.'[33]
- The opportunity to express different degrees of depression, to acknowledge that grief is normal and that it might take time. The service begins, not with the triumphant prayer of the *ASB* service but with a reminder of Jesus' tears at Lazarus' grave, and includes, in the prayers of penitence and elsewhere, a chance to look at the guilt which sometimes causes grieving to get stuck, e.g., 'we are mindful of all that we have failed to do', and 'as we mourn . . . we also remember times when it was hard for us to understand, to forgive and be forgiven. Hear our memories of hurt and failure'[34] or 'Often you weep over our sins and our pride; Tenderly you draw us from hatred and judgement.'[35]
- A look at the future of acceptance and relocation, for example in the prayer at home after the funeral: 'Now we ask for your presence to be recognised in this home; bring your peace and joy to each place which stirs the memory; give your strength and presence in those daily tasks which used to be shared, and in all the changes of life give us grace . . .'[36]

The Funeral Service journey, in the company of others at different stages on the road, is part of a journey in the hope of eternal life, and experience of that life now, in the course of which grieving is resolved into acceptance. It is a long and almost eternal perspective.

Notes

1 The text of this single sheet of paper, 'Draft Funeral Service', is in General Synod House of Bishops HB(97)10. This is an unpublished document in the House of Bishops' archives.

2 '(a) To secure the reverent disposal of the corpse.

(b) To commend the deceased to the care of our heavenly Father.

(c) To proclaim the glory of our risen life in Christ here and hereafter.

(d) To remind us of the awful certainty of our own coming death and judgement.

(e) To make plain the eternal unity of Christian people, living and departed, in the risen and ascended Christ.' *Alternative Services Second Series*, London: SPCK, 1965, pp. 105–6.

3 *Alternative Services Second Series*, London: SPCK, 1965, pp. 105–6.

4 Michael Perham's chapter 'Anglican Funeral Rites Today and Tomorrow' in this book's predecessor, Peter C. Jupp and T. Rogers (eds), *Interpreting Death: Christian Theology and Pastoral Practice*, London and Washington: Cassell, 1997, pp. 157–69, indicates some of this dissatisfaction, and reflects the thinking behind the Commission's new text taking shape in 1995–6. In its 1993 brainstorming session the Commission mentioned:

- The lack of flexibility in the 1980 rite which meant it could not meet the wide variety of needs.
- The absence of any rites focusing on the different moments in the process of dying.
- The failure to address the grieving process in a rite focused strongly on resurrection, for example in the way the 1980 rite begins.
- The 'lowest common denominator' approach to prayer and the departed.
- The absence of provision for symbols.

5 *Church Times* and *Church of England Newspaper*, December 1993: 'I chair a group of the Liturgical Commission which is currently looking at the shape of Church of England funeral services after the year 2000. We are at the stage of collecting resources, prayers, introductions, words for committal and blessing etc., and would be grateful if your readers could send us, or draw our attention to, anything they think ought to be included. . . . We are also open to general comments and advice!'

6 Position papers circulated before these meetings were from Dr Christopher Cocksworth and Dr Kenneth Stevenson (1995) and Revd Andrew Burnham and Ven Pete Broadbent (1996). The substance – amplified – of Dr Cocksworth's paper may be found in Christopher Cocksworth, *Prayer and the Departed*, Grove Worship Series 142, Cambridge: Grove Books, 1997.

7 *Pastoral Rites: Responses from the Experimental Parishes*, GS Misc 531, London: Church House, June 1998, p. 3.

8 *Draft Funeral Service*, above.

9 *Common Worship: Pastoral Services*, London: Church House Publishing, 2000, p. 3.

10 *Common Worship*, p. 5. See Chapter 5, and note 26, below.

11 *Common Worship*, pp. 51–92.

12 *Common Worship*, pp. 216–35.

13 *Common Worship*, pp. 236–9.
14 *Common Worship*, pp. 240, 241.
15 *Common Worship*, pp. 242–6.
16 *Common Worship*, pp. 247–54.
17 *Common Worship*, p. 5.
18 *Common Worship*, p. 6.
19 *Common Worship*, p. 260.
20 *Common Worship*, p. 291. The next note distinguishes the tribute from the (mandatory) sermon: 'The purpose of the sermon is to proclaim the gospel in the context of the death of this particular person.'
21 HB(97)10. This is an unpublished document in the House of Bishops' archives.
22 *Common Worship*, p. 257.
23 See Jupp, this volume chapter 6.
24 So, for instance, intercessions and words for Commendation can be chosen to reflect the heavenward theme, and there is a rubric before the Committal: 'If the Committal does not follow as part of the same service in the same place, some sections of the Dismissal (pages 270–273) may be used here', *Common Worship*, p. 267. And Note 8 (p. 292) says, 'The Committal is used at the point at which it is needed'.
25 I have looked briefly at some of the reasons for this, and how the growth of this awareness can be traced across the Anglican Communion, in my chapter, 'Prayer Book Services across the Anglican Communion: Funeral Services' in *The Oxford Companion to the Book of Common Prayer*, New York: Oxford University Press, 2006, p. 519 – the reaction against the commercialization and de-humanization of the processes of dying and bereavement which in the West had transferred the ownership of the funeral to the professionals; the hospice movement and the growing understanding of bereavement; the awareness of different cultural approaches to funerals.
26 See the quote from note 4 and note 20 above.
27 See Valentine, this volume. The Commission was well aware of criticisms of those who took Elisabeth Kübler-Ross's stages as some kind of blueprint, and of recent developments in grieving 'theory' summarized here in Chapter 6, this volume. That is what led to the scattered approach to echoes which may or may not be picked up, outlined in the next paragraph.
28 *Common Worship*, pp. 238, 240, 244.
29 *Common Worship*, p. 246.
30 *Common Worship*, pp. 302, 355.
31 *Common Worship*, p. 307.
32 *Common Worship*, p. 355.
33 *Common Worship*, p. 355.
34 *Common Worship*, p. 354.
35 *Common Worship*, p. 401, A Song of St Anselm.
36 *Common Worship*, p. 321.

The Roman Catholic Experience:
Change in a New Century

TONY ROGERS

Changes and trends

The funeral of Princess Diana was undoubtedly something of a turning point in terms of the public expression of grief for a member of the Royal Family. The plethora of flowers, the books of condolence, the candles and, perhaps most striking of all, the applause as the hearse passed through the streets following the service, were all indications that the British people were not only in shock and grief, but also that they were responding differently. There were similar elements at the funeral of Pope John Paul II, including applause which, at the end of the Mass, was intensified as the coffin was lifted and rotated in front of the crowd prior to burial in the crypt of St Peter's.

Ten years on from Diana's death, the world's press seems to imply that for some British people there is an ongoing agenda of mourning. One interesting recent contribution for those who still grieve about her took the form of a prayer for use in churches; this spoke directly of her vulnerability, as well as her reaching out to those on the margins. In using the word 'vulnerability', there is an acknowledgement of human frailty, perhaps obscured for many at the time of her death.

Some of these expressions are connected with genuine affection for two very different people, but there is another side; this speaks of a confusion about what is the appropriate response in an age beset by its own uncertainties about death and the hereafter. Elements of these two very public occasions are now mirrored to some extent in other funerals, and present something of a challenge to all Churches. The Diana event was perhaps, in its own way, a revival of the wake tradition even if, for some, it lacked the element of prayer. It certainly happened with spontaneity, but the extent to which the risen Christ was at its heart is something to which we might never know the answer until the day of resurrection. Just as English law works on precedent, so does liturgy and human ritual. What has happened once – especially if it was in a very public setting – will undoubtedly happen again and again. The assimilation of certain practices in our changing religious culture need not necessarily be viewed negatively. Take, for example, the question of symbolism.

In the months leading up to the fall of Communist regimes in Eastern Europe, candles were lit in city squares by those who saw in the flickering flames both an expression of hope for the future and solidarity for the present. But for some who lit them there was also the traditional dimension of prayer that God would be able to do for us and our world what we cannot hope to achieve alone. Here is an example of Christian symbolism which has taken on a wider meaning without necessarily losing its religious significance. Conversely, the use of flowers – popular since the mid-nineteenth century as an expression of condolence at the time of a funeral[1] – has also taken on a new meaning at the graveside. The Catholic custom of sprinkling holy water or throwing earth onto the coffin has, in recent years, been supplemented or in some cases supplanted by family members and close friends stepping forward and dropping a single rose or other flower into the grave. At one level this is an apparently secular gesture, but surely one that reminds us of the words of scripture: 'All people are grass, their constancy is like the flower of the field. The grass withers, the flower fades' (Isaiah 40.6–7).

Pastoral issues in the twenty-first century

As faithful and observant Catholics approach the end of their lives, a common cause of concern is what will happen when they die, especially if those closest to them – even their children – are not religious. How will they know what to do? In a secular and geographically mobile society, there is a growing practice of planning and preparing the funeral liturgy before death, and of leaving instructions with the family, alongside the will, or with the local church. The trend towards pre-paid funeral plans will enable people to sort these matters out beforehand, though not all will be aware of what is involved in each plan on offer. This is an area where parish communities can heighten awareness through the use of leaflets, references in preaching and newsletter inserts.

Burial of ashes

Many churches have, in recent years, set aside part of their grounds as a 'memorial garden' for the burial of ashes. Others have built or set up a columbarium – niches in a wall into which ashes can be placed. These spaces are often tended as lovingly as graves, with flowers and plants placed regularly near the memorial tablets.[2] For many Catholics, visiting graves on birthdays or anniversaries, or during the month of November, has been an important prayer focus. The practice of cremation, while more widespread among our own community nowadays, does however often leave people with a sense of unfinished business.[3] Families leave the crematorium, knowing that others will complete the task; and the ability to reclaim the ashes and bury or strew them in a piece of ground near the church is a source of comfort and a powerful link with Christian burial. Associated with this growing custom is an annual parish visit to a local cemetery or the burial ground or columbarium – a time of prayer for the whole community, and a particular opportunity for those who have lost relatives or friends over the past year to bring them to God in prayer with others. In many communities this is becoming popular in the month of November, and while it may not be a familiar practice for many English Catholics, it is one well known in Ireland and on the European mainland. The revival of an ancient custom is welcomed by many and is part of the 'counter-culture' of Christianity – in which we are able to focus on death and eternal life, not only at the time of the funeral, but repeatedly, and until the Eschaton.

Recent immigration

The recent waves of immigration from Eastern Europe, the Philippines, Africa and India, have brought us face to face with customs and practices unfamiliar to us in the United Kingdom.[4] Time is one factor which impacts in different ways. For many people the delay between the time of death and the funeral seems unnecessarily prolonged. They may be used to a funeral within a day or two, and find the gap unhelpful in the whole process of grief. On the other hand, time has different implications when it comes to the length of a funeral. In our culture we are attuned to constraints set by funeral directors, churches, crematoria and cemeteries – restrictions which are often very difficult for those whose grief is expressed in a more overt manner, and who may want to spend time round an open coffin. Increasing multiculturalism helps undertakers to be wise in the time allotted. The spontaneous grief displayed by many from immigrant communities often contrasts with the restraint which characterizes many an English funeral,[5] and the coming together of different communities for a funeral will highlight this difference.

The funeral liturgy

The publication of *The Order of Christian Funerals*[6] took into account the pastoral situations current in Great Britain at that time. As well as the option, which has always been in place, for a funeral liturgy with or without Mass, there was a recognition that, increasingly, nothing will take place in church, but the funeral will be centred solely on the cemetery or, more likely, the crematorium.[7] Thus, provision was made for a rite which would include a reception of the body, a liturgy of the word, a commendation and a committal. Such an optional provision does not take away the centrality of the Eucharist as the normative form of celebration. But perhaps one of the most attractive features of the book is the number of opportunities prior to the funeral when it is appropriate to come together for prayer, for example, when the family gathers for the first time in the presence of the body. These simple rites may be led by ordained or lay ministers.

Planning the funeral

In an age when some people find it possible, according to surveys and research,[8] to believe in God without believing in an afterlife, it is clear that nothing can be taken for granted when it comes to the planning and celebration of a funeral in a Catholic, or any other church save the Orthodox.[9] When *The Order of Christian Funerals* was published in 1990, the funeral rites were set out in the form of a journey – from the moment of death to the burial – either of a body or of cremated remains.[10] Many of the options set out in the book, including low-key, domestic occasions when families gather for prayer, have proved an invaluable and welcome asset to those in need of a structured outline at a time when words fail. But it is probably true to say that the riches of this book lie largely undiscovered, even after almost 20 years of use. For every family that comes with a *tabula rasa*, seeking and welcoming guidance from those involved in funeral ministry, there will be another which has fixed and firm ideas as to what is appropriate, and this can be difficult to resist.

Because there is often a greater familiarity with the favourite poems or songs of the deceased, family and friends may have more to offer by way of suggestions for the funeral from these sources.[11] There is need for greater sensitivity on the part of priests or members of the parish community involved in funeral planning. The bereaved are easily offended if their requests are not granted, but there are other opportunities besides the funeral liturgy for poems and songs to be included,[12] not least during the words spoken in memory of the deceased.

On the plus side, helpful publications have been produced[13] to assist the bereaved in the planning of a funeral liturgy, and even among those unfamiliar with the scriptures they have proved invaluable. The word of God often speaks louder than we imagine. Unfamiliar passages from the Old Testament – particularly from the Wisdom literature – will often be chosen because they are so appropriate to the circumstances of death. Verses such as 'In the eyes of the foolish they seemed to have died, and their departure was thought to be a disaster' (Wisdom 3.2) or 'For old age is not honoured for length of time, or measured by number of years' (Wisdom 4.8) will resonate loudly both in the choosing and on the day of the funeral.

Participation by the funeral congregation is made so much easier when suitable leaflets are prepared. In a gathering where it is quite likely that the majority will be unfamiliar with liturgy, it is important that the 'pew leaflets' are prepared with the necessary texts for full participation. An Order of Service leaflet which contains only hymns is less than useful. It is no major task for a church to be able to prepare tailor-made material for each funeral. Computerization and desktop publishing have made this all so much easier, even though copyright laws must be observed. It not only makes it easier for all concerned not to have to switch from one book to another, but it is also something of a tribute to the one who has died.

Even when care has been taken in the planning of the funeral, unfamiliarity with a church setting can be a problem on the day itself. For this reason it is helpful if clergy or lay leaders in their words of welcome acknowledge something of the unease which people may be feeling. This sensitivity should pervade the whole service. Coming from a liturgical tradition, we need to speak quite deliberately to non-believers and searchers who, in all probability, will make up a considerable percentage of the mourners.[14] While it is right that we pray unashamedly according to our tradition, and that we proclaim what we believe without embarrassment, it is also important to acknowledge that not everyone will be in tune with what we say.

Even the simple invitation 'Let us pray' needs a bit of unpacking. What do non-religious people do at this point? Perhaps they need a simple encouragement at the start of the liturgy to use those moments when others pray as an opportunity to recognize their own hopes and longings? There is also the issue of the hope we proclaim in our preaching of the Lord's promise of eternal life. For many,[15] this will not be a hope that they share. Nonetheless, it is important that their memories and emotions are something which they have in common with others present, and that itself enables them to share in the celebration. Recognition of this fact can go a long way, and mourners will welcome the inclusivity. Above all, a funeral should never be an occasion to make people feel guilty for their absence from active church life. The American writer, Joseph Champlain, wrote passionately in his book *The Marginal Catholic*[16] about the way in which bad experiences of church for the occasional attender will always reinforce their negative feelings, while a good experience *may* help to open the door and ease the return.

Speaking in memory of the deceased

The Order of Christian Funerals made provision at the end of the funeral liturgy for a family member or friend to speak in memory of the deceased. When the book was compiled, this option was included because of fairly rare occasions when this had been requested. No one could have guessed how popular the practice would become, to the extent that those unwilling or reluctant to read from scripture would feel honour bound to speak in memory of someone they loved. Perhaps the reason why the practice has caught on so quickly may be connected with the desire to celebrate what has happened, because faith in what is to come may be absent. Like all practices that are welcomed and encouraged, there are drawbacks. While the preacher's task is to relate the scriptures that have been proclaimed to the death of the person whose funeral rites are being celebrated and to the mourners, the tribute may take a number of forms. It may be an immensely powerful and sensitive tribute, but it might be a read obituary, with little more than a string of dates and events joined together. It may almost amount to a canonization, the deceased being spoken of as if no one else could ever match their high standards. Again, it may not be too far removed from a best man's speech, with innuendos and in-jokes that will only resonate for a small percentage of the congregation. Time and unfamiliarity with public speaking can also be a problem. It is by no means unknown for what was promised to be a tribute of 'no more than five minutes' to last three times that length and be delivered either at breakneck speed or without any attention to a perfectly good public address system.

Lay-led liturgies

Though the *Order of Christian Funerals* made provision for elements of the funeral liturgy other than the Mass to be led by deacons or lay leaders, lay presidency of funerals was seen from a theoretical rather than a practical perspective. But within a few years of its publication in 1990 a book designed specifically for lay leaders was produced by the Bishops' Conference of England and Wales. Entitled *In Sure and Certain Hope*[17] it sets out both the adaptations needed as well as some helpful guidelines for those involved in this ministry.

Neo-natal deaths, stillbirths and miscarriages

The death of a newly born baby, a stillbirth or a miscarriage will have a focus of a different kind.[18] It is in these circumstances that the expression 'celebration of life' can have a hollow ring, because there are few memories to share and no stories that will enable tears and laughter to mingle unashamedly and naturally. Yet, strangely enough, there is an element of memory as well as of promise. The miscarried or stillborn baby or one whose life was short is still part of parents' history. Only recently a young couple who had lost their first child quite early in the pregnancy asked me to conduct a short graveside service while they lovingly laid a tiny casket to rest. They also took the opportunity of giving that child a name – a child whom they had never seen or cradled in their arms. They wanted to be able to speak to any children born to them in the future of this member of the family – an older brother or sister who had gone before them. There is nothing artificial about this exercise, because, though the memories are of a different kind, a short burial service will evoke thoughts and emotions of the joy and delight associated with the confirmation of a pregnancy.

In the grounds of the church to which I am attached, a 'memorial to the unborn' was put up a few years ago and, while dedicated to no one in particular, it has proved to be a source of catharsis for some people who have never grieved – or who perhaps have never properly come through their grief. If death is a taboo, then the death of the unborn is perhaps an even greater taboo, precisely because of a confusion in our culture about the reality of human life in the first place. The Roman Catholic Church, alongside many Evangelical Christians, has through its consistent stand against abortion been clear in its proclamation of the sacredness of life from womb conception till death. Thankfully, in terms of pastoral response, it is an area where all Churches have responded in recent years, making provision for prayer and ritual where previously there was nothing. Sadly, stories still appear in the press which reveal an insensitivity or inability on the part of priests and ministers to respond appropriately in these circumstances.

The widespread belief among Catholics that we had to be circumspect when speaking of unbaptized children has now been eased by the recent declaration from Rome[19] that while 'limbo' was a genuine theological attempt to find an answer to the question of their fate, it was never formally part of our teaching and was a product of another age. The texts used for the funerals of unbaptized children are a reminder of the truth that if we want to know what the Church believes about a particular issue, we look to see how we pray. These prayers are an expression of our firm hope that unbaptized babies are in God's care and keeping and part of his plan.

'In my Father's house there are many dwelling-places' (John 14.2)

As part of society, Catholics are caught up in the culture which sees death as defeat and which can be reluctant to focus on its reality. So, in the preparation of participation aids for a funeral liturgy, it is not uncommon to see the liturgy described as 'A celebration of the life of . . .' or 'A thanksgiving for the life of. . .'. Understandably, this is something which most people at the time of death would want to do. At the same time, we need to be careful that we do not lose sight of the fact that we are gathering to proclaim our faith and hope in Christ's promise of eternal life. The model for Catholic funerals is the Easter journey of Jesus Christ from death to resurrection,[20] and our prayer is made in that context. It is right to be grateful for all that has been good and positive. It is not appropriate to dwell on the negative aspects of their life, but equally it is good for us to remember that all of us are daily in need of God's mercy for those things which have not been right.

Before he became Pope, Cardinal Joseph Ratzinger wrote:

The purpose of Christ's campaign was to eliminate death, that death which devours time and makes us cultivate the lie in order to forget or 'kill' time. Nothing can make man laugh unless there is an answer to the question of death. And conversely, if there is an answer to death, it will make genuine joy possible – and joy is the basis of every feast. At its very heart the Eucharist is the answer to the question of death, for it is the encounter with that *love which is stronger than death*. (Song of Songs 8.6)[21]

This truth lies at the heart of every funeral. The death of a Christian who lived with that belief, and whose family shares it, will give a dimension that somehow makes sense of death and comprehends it, whatever tears may be shed. Just as Paul was nearly stoned to death in Lystra (Acts 14.19) but was still able to put new heart into the believers and encourage them to continue in the faith, so the Christian in the midst of tears will still be filled with an unshakeable hope and be encouraged too. If the life we have lived is essentially more precious than the hope held out to us, then it is inevitable that the focus will be backwards rather than forwards. Often, of course, the kind of funeral which has this focus will not be a reflection of the faith of the deceased, but of the mourners. They will be seeking comfort from the sources which are real for them. But this is the paradox facing the minister at a funeral. The Introduction to *The Order of Christian Funerals* speaks of what we are about:

In the face of death, the Church confidently proclaims that God has created each person for eternal life and that Jesus, the Son of God, by his death and resurrection, has broken the chains of sin and death that bound humanity.[22]

Notes

1 J. J. Farrell, *Inventing the American Way of Death 1830–1920*, Philadelphia: Temple University Press, 1980.

2 See Kellaher, this volume, especially the section, 'Burial in the twenty-first century'.

3 See Lampard, this volume, especially the section, 'What should the Christian Church do?'

4 See Hilborn, this volume.

5 T. Walter, 'Emotional Reserve and the English Way of Grief' in K. Charmaz, G. Howarth and A. Kelleher, *The Unknown Country: Death in Australia, Britain and the USA*, Basingstoke: Macmillan, 1997, pp. 127–40.

6 *The Order of Christian Funerals*, London: Geoffrey Chapman, 1990; Ann Ball, *Catholic Book of the Dead*, Huntington, Indiana: Our Sunday Visitor Publishing Division, 1995.

7 For a contrasting emphasis, see John Lampard, this volume and 'Cremation: How the Churches Got It Wrong', *Pharos International*, forthcoming.

8 See D. J. Davies and A. Shaw, *Reusing Old Graves: A Report on Popular British Attitudes*, Crayford: Shaw & Sons, 1995; D. J. Davies, 'Contemporary Belief in Life after Death', in P. C. Jupp and T. Rogers, *Interpreting Death: Christian Theology and Pastoral Practice*, London: Cassell, 1997, pp. 130–42.

9 See Nankivell, this volume.

10 See the chapters by Kellaher and Nankivell, this volume.

11 J. W. Willson, *Funerals without God*, 6th edn, London: British Humanist Association, 2006; and Dally Messenger, *Ceremonies and Celebrations*, Melbourne, Victoria: Lothian Publications, 1999.

12 P. P. J. Sheppy, *In Sure and Certain Hope*, London: Geoffrey Chapman, 1999.

13 An invaluable publication in widespread use is *Into Your Hands: Planning a Catholic Funeral, Readings and Prayers*, Mildenhall: Decani Books, 1999. Also useful are: Sarah O'Malley, *In the Potter's Hands*, San Jose, California: Resource Publications, 1988; Flor McCarthy, *Funeral Liturgies*, Dublin: Dominican Publications, 2003; Michael Marchal, *Parish Funerals*, Chicago: Liturgy Training Publications, 1987; *The Order of Christian Funerals: Mass and Vigil Service: People's Book*, Great Wakering: McCrimmon, 1990.

14 An issue dealt with in considerable detail by Paul Sheppy in *Death, Liturgy and Ritual: A Pastoral and Liturgical Theology Vol. 1*, Aldershot: Ashgate, 2003.

15 Of the 1603 people interviewed by Davies and Shaw, 28.8 per cent, *Reusing Old Graves*.

16 Joseph Champlain, *The Marginal Catholic*, Notre Dame, Indiana: Ave Maria Press, 1989.

17 *In Sure and Certain Hope*, London: Geoffrey Chapman, 1999. Also *The Order of Christian Funerals: Rites of Committal*, London: Burns and Oates, 2004.

18 See Dent, this volume.

19 Report of the International Theological Commission, *The Hope of Salvation for Infants Who Die without Baptism*, 8 May 2007.

20 Cf. General Introduction to *The Order of Christian Funerals*, 1990, especially #3.

21 Cardinal Joseph Ratzinger, *The Feast of Faith: Approaches to a Theology of the Liturgy*, E. T. Graham Harrison, Ignatius Press, San Francisco, 1981, p. 130.

22 Cf. General Introduction to *The Order of Christian Funerals*, 1990, especially #3.

17

Free Church Liturgies

PAUL P. J. SHEPPY

Introduction

This chapter offers a brief consideration of the funeral liturgies of three Free Church traditions: the Baptist Union of Great Britain, the Methodist Church and the United Reformed Church. The most recently published liturgical texts will be discussed and some comment made about the pastoral practice implied and expressed in them. In the predecessor to this book, John Lampard wrote about funerals in the black majority traditions;[1] I do not feel competent to do this, and interested readers should consult Lampard's excellent article in that earlier collection of essays.[2] It might also have been within the scope of this review to have looked at the funeral service provided by the Joint Liturgical Group (JLG) for use by Free Church ministers at cemeteries and crematoria.[3] However, JLG is currently preparing material to replace the current texts and so it seems better at this juncture to await the publication of the new without further comment.

Death comes to us all; but funerals do not come to the average Free Church congregation with the same regularity as the weekly Sunday worship. Ministers and other worship leaders, who are quite comfortable to follow unwritten liturgical forms shaped by local custom and practice, almost all feel less sanguine about leading funerals without the support and guidance of service books.[4]

Free Churches have not traditionally had books of liturgical texts that they were obliged to use. This is not to suggest that they have not published service books, but ministers and congregations have generally been able to decide where and when they will use them. Typically, Methodists have used their books more frequently at Sunday worship (especially for Holy Communion) than either Baptists or the United Reformed Church. However, most Free Church ministers within each of the three traditions will use some collection of written texts for occasional offices – and particularly for weddings and funerals.

The Baptist Union of Great Britain

In 2005, the Baptist Union of Great Britain (BUGB) launched its most recent service book, *Gathering for Worship*.[5] Subtitled 'Patterns and Prayers for the Community of Disciples', it offers exactly that. The book has no juridical authority and (like its predecessors) will probably be used irregularly and patchily across its intended denominational constituency.[6]

The section relating to funerals and the pastoral care of the bereaved is entitled 'Confronting Death – Celebrating Resurrection'. The editorial panel settled on this phrase as a means of addressing what it saw as two major matters in contemporary funerary practice (both within and beyond the church context).[7] The move to make funerals more celebratory has led some to believe that the sharpness and darkness of death is being avoided in the frequently expressed wish of families that the funeral should celebrate the life of the deceased.[8] The texts provided were meant to remind ministers and others that to airbrush out the pain of death may have aggravating consequences in the later experience of those who are bereaved, and that the life that the Church celebrates at a funeral is primarily the resurrection life of Christ. The sectional title encourages those leading funeral services to see that within the Christian tradition funerals are not merely occasions for honouring the dead, they are acts in which we worship the God who raised Christ from the dead.

As with the immediately previous Baptist worship book,[9] two basic patterns of funeral rite are offered. However, the order in which they are presented has been reversed. The first form now begins with the service in church followed by a committal; the second begins with a committal followed by a service of thanksgiving. The editorial panel accepted the view that placing the committal first implicitly privatizes the funeral and privileges the biological family over the household of faith.[10] The most common arguments in its favour are twofold: that it enables the family to be with the congregation immediately after the service in church, and that it stresses the Christian sense of thanksgiving and hope in the face of death: a sense arising from the promise of resurrection for the believer guaranteed by the resurrection of Christ. These arguments are not without force, and it is not the purpose of this chapter to take sides in the matter.[11]

In common with most other Christian Churches, Baptists no longer offer one set order of service but propose a menu of provisions allowing for varieties of funerals (including an order to mark perinatal death and another for the funeral of a child) and for multi-stage rites of death and bereavement (including a rite for the burial of ashes).[12] The committal-thanksgiving order is effectively the same as that provided in the previous book – although the prayer 'Go forth, Christian soul' no longer appears.[13] The church service-committal form is more consciously shaped in a formal liturgical tradition (and includes an extended litany for optional use) and its language is similarly more formal. The contrast reflects the book's overall aim to meet the needs of a tradition in which most funeral congregations are more comfortable with informal and extempore styles and at the same time to bring to the notice of ministers and others resources from other confessional groupings. Both main patterns include prayer texts from other Christian traditions.

A series of occasional texts, provided as a sort of appendix, includes material for the funerals of the newborn and stillborn and of children, and for funerals following suicide and other sudden or violent death. Some of this material (as with the first main pattern) draws on a wider range of provision by the present writer upon which others may more appropriately comment.[14]

What seems to be a significant gap in these provisions (compared with those of other church traditions) is the apparent lack of prayers with the dying or at the time of death. In fact, two prayers referring to those near death are included in the section of the book that relates to visiting the sick.[15] The first prayer reference is built on Romans 14.8 ('If we live, we live to the Lord, and if we die, we die to the Lord; so then, whether we live or whether we die, we are the Lord's') and seeks to plant that reassurance in the mind and heart of the one close to death. The second prayer is more specifically a prayer for the sick but contains the following closing reference:

In the hour of death hold *her/him*
and all *she/he* loves, safely in your hands
now and for ever.

Given Baptist reservations about praying for the dead, one would not expect to find prayers for someone post-mortem. Even so, the provision for those close to death is minimal. This may reflect a theological hesitancy; but we might feel that it also reveals a pastoral omission. Users of *Gathering for Worship* will have to look elsewhere for prayers with the dying and those close to them.[16]

My own view is that this creates a pastoral gap of which many Baptist ministers may be unaware and to which they may be ill-equipped to respond beyond the reading of scriptures promising the hope of eternal life. In the collection *In Sure and Certain Hope*, I offered prayer texts for use 'at (or immediately after) the Time of Death'.[17] With the benefit of hindsight, I wish now that the heading read 'at (or near) the Time of Death'. What I was hoping to do was to provide such a resource as is not found (published subsequently to my own work) in *Gathering for Worship*. Baptist hospital chaplains will have to make the decision about whether they can find a way of praying for those who have just died (whether with the family or not) which squares with a rigorous adherence to their theological reservations.[18]

The Methodist Church

The Methodist Worship Book offers a more explicitly delineated range of services.[19] Included here are 'Prayers in the Home or Hospital after a Death', 'An Office of Commendation', 'A Vigil', 'A Funeral in a Church, a Crematorium or a Cemetery, leading to Committal', 'A Funeral Service at a Crematorium or Cemetery, followed by a Service of Thanksgiving in Church', 'A Funeral Service for a Child', 'A Funeral Service for a Stillborn Child' and 'A Service for the Burial of Ashes'.

The 'Office of Commendation' is of particular interest in that it offers a service for those who cannot be at the funeral itself. The introductory note observes that the Office 'is particularly appropriate when a person dies abroad and the immediate family is not able to attend the funeral service'.[20] The present writer imagines that with one or two additional prayers it might also prove effective when there is a funeral without a body: air-crashes, loss of life at sea, situations where family and/or friends want to mark the death but cannot travel to the 'proper' funeral which is geographically remote – and so on.[21]

Vigils have not traditionally been a Free Church usage,[22] and it is interesting to see how *The Methodist Worship Book* provides a rite for use on the evening before the funeral. The vigil may be at home, in church or in a chapel of rest, and the body may or may not be present. The mood, which is quiet and reflective, is set by the proposed readings – in particular Psalm 27. Prayers and the concluding blessings offer the congregation a reminder of the hope found in Christ the crucified Saviour, risen Lord, gentle Shepherd, Lamb of God and son of Mary.

The two orders of funeral service are the same in structure as those provided by the Baptists: church service followed by committal, or committal followed by service of thanksgiving. Much of the material is simply the same but differently ordered. The prayers of committal are all drawn from the Christian tradition beyond Methodism. The orders for the funeral of a child and for the funeral of a stillborn child do not offer a different structure, but the pastoral sensitivities of the special circumstances are met by the choice of scripture readings and by the nuances of the prayers.[23]

What is immediately noticeable in reading *The Methodist Service Book* is the consciously liturgical tone of the orders of service.[24] This is clearly expressed in the choice of texts from the ancient prayers of the Christian Church. Whether or not all Methodists will recognize the sources being used, the editorial panel displays a greater confidence in its use of the patristic and medieval traditions than the Baptists, whose primary concern is to engage with those who normally eschew written texts and who have generally been less attached to the extra-canonical heritage. The Baptist editors openly encouraged the writing of new texts in a way not found in the Methodist book – with a greater resultant informality and a less careful attention to literary expression.

The United Reformed Church (URC)

The pastoral offices of *Worship: From the United Reformed Church* are to be found in the second volume of worship texts and resources.[25] Once again, a range of services and staged rites is provided from which the minister may choose. The services include: 'Prayers with the Dying', 'Service before a Funeral', 'A Service of Witness to the Resurrection' and 'Committal', 'A Service of Committal' (to precede a service of thanksgiving and release), 'A Service of Thanksgiving and Release', 'Committal' (to follow such a service), 'A Service of Thanksgiving for One who has Died', 'Interment or Scattering of Ashes' – an appendix of funeral readings is also included.

'Prayers with the Dying' may be used with members of the family present or not; it is commendably brief and designed to offer comfort and hope. The primary 'proper' prayers are of commendation (a shortened version *Proficiscere Christiana anima* and 'Acknowledge a sheep of your own fold, a lamb of your own flock . . .') and the *Nunc Dimittis*.[26] Two additional prayers with the family follow the moment of death.

The 'Service before a Funeral' may be held (on request) at home or the chapel of rest or in church. It is brief and is designed as a sort of vigil rite. The service allows for the expression of grief (particularly in its sharpness) and seeks the comfort of Christ who 'wept at the grave of a friend'.

'A Service of Witness to the Resurrection' and 'Committal' combine as the first form of funeral – that is, in church followed by burial or cremation. The explicit reference to the resurrection signals that the pastoral agenda is controlled by theological considerations. How the minister is to deal with the funeral of one who has only been remotely attached to the worshipping congregation or where the mourners have not had regular contact with church is left unremarked.

It may be that the 'Service of Thanksgiving and Release' is more flexible in this regard. Certainly, the introductory notes refer to this newly written text as not assuming what people feel but seeking to provide 'a space for the expression of what they genuinely experience'.[27] 'A Service of Thanksgiving for One who has Died' is even simpler. However, the overt theological perspective strongly shapes the rite; and the minister who wants to be open to a wider pastoral sensitivity may well feel that the final comment in the introductory notes is most apposite: 'There is always more to do than read from "the book".'[28]

In mood, the URC service texts feel close to their Baptist counterparts; in liturgical articulation, they are (like the Methodist rites) more literary – more polished. The Baptist book is determined to engage ministers and congregation who are customarily more 'Radio Two' in their liturgical performances. The URC book feels more formal; yet its presentation in typeface, use of colour and page-setting is less traditional than either the Methodist or the Baptist provisions. All three books unapologetically offer Christian funeral rites; how well they adapt to the funerals of those without faith or to mourners of different faiths or none is problematic.

General conclusions

Those preparing service books do not work in hermetically sealed spaces. The Free Churches have frequently drawn on texts from other traditions. In part, this reflects the recognition that the texts are quite simply available. It also is a sign of general ecumenical convergence – not least in liturgical scholarship and performance. In all three books there are echoes of older literary liturgical strands. This is seen not only in individual prayer texts but also in the way that rites are shaped and structured. This convergence arises from the closer ecumenical contacts developed over the past 40 years. It also indicates how social pressures shape Christian worship – not least in the pastoral offices.

The old anonymity of the 1662 *Book of Common Prayer* has been replaced by personalized texts. The earlier understanding of death as our common lot produced a short service fitted for 'all sorts and conditions of men'. The concerns of late modernity and postmodernity have been with individuality and identity, differentiation and distinctiveness.[29] As infant mortality rates have dropped, the death of children has become more remarkable. It is far more difficult now to justify the absence of separate texts for funerals of children.[30] Nor can anyone drafting liturgical texts allow gender-exclusive language to stand – certainly as it relates to human beings.[31] Liturgical language is generally slower to move to the most recent beat because it rests in a historical development from which it can only detach itself at the risk of losing continuity with the tradition from which it springs. Nonetheless, the language of funerals is changing as those who minister at the time of death meet the changing milieu.

The service books discussed here offer services of Christian worship. In so doing, they assume (to greater or lesser degree) a Christian understanding of what is to happen. In an increasingly secular society this draws attention to the gap between what the texts take for granted and what the person in the pew apprehends. In 2003, I wrote:

> The remoteness of much of the Christian faith to contemporary people ought to challenge liturgists and pastoral officiants to be particularly sensitive to the language and ideas in which pastoral liturgy seeks to express itself. A funeral service is not always an unequivocally good example of user-friendliness. Much of what is said must sound strange – even alien – to those who hear it.
>
> Frequently the first words which are spoken are the sentences of scripture as the coffin is borne into the crematorium chapel.
>
>> I am the resurrection and the life, says the Lord; he who believes in me, though he die, yet shall he live, and whoever lives and believes in me shall never die.
>
> If the deceased person was indeed a member of a Christian tradition, those who hear these words are entitled to wonder why their relative or friend is dead. Yet beyond the awkwardness of the apparent equation between belief and not dying, there lie the difficulties of using male pronouns when the deceased is female, and of using such a text where no Christian belief was expressed by the deceased in life.
>
> Similarly, in a burial as the coffin is being lowered, these words are heard at the graveside:
>
>> To the One who is able to keep you from falling . . .

When asked about the appropriateness of such texts, ministers suggest that people know what is meant and that they understand that such words are not to be taken literally. It is uncertain to me that this can be universally assumed. Some mourners are acutely sensitive to the least infelicity of expression, and one detail may colour their recollection and, indeed, the effectiveness of the entirety.[32]

The comment still stands.

Moreover, there is almost no reference in the service texts examined in this chapter to the pastoral circumstances which involve funerals where there is little or no previous contact with chapel, congregation or Christian profession of faith.[33] Since this category forms a not inconsiderable proportion of funerals taken by Christian ministers, the lack of discussion in the pastoral notes accompanying service texts is (to put it mildly) unhelpful. I suspect that it represents a failure to tackle a considerable pastoral difficulty. If we wish to suggest how the Christian minister is to conduct a funeral, we surely ought not to neglect some sort of explanation of how we understand the Church's ministry at the funeral when those who gather have no familiarity or connection with the underlying presuppositions of the liturgy which is to be provided. What, of course, happens in practice is that in most cases the minister and the mourners negotiate a mutually acceptable 'halfway house'.

There is (it seems to me) a gap between the Church's desire that a funeral should be a service of Christian worship and the secular demand for something cheerful and celebratory. A newspaper survey conducted in 2006 asked the question, 'Would you prefer your funeral to be a celebration of life, or sombre?' It is not very surprising to report that 86 per cent of those answering said that they wanted a celebration of life. Of course, the way the question is asked can skew the answer you receive. Imagine that the question had been, 'Would you prefer your funeral to be dignified or a bit of a giggle?' It is unlikely that 86 per cent would have opted for the giggle.

Nonetheless, the fact remains that the darkness of death is not where most people now want to place the emphasis at the funeral. The texts we have reviewed share in common a proclamation of hope in the midst of death. That hope is founded on the resurrection of Christ from the dead and the consequent promise of eternal life. Where the minister is dealing with the community of faith, this message is known and understood. In such a context the kerygmatic task is to call upon the congregation to make it their own.

On many occasions, however, the death being marked has occurred outside the community of faith. It is doubtful whether the celebration the family wants is exactly what the liturgical texts offer. At such times, the minister is called on to exercise complex pastoral judgements which the texts know not of – or, at least, for which they do not directly provide. In the visitation preceding a funeral, officiants have not only to gather the history of the deceased, they have to build a sense of trust and confidence which will enable the personal sensitivities of the mourners to express themselves. They may have to negotiate between competing claims around the 'ownership' of the funeral and they will have to find a way in which they can tell the story of the deceased without obscuring the story of Christ.

As ever, liturgy is never simply the text; and it may be a strength among the Free Churches that they are not bound to their texts by obligation to ecclesial authority. Whatever the liturgical purist may think, it may be that the ability to 'pick and mix' gives a flexibility to ministry at the time of death which enables the minister to build a bridge between the hopes of the bereaved, the wishes of the deceased and their own sense of calling in these circumstances (as in all) to be ministers of Jesus Christ – way, truth and life.

Notes

1 P.C. Jupp and T. Rogers (eds), *Interpreting Death: Christian Theology and Pastoral Practice*, London: Cassell, 1997. See Lampard's essay, 'Funeral Liturgies of the Free Churches', pp. 185–96. Lampard also described the texts and pastoral guidance provided by the Salvation Army in *Salvation Army Ceremonies*, London: International Headquarters of the Salvation Army, 1989. This book was reprinted in 2004 with some revisions. None of these applied to the section relating to funerals and I have nothing to add to Lampard's excellent and succinct essay in respect of the guidance and proposed texts.

2 See also the comments on African and Caribbean funerals in Hilborn, this volume.

3 See *Funeral Services of the Christian Churches in England*, Norwich: The Canterbury Press, 2001, pp. 1–21.

4 I have written extensively about this in *Death Liturgy and Ritual: A Pastoral and Liturgical Theology* Volume 1, Aldershot and Burlington, VT: Ashgate, 2003. See particularly chapter 2, 'Ritual Blunder' (pp. 10–21) and chapter 5, 'Death in the Community', pp. 43–60.

5 C. J. Ellis and M. Blyth (eds), *Gathering for Worship: Patterns and Prayers for the Community of Disciples*, Norwich: The Canterbury Press, 2005.

6 If we ask what material Baptist ministers will use for the conduct of funerals, the answer will probably be that they will glean from whatever sources they have encountered in their ordination and in subsequent ministerial experi-

ence. Many, though not all, will use texts from *Gathering for Worship* or its predecessor books; others may borrow from the books of other traditions or use the JLG text provided in *Funeral Services*, Norwich: The Canterbury Press, as found across England and Wales in cemetery and crematorium chapels.

7 The editorial panel for *Gathering for Worship* worked slightly differently from the Church of England's Liturgical Commission (see Lloyd's chapter, this volume). It gathered a group of interested ministers together and through that group it invited anyone interested to submit texts for consideration. There was much less 'road testing' of what was sent in. In large measure this reflects a less hierarchical way of being Church. Baptists are like an omelette: it is impossible to control the edges from the middle!

8 It is extremely doubtful whether the service at Westminster Abbey for Diana, Princess of Wales, began this move to celebrate the life of the deceased; however, it certainly articulated it very publicly. Diana's celebrity and the publicity or the service gave great impetus to the request that funerals should celebrate (rather than give thanks for) the life of the one who has died. See also Rogers, this volume.

9 *Patterns and Prayers for Christian Worship*, Oxford: Oxford University Press, 1991.

10 Many Baptist churches have adopted the language of family when referring to themselves: 'The church family at Little Fidget welcomes you to worship.' The model is often that of a nuclear family and can be rather inward-looking. The scriptural model of a household is somewhat different, since it includes those who are not tied by kinship but who are part of the common enterprise. Insofar as families are kin-related, they are exclusive. This can be extremely problematic when the deceased was closer to friends than to family. See my discussion in *Death Liturgy and Ritual, Volume I*, pp. 51–2.

11 For members of the Christian faith, I favour a public service in church. I do so for two reasons. Cemeteries, crematoria and funeral parlours are places of death and death alone. They have no other purpose. The church building is dedicated to the worship of God and is where the community of faith gathers to celebrate birth and death, sacrament and rite. To this place the deceased came to receive Christ; to this place we bring the deceased that they may be received by Christ.

Nonetheless, the practicalities of keeping the congregation together when close mourners go to the graveside or to the crematorium are considerable. It may be that not all need to go for the inevitably short obsequies; it may be enough for one or two to accompany the coffin while others stay to start the gathering after the funeral. It may also be possible (though perhaps with other considerable practical difficulties of time and distance) for the move to the graveside or crematorium to happen *after* the gathering following the funeral.

12 The sense of staged rites is hinted at but is not as clearly articulated as in other traditions – or, indeed, as in my own work – P. P. J. Sheppy, *In Sure and Certain Hope*, Norwich: The Canterbury Press, 2003.

13 The *Proficiscere Christiana anima* was a strange prayer for Baptists to be saying (even in the pared-down version in which it appeared). It was included in the committal rite of the funeral rather than at its 'proper' place at or near death. This liturgical incongruity has not survived into the current service book; nor has the prayer text itself.

14 Sheppy, *In Sure and Certain Hope*.

15 *Gathering for Worship*, pp. 282–5. The specific prayers are found on p. 283.

16 This might have been the place to include 'Go forth, Christian soul' (see note 6), but it is absent.

17 Sheppy, *In Sure and Certain Hope*, pp. 5–8.

18 See also my discussion of this issue in 'What, No Saints? A Dissenter Considers the Place of God's Holy People of Past Days in the Worship of the Chapel', in M. Barnard, P. Post and E. Rose (eds), *A Cloud of Witnesses: The Cult of Saints in Past and Present*, Leuven, Paris, and Dudley, MA: Peeters, 2005, pp. 345–52.

19 *The Methodist Worship Book*, Peterborough: Methodist Publishing House, 1999, pp. 433–502.

20 *The Methodist Worship Book*, p. 437.

21 See also Eyre, this volume.

22 I provided a rite for the reception of the body into church in my collection *In Sure and Certain Hope*, pp. 9–14.

23 See *The Methodist Worship Book*, p. 474. The occurrence of 'abnormal' raises the interesting question as to whether we need special orders of service (as such) for such deaths. What changes is the pastoral circumstance, rather than the structure of the rite. Normally, we provide different readings and prayers to meet specific circumstances of death (train crash, suicide, homicide and so on). In these cases, it is common to print special service sheets. See Eyre, this volume.

24 It will, of course, depend on individual ministers as to how the rites are *performed*. Insofar as this present chapter examines texts, the principal focus is upon what is written. But see in my general conclusion some reflection upon the importance of rite as performance.

25 *Worship: From the United Reformed Church*, London: United Reformed Church, 2004, pp. 189–250.

26 See John S. Lampard, *Go Forth, Christian Soul: The Biography of a Prayer*, Peterborough: Epworth Press, 2005. Lampard is vice-chair of the Churches' Funeral Group. His commentary on *Proficiscere* is a most important study of this historic prayer text.

27 *Worship: From the United Reformed Church*, p. 189.

28 *Worship: From the United Reformed Church*, p. 190.

29 See P. A. Mellor, 'Death in High Modernity: The Contemporary Presence and Absence of Death' in D. Clark (ed.), *The Sociology of Death*, Oxford: Blackwell Publishers/The Sociological Review, 1993, pp. 11–30; also Philippe Ariès, *Western Attitudes towards Death*, Baltimore: Johns Hopkins University Press, 1974; and *The Hour of Our Death*, London: Penguin Books, 1981, reprinted 1987.

30 Though see Anne Dent's comments (this volume).

31 There is still resistance among many to gender-inclusive language relating to God – or even to varied-gender language (God as 'she'). There is no real opportunity here to review the argument in detail, but we should note that the language we use in worship can be deeply alienating to some.

32 *Death Liturgy and Ritual, Vol. I*, p. 15.

33 This problem is more acute for the Church of England. Most Free Church ministers in charge of local congregations will only take the funerals of those with whom they have some direct or historic connection ('Mum used to come to your Sunday School') whether through the congregation or by some chaplaincy role they may exercise within the local community.

18

Orthodox Liturgy, Theology and Pastoral Practice

JOHN NANKIVELL

Introduction

Orthodox funeral and memorial services and related practices have remained unchanged for centuries. The prayers of the fourth-century Apostolic Constitutions,[1] for example, have parts that are identical with those in use today. Such continuities are seen by the Orthodox to express the essential unity of the Church in its antiquity and universality.

In this respect, the Church of the patriarchates of Jerusalem, Antioch, Alexandria and Constantinople, together with their daughter Churches, differs from that of Rome. The medieval Roman innovations of purgatory and indulgences represent significant departures. But in eliminating these, the Churches of the Reformation removed also some of the most ancient beliefs and practices of the early Church, in particular the prayers for the departed. The impact of the Renaissance, the Counter-Reformation, the Enlightenment, Modernism and Fundamentalism and other movements have all contributed to the diversity of tradition within the Roman Catholic and Reformed churches.

With its different self-understanding and historical experience, the Orthodox Church has retained ancient practice. For non-Orthodox the period of the Apostles and the Fathers is often seen as remote: for the Orthodox, the saints of the early Church are daily invoked and vividly present. The funeral rites and their associated theology characteristically express this continuity with the early Church.

The pattern of Orthodox services for the departed

The prayer books of the Orthodox Church include prayers and services for the following situations: at the point of death; at the home of the departed; for the procession of the bier from home to church; in the church; for the procession to the grave; at the interment; for the third, ninth and fortieth days after the death;[2] at the end of the third, sixth and ninth months after the death; and on the anniversary of the death.[3]

The services were established by the eleventh century, but most of the material is much more ancient. Italo-Greek and Palestinian manuscripts of this time have a close family resemblance to those from Sinai and Constantinople,[4] indicating a broad unity of practice throughout the Greek-speaking world. Such changes as have been made in modern times tend towards a shortening of the services, for example by intoning only parts of Psalm 118 [119]. There are other minor variations, such as the emptying of the ashes from the censer onto the coffin as it lies in the grave. This appears in the printed texts, but has no manuscript authority.[5]

The service in the home is the same as that used for the memorial services. Often called the *Trisagion*, it starts with the threefold repetition of the prayer 'Holy God, Holy Mighty, Holy Immortal have mercy on us'. It is probably the best known of all Orthodox services, as even those with minimal contact with the Church are likely to have attended anniversary memorials for departed members of their family throughout their lives.

The prayers that follow the 'Our Father' are the oldest of all the funeral prayers, and include the following:

With the spirits of the righteous made perfect in death give rest, O Saviour, to the soul of your servant, keeping it for the life of blessedness with you, O Lover of mankind.

You are our God who descended into Hell and did away with the pains of those who had been bound; give rest, O Saviour, also to the soul of your servant.

Deacon: The mercies of God, the kingdom of heaven and the forgiveness of his/her sins, let us ask of Christ, our immortal King and God.

Priest: O God of spirits and all flesh who trampled down death and crushed the devil, giving life to your world; do you, Lord, give rest to the soul of your servant N., who has fallen asleep, in a place of light, a place of green pasture, a place of refreshment, whence pain, grief and sighing have fled away. Pardon, O God, as you are good and love mankind, every sin committed by him/her in word or deed or thought, because there is none who will live and not sin, for you alone are without sin; your righteousness is an everlasting righteousness, and your word is truth.

For you are the resurrection, the life and the repose of your servant N., who has fallen asleep, Christ our God, and to you we give glory, together with your Father who is without beginning, and your all-holy, good and life-giving Spirit, now and for ever, and to the ages of ages.

The presence of the name of the departed, for whom Christ is 'the Resurrection, the life and the repose', makes these ancient prayers profoundly personal.[6]

The *Trisagion* is sung during the procession to the church to a funeral melody, identical, in some traditions, with that used at the Great Friday procession to the tomb of Christ. As in the house, so also in the church, the coffin is uncovered and the person is clothed in normal churchgoing clothes; a priest is therefore vested and holds the Gospel book. An icon depicting the resurrection – in particular, the harrowing of hell – is placed on the lay-person's chest.

There are different funeral services for a child,[7] a priest, a monastic and a lay-person. In the week after Easter the services, based on the Paschal Matins, are quite different. This short chapter will discuss the service outside Pascha for a lay adult, with some reference to that for a child. All funeral services are based on Saturday matins, the Sabbath being the day on which Christ descended into hell, destroyed the power of the evil one and overcame death.

The service starts with the singing of Psalm 118 [119] in three sections to special melodies; each section concludes with the short litany of the departed. Then come the *Evlogitaria* of the Dead, so called because each verse is introduced with the words 'Blessed [*Evlogitos*] are you O Lord, teach me your statutes'. Some of the verses are put in the mouth of the departed:

Of old you formed me from nothing and honoured me with your divine image but, because I transgressed your commandment, you returned me to the earth from which I was taken; bring me back to your likeness, my ancient beauty.

The music is identical with that of the well-known Resurrection *Evlogitaria* used at every Sunday matins, which recall and celebrate the resurrection of Christ; death is always seen in the light of the resurrection. The Canon, a characteristic feature of matins, follows and includes the *kontakion* of the dead:[8]

> With the saints give rest, O Christ, to the soul of your servant,
> where there is no toil, nor grief, nor sighing, but life everlasting

The deeply moving music engenders a sense of calm.

Then come the eight hymns of St John of Damascus (655–750), sung to special, haunting melodies. In these, the stark reality of death and the transience of earthly life are emphatically laid before us, and each hymn concludes with a prayer to God that he grant rest to the one who has fallen asleep. The first hymn is characteristic:

> What pleasure in life remains without its share of sorrow? What glory stands on earth unchanged? All things are feebler than a shadow, all things are more deceptive than dreams; one instant, and death supplants them all. But, O Christ, give rest to him/her. You have chosen in the light of your countenance and the sweetness of your beauty, as You love mankind.

The dominant theme of the verses sung with the Beatitudes is that Christ remember us in his kingdom, as he promised the penitent thief on the cross:

> May Christ give you rest in the land of the living,
> open to you the gates of Paradise, make you a citizen of the Kingdom and grant you forgiveness of sins you committed in life, O Lover of Christ.

The epistle is introduced by the prokeimenon:

> Blessed is the way on which you journey today
> for a place of rest has been prepared for you

sung to an assured melody. The epistle for a lay funeral is 1 Thessalonians 4.13–18; that for a child is Romans 6.9–11, which concludes 'you must consider yourselves alive to God in Christ Jesus'. The Gospel is John 5.24–30; that for a child is Luke 18.15–17, 26–7, which includes Christ's words, 'Let the children come to me . . . for to such belongs the kingdom of God'.

The service in the church concludes with the Last Kiss. As each person comes to venerate the icon in the coffin and kiss the departed on the forehead, the singers intone verses on the grim reality of death:

s/he is being entrusted to the grave . . . the beauty of the face has rotted and death has withered all the flower of youth . . .

And, in the final verse, the departed addresses his/her friends, relatives and acquaintances:

Only yesterday I was talking with you, and suddenly the dread hour of death came upon me . . . come, all who loved me, and kiss me for the last time; for I shall not walk with you again, nor speak with you any more; for I am on my way to the Judge . . . slave and master stand alike before him, king and soldier, rich and poor . . . pray for me without ceasing to Christ God that I may not be condemned because of my sins to a place of torment, but that he will establish me in the place of the light of life.

The verses for a child differ and include:

Like a sparrow have you flown swiftly from your mother's arms, to take refuge with the Creator of all . . . who would not weep and cry aloud at the beauty of your pure life?[9]

The Dismissal begins, as on Sundays, 'May He who rose from the dead, Christ our true God'. It continues 'and has dominion over the living and the dead', and includes among the named intercessors 'the holy and glorious forefathers, Abraham, Isaac and Jacob' and the 'holy and righteous Lazarus, dead for four days, the friend of Christ'.

At the Interment, the priest scatters dust crosswise over the remains, saying:

The earth is the Lord's and its fullness; the world and all who dwell in it.

He then pours the oil of the lamp and the ash of the censer over the remains. The people also scatter earth on the coffin as the final *Trisagion* is sung.

The underlying theology[10]

Death and resurrection

Throughout the funeral service the brutal reality of death[11] is juxtaposed with Christ's triumphant conquest of death. The overwhelming experience of grief and loss is fully expressed, but it is set alongside the vital presence of the risen Christ. The departed one whom we mourn, with whom 'but yesterday we walked and talked', lies in the open coffin, cold to the touch and to the lips at the last kiss. But this same departed one takes part in the liturgy; s/he cries out, 'give me the longed-for fatherland, making me once again a citizen of Paradise'. These dualities of loss and hope are understood in the context of the fundamental realities of death and of Christ's trampling down of death.

Christ's descent into hell (1 Peter 3.18–20; Acts 2.27, 31) is an ever-present reality in Orthodox worship. The Easter hymn celebrates it: 'Christ has risen from the dead, by death He has trampled on death and to those in the graves given life'; the icon of the resurrection depicts it in colour; the hymns in the eight tones for Vespers and Matins for the Lord's Day, the first of the week, the day of resurrection,[12] extol it; it is explicit in many parts of the daily and weekly services and implicit throughout.

This underlying confidence in the resurrection pervades the funeral service. It explains the primary metaphor for death, the biblical metaphor of sleep. The deceased is most commonly called 'the one who has fallen asleep',[13] and the burial ground is called a 'cemetery', *koimitirion*, a 'sleeping-place' in which the dead await the final awakening. The processions are, in one sense, a practical expression of another metaphor, that of a journey, which appears most clearly in the *prokeimenon*.

Soul and body

Orthodox liturgical texts are thoroughly biblical, and references to 'soul' (*psyche*) and body should be understood in this light. Death is sometimes portrayed as the wrenching of the soul from the body. In one prayer,[14] the soul is said to proceed to where it had received its being until the general resurrection, and the body left to be decomposed and dissolved. But there is none of the speculative discussion about the nature of the soul, of its immediate and medium-term fate, nor of the relation of soul and body, such as can be found in some of the writings of the Fathers. The Orthodox Church has not made definitive statements on these matters, and the liturgy, remaining true to its biblical roots, preserves a similar taciturnity.[15]

Sin and death

The biblical understanding of the origins of death, and of its ultimate overthrow by Christ, undergirds the whole rite. 'Of old you formed me from nothing and honoured me with your divine image, but because I transgressed your commandment, you returned me to the earth from which I was taken' [*Evlogitaria* of the dead]. Turning away from God, the source of Life, leads to the loss of 'our ancient beauty', exile from paradise, and a hastening towards death.

Late medieval Latin theories of the atonement, which live on in some 'evangelical' traditions and which focus on the cross as a sacrifice of substitution for the appeasement of a wrathful Father, form no part of the Orthodox liturgy. Death is seen rather as a blessing than as a punishment. It is a gift which ensures that the evil state, in which we have not preserved the divine image, should not endure.[16]

Penitence and paradise

Christ, the image of God, the second Adam, is without sin. By his sinless life, the power of death is overthrown, and by his death, death is trampled down and destroyed. Once more, the gates of paradise are opened to those who have found the way of repentance. So the dead cries out: 'The choir of Saints has found the source of life and the door of Paradise; may I too find the way through repentance; I am the lost sheep, call me back, O Saviour, and save me' (*Evlogitaria*).

Heaven and hell

The term 'heaven' occurs only in the Lord's Prayer, but it is described in such biblical terms as 'the bosom of Abraham', 'a place of green pasture', 'paradise' and, from the prayer of the thief, 'Remember me Lord in your kingdom'. Hell occurs as the place despoiled by Christ.

Christ's teachings about judgement and everlasting fire are explicit, and the funeral rites can be seen as the final steps in the human journey of preparation for 'a good defence before the dread judgement seat of Christ', to use the words of a litany that occurs in most Orthodox services.

Christ's parable refers to a 'great gulf' between Lazarus, safe in the 'bosom of Abraham', and the rich man (Luke 16.19–31). St Mark Evgenikos, in his Responses to the 'Latins' at the Council of Ferrara-Florence 1438–1439, says there is no third place, no purgatory. The everlasting fire is the same light of Christ that illumines the blessed, experienced as fire by those on the other side of 'the great gulf'.[17]

The mysterious truths dealt with in the funeral services – death, Christ's descent into hell, the Last Judgement – cannot easily be expressed in words. The Fathers are consistently clear about the partial nature of our understanding, our incapacity to express in words even that partial understanding, and the dependence of both understanding and words on the incarnation of the Word. The paradoxical nature of our situation is captured by St Ephrem:

> By means of what belongs to us did He draw close to us
> He clothed Himself in our language,
> so that He might clothe us in His mode of life . . .
> It is our metaphors He put on – though He did not literally do so;
> He then took them off – without actually doing so . . .[18]

The musical expression of words used in worship and their setting in the liturgical drama give them an added dimension. It is difficult to recognise in all this the naive literalism of 'traditional beliefs' described elsewhere in this volume.[19]

Prayers for the dead

Prayers for the dead were part of the Church's earliest practice; the earliest liturgies have commemorations of the dead, and the walls of the catacombs have many prayers for the souls of the departed. The absence of debate on the matter in the early Church argues for their having always formed part of Christian life. Their absence from most post-Reformation Churches strikes an Orthodox, unfamiliar with the religious conflicts of sixteenth-century Western Europe, as extraordinary; one of the more baleful consequences of Roman teaching on purgatory and indulgences.[20] The vacuum left has often been filled with anthropocentric material of doubtful connection with the gospel.

Pastoral practice

The funeral and the memorial services are central for a bereaved Orthodox Christian. The daily practice of praying for the departed at home; the prayer of the whole Church on the third, ninth and fortieth days, after three, six and nine months, annually on the anniversary and on the Saturdays of the Souls (*Psychosavvata*); the practical work of making the boiled wheat (*kolyvo, zhito*), of praying with the rest of the parish and the sharing of the wheat – St Paul's symbol of the resurrection – at the end of the service, possibly followed by a communal meal; and the memorial prayers at the grave on the anniversary, all provide opportunities for the expression of grief, for the support of family, friends and the community, and for the continuing prayer for the departed. Modern research on bereavement[21] shows the value of this recognition of the continuing reality both of grief and of 'the one who has fallen asleep'.

The services express the mourners' sense of loss. This in itself is supportive: the searing reality of loss and grief is recognized and shared by all, including the children.[22] The prayer that the departed find rest 'in a place of green pasture' resonates with the mourners' longing that the one for whom they grieve suffers no more.

The ways in which modern British approaches to death impact on the work of the Church as described by Peter Jupp[23] are significant for the Orthodox Christians of Britain. The extent of their influence in any particular case depends largely on the degree to which the family concerned has retained its ties with the Church. For example, those responsible for the funeral arrangements may contact the church at the last minute, when a 'slot' has already been booked at the cemetery chapel: only a very truncated version of the Orthodox funeral can be celebrated in the time allowed in such a slot.

More seriously, arrangements for a cremation may already have been made. Cremation is not permissible in the Orthodox Church.[24] It is not possible in this short chapter either to discuss the arguments for burial[25] or to outline the practical, emotional and ecological problems with cremation.[26] Where space is an issue, exhumation is possible, and is the norm in Greece.[27] Exhumation also allows confirmation of incorruption, a sign of sanctity, to be confirmed, as in the cases of the seventh-century Northumbrian saint Cuthbert,[28] of St Alexis of Ugine in France from the last century,[29] and of many others in the life of the Church. Cremation is still illegal in Greece, and has therefore been a matter for political discussion, leading successive synods of the Church of Greece to reaffirm the Church's position.[30] Whatever the political outcome, there is no reason for the Church's position to change.

An important pastoral issue in Britain is the question of the language to be used in the services. The Greek, Slavonic, Arabic and Romanian services are established, and there are several translations into English. Congregations are usually mixed, and it is often important that the priest, or priests, celebrate in more than one language. It is also important for some exposition, particularly when the congregation includes non-Orthodox. Sadly, this is not always done.

The funeral and memorial services developed during the early life of the Church. They embody many centuries of the Church's experience of care for the dead and bereaved. For the Orthodox they are a given, a gift. They express the Church's response to the gospel, at the heart of which lies the cross, the descensus and resurrection of Christ, in whose light death is always placed.

Notes

1 *Les Constitutions Apostoliques Tome II Livre* 6.30 and *Tome III* 8.41, Sources Chrétiennes No. 336, Paris 1987, critical text and translation by M. Metzger. English translation in Alexander Roberts and James Donaldson (eds), *Ante-Nicene Fathers*, Vol. 7, Massachusetts, 2004 (reprinting an 1886 edition).

2 For a discussion of the significance of these days in the early Church, see G. Dagron, *Troisième, neuvième et quarantième jours*, Colloques Internationaux du CNRS (Centre National de la Récherche Scientifique), 1984, p. 604. The grave may be visited at any time, of course, and the *Trisagion* prayers said. Kellaher (this volume) refers to visits made on the name day.

3 The most complete recent texts in English were published in 1999 by St Tikhon's Seminary Press, vol. III of *The Great Book of Needs*. This is a translation of the *Veliki Trebnik* published at the Kiev-Caves Lavra in 1902, supplemented from other 'books of needs' published in Moscow and St Petersburg between 1884 and 1962. In essentials, it is identical with the Greek texts of the *Great Euchologion, Μέγα Ευχολόγιον*, available in the 1980 edition published in Athens by Astir, itself based on the 1862 edition published in Venice. The English texts used in this article are taken from the provisional translation of Archimandrite Ephrem Lash which can be found on <www.anastasis.org.uk/funeral.htm>.

4 See Elena Velkovska, 'Funeral Rites according to Byzantine Liturgical Sources', Washington, DC: Dumbarton Oaks Papers No 55, 2001, pp. 21–51.

5 Ιωάννης Μ Φουντούλης, *Απαντήσεις εις Λειτουργικάς Απορίας* Vol. 7, Τομ 4 σ. 185–187 Αποστολική Διακονία έκδοσις Τρίτη 1989 (J. M. Fountoulis, *Answers to Liturgical Queries*, Vol. 4, *Apostoliki Diakonia*, 1989, in Greek).

6 See Lloyd, this volume.

7 See Dent, this volume.

8 This is perhaps the best-known verse of the Orthodox funeral service. It occurs in *The English Hymnal*, No. 744 in the 1933 edition, where it is set to a Russian melody and is entitled 'Russian Contakion of the Departed (Kieff Melody)'.

9 Author's translation.

10 For a discussion of patristic teaching on these issues, see B. E. Daley, *The Hope of the Early Church*, Cambridge: Cambridge University Press, 1991; Nikolaos P. Vassiliadis, *The Mystery of Death*, E. T. Peter A. Chamberas, Athens: Sotir, 1997; Hierotheos Metropolitan of Nafpaktos, *Life after Death*, E. T. Esther Williams, Levadia: Birth of the Theotokos Monastery, 1996.

11 The danger of 'airbrushing out' the pain of death is referred to by Sheppey (this volume).

12 The Greek for Sunday is *Kyriaki*, the Lord's Day, corresponding to *Dimanche*, *Domingo* etc. in the Latin languages. The Russian is *Voskreseniye*, the Day of Resurrection.

13 This is not always obvious in English translations which sometimes use the verb 'depart', to represent *koimoumai*.

14 The prayer said at the parting of the soul from the body.

15 See Davies, this volume.

16 For the patristic understanding, see Vassiliadis, *The Mystery of Death*, pp. 99ff.

17 See Nicholas Constans, '"To Sleep, Perchance to Dream": The Middle State of Souls in Patristic and Byzantine Literature', Washington, DC: Dumbarton Oaks Papers 55, 2001, pp. 71–124, which makes an illuminating comparison between Byzantine eschatology and the language used of the ascetic life. See also Hierotheos, *Life after Death*, and Vassiliadis, *The Mystery of Death*, pp. 99–102.

18 Sebastian Brock, *The Luminous Eye*, Kalamazoo: Cistercian Publications, 1985, pp. 60–1. Such sophisticated awareness of the relationship between language, thought and reality runs throughout the writings of the Fathers. They would be at home with the complex metaphors used in sub-atomic (itself a paradox) physics.

19 See Badham, this volume.

20 See Jupp, chapter 7; and Sheppy, this volume.

21 See Valentine, this volume.

22 The contemporary importance of this is clear from Dent, this volume.

23 P. C. Jupp, 'The Context of Funeral Ministry Today' in P. C. Jupp and T. Rogers (eds), *Interpreting Death: Christian Theology and Pastoral Practice*, London: Cassell, 1997, pp. 1–16; and Jupp, chapter 2, this volume.

24 See *The Year-Book of the Archdiocese of Thyateira and Great Britain*, London: Thyateira House, published annually. This permits the funeral to take place in the church, where the relatives are bound by the wishes of the departed to be cremated; at the end of the service, the remains are handed over to the relatives. See also P. Loizos, 'Why Greek Orthodox People Do Not Like Their Dead Cremated', *Pharos International*, Vol. 71, No. 4, Winter 2005, pp. 14–15.

25 See the arguments for burial in McGinnell and Kellaher, this volume.

26 For a discussion upon cremation and ecological issues, see K. West, 'Ecology' in Douglas J. Davies with Lewis H. Mates (eds), *Encyclopedia of Cremation*, Aldershot: Ashgate, 2005, pp. 172–4.

27 See, for example, the study by Loring Danforth, *The Death Rituals of Rural Greece*, Princeton: Princeton University Press, 1982. The photographs by Alexander Tsiaras are striking and, *mutatis mutandis*, could be of an Orthodox funeral in any part of the world.

28 Bede, *A History of the English Church and People*, IV: 30.

29 *The Life of Our Father among the Saints Alexis of Ugina [1867–1934]*, published by the Monastère Orthodoxe Notre-Dame-de-Toute-Protection (Orthodox Monastery of the Protecting Veil of the Mother of God), 11, Rue de la Forêt, 89400, Bussy-en-Othe, France, where his relics now rest.

30 See the three articles under 'Greece' in the *Encyclopedia of Cremation*: Magdalini Dargentas, 'Cremation and Modern Greece', pp. 223–5; Panagiotis J. Boumis, E. T. Revd Anastasios Barkas, 'Greek Orthodoxy', pp. 225–6; and the Revd Anastasios Barkas, 'Greek Orthodoxy in Great Britain', pp. 226–7.

Music at Funerals:

The Challenge of Keeping in Tune with the Needs of the Bereaved

BRIAN PARSONS

Introduction

Music occupies an important place in funeral services. Through singing or simply listening to favourite pieces, it provides emotional engagement by linking past associations with the deceased to those attending funerals. But the role and choice of music has been changing in an attempt to meet new demands. No longer is 'church music' – be it hymns or organ music – the only type of work performed, despite the fact that most funerals are still religious.

This chapter charts the change in music used at funerals in churches, cemeteries and crematoria in the UK over the past 150 years, but with particular reference to the past two decades. Commencing with a historical sketch which embraces the shift away from funerals taking place in the church, it moves towards the trends occurring in the past 25 years attributable to what can be termed the 'funeral reform movement'. The final section explores issues confronting funeral directors, cemetery and crematorium managers, along with funeral officiants.

Burial

The rubrics contained in the Book of Common Prayer make provision for the priest and clerks to sing during the Order for the Burial of the Dead. Music composed by William Croft, which incorporates Henry Purcell's setting of 'Thou knowest, Lord, the secrets of our hearts' was intended for singing when the corpse is met at the entrance to the church and also 'while the corpse is made ready to be laid into the earth'. It is a work that continues to occupy an important position in the repertoire. Psalms were also sung, but it was not until the nineteenth century – a period of considerable change in respect of the disposal of the dead – that the congregation participated by singing hymns. The primary thrust was from proprietary cemeteries which challenged the established Church's monopoly of burial provision by opening commercial burial grounds. Further support to their development was given from the 1850s following the prohibition of interments in and under churches located in urban areas. Burial grounds such as All Souls at Kensal Green in London and Liverpool's St James's Cemetery presented the opportunity for interment away from the parish churchyard in addition to funeral services held in the cemeteries' own chapels. Many were consecrated for the use of Church of England clergy while some also had a chapel for Dissenters and Roman Catholics. However, they did not possess organs to accompany hymn singing (although an advertisement for Kensal Green Cemetery published in *The Undertakers' Journal* of 1897 does mention the availability of an instrument in their Anglican chapel). The effect of this shift in place of burial was a decline in the use of churches for funeral services, a situation aggravated as Burial Boards (the precursor of local authority cemetery departments) also established cemeteries with chapels.

For services held in an Anglican church, however, a choral service including congregational hymns would often be held before the burial in the churchyard or before departure for a cemetery. Although hymn books had been available from the early eighteenth century, particularly in Nonconformist churches, it was not until the publication of *Hymns Ancient and Modern* in 1861 that congregations were encouraged to participate in singing. However, accounts of services taking place in the late nineteenth and early twentieth centuries indicate that the hymns tended to be chosen from the 'General' or 'Eastertide' category, as 'O God, our help in ages past', 'Lead kindly light', 'On the Resurrection morning'. 'Now the labourer's tasks are o'er' was included at the funeral of Baroness Burdett-Coutts in 1907.[1] Services were often preceded by or concluded with pieces from the classical repertoire such as the 'Dead March' from *Saul* by Handel, and Chopin's 'Funeral March'. Where funerals were conducted away from a church, brass instruments were used to accompany hymn singing. At the funeral of Dr Barnado in September 1905, a brass band led the hymns 'For ever with the Lord', then 'Lead, kindly light' and 'There's a friend for little children, above the bright blue sky'.[2] The music at Roman Catholic funerals was largely restricted to the singing of plainsong.

Cremation and the myth of 'canned' music

An important late-nineteenth-century development which would have an impact on funeral services and their music was cremation. The Cremation Society of England was founded in 1874 and the first cremation took place at the Society's crematorium at Woking 11 years later.[3] Funeral services were either conducted in a church before the coffin was taken to the crematorium or read in the presence of the coffin immediately prior to cremation. Alternatively, the burial service was read when the ashes were interred. No organ was provided at Woking until 1922, but at Manchester, England's second crematorium, an instrument was installed in the gallery at the time of opening in 1892.[4] Of the 50 crematoria opened between 1900 and 1939, many made no provision for music; this could be attributed to the expense of purchasing a pipe instrument, especially since by 1939 under four per cent of all deaths in the UK were followed by cremation.

In the 1930s there was increasing experimentation with the installation of recorded music facilities in cemetery and crematorium chapels. During the second Joint Conference of Cemetery and Crematorium Authorities in July 1933, over 200 delegates visited Tottenham and Wood Green Cemetery to experience the sound of HMV equipment playing 78 rpm recordings of Handel's 'Largo' and Chopin's 'Funeral March'. A report commented,

> One needs but little imagination to realise what a lasting impression it leaves upon the mourning relatives. It brings for the first time beautiful music into the burial service for every class, rich and poor ... It is needless to say that the funeral public fully appreciate what is perhaps the finest thing that could have been introduced to take away the cruel silence that precedes a funeral service.[5]

However, while recorded music provided an economical alternative to an organ and the services of an organist, it was not intended to accompany hymn singing. Furthermore, although crematoria continued to embrace technological advances by installing gramophones, then continuous loop cartridges and cassette tapes, both the quality of reproduction and the choice of music often left much to be desired. A contributor to the Cremation Society of Great Britain's conference in 1964 said that he knew of one crematorium where Handel's 'Largo' and 'Abide with Me' were played at the commencement and conclusion respectively of every cremation service.[6] As the number of cremations increased in the post-war years, tight time schedules were introduced to cope with demand; services were often held at 20-minute intervals. The impact was such that, when in 1995 Douglas Davies conducted his survey of crematoria, he observed,

> If the conveyor belt image is one leading popular motif of modern cremation then 'canned' music is another. Such taped and recorded music is often invoked as one of the clearest signs of the impersonal, mechanical and least desirable aspects of crematorium operation . . . indeed the very idea of 'piped' music has almost entered into popular language in connection with crematoria as an expression of inappropriateness.[7]

However, what had become a popular myth could not be supported by the evidence; at least 82 per cent of crematoria surveyed offered the option of the service being accompanied by an organ. Although pipe organ builders advertised in Cremation Society literature from the 1940s onwards, advancements during the 1960s in the quality and affordability of electronic organs made this type of instrument ideal for crematorium chapels. In cemetery chapels, however, organs tended not to be installed, largely as a result of the lack of use of the building attributable to the declining preference for burial. Today, it is still the case that many burial chapels are without music facilities.

It is at funerals taking place in crematoria where the introduction of music of a non-sacred character has been in evidence. Indeed, the origin of the cremation movement was secularist (the chapel of Woking crematorium was originally termed a 'hall') and in the first 50 years of cremations in the UK many services of a non-religious nature took place, with music reflecting this characteristic. For example, during the service in December 1926 at Golders Green Crematorium for M. Krassin, the Bolshevik Chargé d'Affaires in London, music by Tchaikovsky was performed on the organ; Franz Lehar's 'The Merry Widow Waltz' was also heard at a service earlier that year.[8]

However, despite the availability of organ arrangements of orchestral works and also recordings, the music at funerals tended to be of a 'religious' nature up to the late 1970s. Some crematoria published music lists to help clients make a selection, and examination of those produced by Golders Green Crematorium shows works from oratorios as well as popular classics by composers such as Chopin, Dvořák, Elgar and Mendelssohn.

Contemporary developments

Although hard to date precisely, from around the early 1980s there has been considerable change in funeral ritual in the UK in an attempt to ensure that the service reflects the personality and beliefs of the deceased and the preferences of the family.[9] Attributable to a combination of increasing interest in dying, death and funerals, together with a proliferation of literature along with a shift in attitude by those working with the bereaved, the effect of these developments has been considerable. In general terms this interest has created a culture where alternatives available for inclusion in a funeral service are increasingly embraced by families. Differing types of coffins (such as wicker, bamboo, cardboard, painted, etc.); part-religious or non-religious services; elements of participation such as reading prose, giving a eulogy, carrying in the coffin or playing instruments; interment in a woodland burial ground: these are some of the possible options. Although the reform movement was already well under way by the time of her death in August 1997, the funeral of Diana, Princess of Wales, indicated to a worldwide audience that funerals did not have to conform to a prescribed ritual. Nowhere has this change been more apparent than in the choice of music.

Tony Walter's groundbreaking book *Funerals and How to Improve Them* has also encouraged a reappraisal of the value of funerals in stating that services 'belong' to the families. He observed, 'When all else fails, there is music, for it can speak the unspeakable',[10] and then illustrated the point by citing examples of secular pieces included at funerals (particularly for those dying from AIDS), communal singing and the range of classical music referring to death.

The process of change was further stimulated by the appearance of two charters highlighting the need to improve the right of the bereaved to have a meaningful funeral ceremony. The National Funerals College's *The Dead Citizens Charter* sets out many 'Rights' and 'Recommendations'. Although not specifically mentioning music, the charter does state that, 'The funeral service should reflect the beliefs of the person who has died while being sensitive to the range of beliefs of the mourners', implying the inclusion of words and music of a personal dimension.[11] The Institute of Burial and Cremation Administration (now Institute of Cemetery and Crematorium Management) published their *Charter for the Bereaved* which encouraged cemetery and crematorium managers to provide permanent or portable equipment for the reproduction of music.[12] As a result, funeral directors – who normally meet with families before clergy – have become increasingly inclined to discuss music preferences more thoroughly with families during the funeral arrangement interview and to reassure them that the choice need not be restricted to religious pieces. Furthermore, there has been greater flexibility with regard to music by those conducting services.

Hymns included in the service books specifically intended for use in cemetery and crematorium chapels now embrace those generally recognized as suitable for funerals in addition to those which are simply well known by those attending church occasionally. The first edition of *Funeral Services*[13] prepared by the Churches' Group on Funeral Services at Cemeteries and Crematoria contained 25 hymns; 15 years later it had increased to 44 with many popular hymns such as 'All things bright and beautiful', 'And did those feet' and 'Be still, my Soul'. (The latest edition does not, however, include 'You'll never walk alone', which is occasionally sung at funerals and appears in the BBC *Songs of Praise*[14] hymnbook.)

Surveys of music played before, during and after services confirm this change. For example, in 1984 it was reported that music on the list at Colchester Crematorium was '. . . a 50–50 choice between hymns and general favourites . . .'[15] A survey carried out at St Helens Crematorium by Kenneth Lysons in 2001 showed that a large number of families brought their own cassette tapes to a crematorium, which is indicative of the increasing consideration given to the place and choice of music.[16] Incidentally, Lysons also discovered that crematorium staff were responsible for the selection of music where nothing specific had been requested by the family. Co-operative Funeralcare has regularly undertaken a survey of music and in 2006 noted that 'Contemporary songs are now almost as likely to be chosen at funerals as hymns, accounting for more than 40 per cent of music.'[17] Their report stated that the 'Top 10 Popular Songs' was headed by 'My Way', the 'Top 10 Classical Pieces' by 'Nimrod' from *The Enigma Variations* by Elgar and the 'Top 10 Hymns' by 'The Lord's my Shepherd'.

Evidence from funeral directors also reveals music choices reflecting the interests or occupation of the deceased. A recording of trains shunting was played for a rail enthusiast, the commentary from the Grand National horse race for a supporter of the Turf, the Pearl and Dean advertising company's signature tune for a cinema projectionist, and the sound of the *ITN News* chimes are some of the imaginative choices heard at funerals.

Issues for funeral officiants

The opportunity for the performance of music at funerals has never been so great. However, this brings challenges for funeral directors, cemetery and crematorium managers and funeral officiants. Although the last in particular will often be concerned with the problem of whether there will be a sufficient number present to sing a hymn, it is the choice of music which may also present problems. Until fairly recently the crematorium superintendent and officiant were joint arbiters of 'unusual' requests. In 1984, the *Daily Telegraph* reported on the banning of Morris Men dancing in a crematorium chapel and the ruling that 'Bridge Over Troubled Waters' was 'unsuitable'. Research in 1986 by Maura Page found that some funerals had

> ... become 'farewell ceremonies' linked not to the central theological strands of the Resurrection, but to the body of the deceased, by means of favourite music, favourite flowers, etc. . . . fieldwork has thrown up instances of where they [the clergy] have walked out of services, [and] demanded an apology from funeral directors over the inclusion of pop songs or creative touches such as grandchildren playing their recorders.[18]

As already noted, today's clergy increasingly adopt a flexible attitude to such participation and to unusual requests. Nevertheless, as Paul Denyer acknowledges, they can be placed in a difficult position:

> If their ministry is asked for, the public must expect and get a Christian interpretation of the meaning and significance of death . . . Because of their established position, their services are the prerogative of all citizens, whatever their faith or lack of it. This link with the unchurched is highly valued by most parish priests; but, in our more demandingly consumerist society, it raises tensions for the minister of tender conscience. Every minister has to draw his or her line.[19]

R. Anne Horton suggests that 'It is perhaps wise not to have a hard and fast rule! A pop song, for example, carefully chosen and consistent with Christian belief, can be both appropriate and intensely moving.'[20] However, what if the song is not consistent with this criteria? (The line 'Nothing to kill or die for/And no religion too' from John Lennon's 'Imagine' comes to mind.) What can be done if there is an impasse between the clergy and the family over the inclusion of a particular piece of music? Reaching a compromise by playing the music after the minister has left might be suggested by an astute funeral director. However, some families may then request that the services of a more amenable officiant be secured. With the funeral director being contractually engaged to arrange a funeral according to the wishes of the client, and in a culture where clients are increasingly willing to challenge convention,[21] this situation cannot be ruled out, particularly during services at a crematorium or in a cemetery chapel over which the clergy have no jurisdiction.[22]

Technological change is also having an impact on music at funerals, as pieces not suitable for performance on an organ can be provided by a recording or by downloading from the internet. However, this can raise the issue of copyright, and in an effort to alleviate this problem a number of crematoria no longer permit 'pirated' or 'burnt' CDs (which may also be of poor quality) to be played on their equipment.

Sound systems installed in an increasing number of crematoria give access to a wide variety of tracks, including combinations of instruments and artists; some systems are sufficiently sophisticated to be programmed to accompany congregational hymn singing, complete with a play-over of the tune along with the facility to determine the number of verses. It is a false economy, however, to replace the 'live' organist, who will have the flexibility, experience and musical sensitivity which are essential when accompanying hymn singing.

An issue particularly relating to services at crematoria is that while ceremonies have become more participative including musical items, they can over-run their allocated time. In noting the increasing number of such services, one crematorium superintendent commented, 'A busy establishment can now expect six out of ten funeral services on any given day to be full-scale productions. Overruns become commonplace and heighten tension between staff and public.'[23] In an attempt to solve this problem a number of crematoria have increased the duration of the service time from 30 to 45 minutes, thereby giving the opportunity for additional musical items to be included. However, it has not always been possible to extend the service time especially at busy crematoria. Technology also gives the opportunity for computer-generated presentations to be shown at funerals. Although few crematoria in the UK currently have this facility, visual tributes with musical accompaniment can easily become 'full-scale productions'. However, as a possible trend for the future, it is essential that these are carefully planned by all involved. Such contributions have already attracted censure in Australia concerning 'inappropriate remarks' made during funeral Masses.[24]

Such developments underline the principle that the construction of funeral services requires thorough preparation and negotiation. Those conducting funeral services must be familiar with local facilities, such as the hymn and service books in use at local cemeteries and crematoria, and the availability of live and/or recorded music.[25] Furthermore, if there is a preference for the officiant to discuss music with a family without the intervention of the funeral director, then the latter needs to be informed. Particularly in the case of secular music used in the context of a religious service, the need to be sufficiently flexible in approach will ensure that music contributes but does not dominate; this is the challenge of remaining in tune with the needs of the bereaved.

Notes

1 *The Times*, 7 October 1907.

2 Brian Parsons, 'The Funeral of Dr Barnardo', *Funeral Service Journal*, Vol. 120, No. 9, 2005, pp. 96–8.

3 Brian Parsons, *Committed to the Cleansing Flame: The Development of Cremation in Nineteenth Century England*, Reading: Spire Books, 2005.

4 Chris E. Makepeace, *Manchester Crematorium 1890–1990*, Manchester: Manchester Crematorium, 1990.

5 'Music in Cemetery Chapels', *The Undertakers' Journal*, Vol. 44, No. 3, 1934, p. 96.

6 *Cremation Society Conference Report*, 'Music For Cremation Services', 25 June 1964, p. 65. Anecdotal evidence shared with the author by a priest working in Coventry during the 1960s reveals that an instrumental recording of 'Meditation' from Massenet's opera *Thaïs* was repeatedly played at cremation services.

7 J. Douglas Davies, *British Crematoria in Public Profile*, Maidstone: The Cremation Society of Great Britain, 1995, p. 23.

8 'M. Krassin Cremated', *The Undertakers' Journal*, Vol. 41, No. 12, 1926, p. 402. See also 'Cremation Notes', *The Undertakers' Journal*, Vol. 41, No. 3, 1926, p. 90.

9 See Alan Billings, *Dying and Grieving: A Guide to Pastoral Ministry*, London: SPCK, 2002, p. 11. See also Denison, this volume.

10 A. Walter, *Funerals and How to Improve Them*, London: Hodder & Stoughton, 1990, pp. 157.

11 *The Dead Citizens Charter: The Complete Edition*, Bristol: The National Funerals College, 1998, p. 9.

12 *Charter for the Bereaved*, London: Institute of Burial and Cremation Administration (now Institute of Cemetery and Crematorium Management), 1996, p. 31.

13 Churches' Group on Funeral Services at Cemeteries and Crematoria, *Funeral Services of the Christian Churches in England*, Norwich: Canterbury Press, 1986.

14 BBC, *Songs of Praise*, Oxford: Oxford University Press, 1997.

15 'Freedom of Choice in Funeral Music', *Funeral Service Journal*, Vol. 99, No. 3, 1984, p. 112.

16 Kenneth Lysons, 'Issues of Music at Crematoria', *Pharos International*, Vol. 70, No. 1, 2004, pp. 44–7.

17 'Tears, Trains and Telly . . . Playing at a Funeral Near You', *Funeral Service Journal*, Vol. 121, No. 1, 2007, p. 18.

18 Maura Page, 'Grave Misgivings', *Religion Today*, No. 3, 1986, pp. 7–9, 8. See also Maura Naylor (formerly Page), 'Crossed Wires, Frustrations and Conflicts in Crematoria Funerals', Churches' Group on Funeral Services, *Report of the Day Conference Held at Carrs Lane Church Centre, Birmingham, on Monday 20 October 1991*, pp. 1–17.

19 Paul Denyer, 'Singing the Lord's Song in a Strange Land' in P. C. Jupp and T. Rogers (eds), *Interpreting Death: Christian Theology and Pastoral Practice*, London: Cassell, 1997, pp. 200–1.

20 R. Anne Horton, *Using Common Worship: Funerals*, London: Church House Publishing, 2000, p. 133.

21 See chapters by Jupp (chapter 2) and Lloyd, this volume.

22 Brian Parsons, 'Conflict in the Context of Care: An Examination of Role Conflict between the Bereaved and the Funeral Directors in the UK', *Mortality*, Vol. 8, No. 1, 2003, pp. 67–87. See also Murray, this volume.

23 Editorial, *Journal of the Institute of Burial and Cremation Administration*, Vol. 64, No. 3, 1996, p. 2.

24 'No PowerPoint at the Funeral Please', *The Times*, 24 February 2007. See also 'Pell Clamps Down on Eulogies', *The Tablet*, 3 March 2007.

25 The chapter 'Music at Funerals' in *The Manual of Funeral Directing*, Solihull: National Association of Funeral Directors, 2007, provides helpful guidance. See also Anthony Caldicott, 'Music at Funerals', *Funeral Service Journal*, Vol. 121, No. 2, 2001, pp. 106–8, and Jane Wynne Willson, *Funerals without God: A Practical Guide to Non-Religious Funeral Ceremonies*, 5th edn, London: British Humanist Association, 1998.

Funerals in the Multi-cultural Metropolis:
A Hospital Chaplain's Perspective

MIA HILBORN

Introduction

This chapter is written from the perspective of an Anglican hospital chaplain, who has spent the last 13 years living and working in hospitals and churches in central London, previously having lived and worked in Nottingham, Birmingham and Oxford. While at Mansfield College, Oxford, studying to be a United Reformed Church minister in the mid-1980s, funeral training was quiet, dignified, liturgical in a Nonconformist way and, above all, deeply pastoral. In the intervening years, moving between and across cities and into healthcare chaplaincy, and having transferred to the Anglican Communion, death and dying and funerals have become one of the more challenging and cross-cultural aspects of ministry.

Looking back at our hospital team's average 40 or more funerals per quarter, there is a cross-section of metropolitan society. Most of the funerals are for pre-24-week gestation foetuses, a few for older babies or children, and some for adults who have no next-of-kin, or no one willing or able to arrange a funeral for them. In 2007, 54 per cent of people in the UK died in hospitals and in London 59 per cent; this is a paradox as hospitals are places where patients are generally expected to get better. There may be a sense of medical and nursing failure, conflict or inadequacy associated with the death.[1] About 5 per cent of deaths occur in hospices, where the standards of palliative care are characterized by a holistic perspective. Other people die at home or in nursing homes. In this geographically mobile world, some people have come to the UK for the health care, so-called 'health tourism'. If the patient dies, there can be frustration and anger by first-generation relatives, who had great faith in the British health system. Sometimes sacrificial sums are paid by families, both here and abroad, for example, living kidney donors who come to this country.

Spiritual care

To help improve the experience of palliative care and dying in hospital for both the patient and the bereaved, there have been various government and charity guidelines recently produced.[2] One of these, the Marie Curie spiritual and religious competencies tool, marks the first time such practice has been seen in the United Kingdom, although it is not unusual in the United States. At Guy's and St Thomas', we have adapted the competencies by adding the word 'cultural', i.e. competencies for spiritual, religious and *cultural* care, which means they can be used for all acute patients, not just in the palliative setting. The Liverpool Care Pathway for the Dying (LCP),[3] a 'gold standard' by the Department of Health, is being used in community and social care, so secular caregivers will need to be taught how to ask the several questions relating to spiritual and religious care within the last days of life.

The LCP audit (at its annual conference in December 2007) revealed that caregivers are finding spiritual care questions some of the toughest to ask, and I would suggest three reasons for this. First, both good and excellent quality spiritual care takes time, it involves listening to the patient and perhaps taking a dying person's or a family's spiritual history or assessment. Non-chaplaincy staff generally do not have this time, especially in these target-driven days.[4] It is also difficult to document accurately and sensitively, especially if there have been aspects of a theological 'confession' as part of the discussion. There are data protection issues, and confidentiality is paramount in such discussions. Entries in patient notes are generally the name of the spiritual care giver, signature and the date.

Second, the secular white English culture, in which many staff have been brought up, does not allow for many 'religious', 'death' or 'spiritual' discussions or experiences to have taken place during the spiritual formation of the staff, either personally or during training. I have observed that many English staff appear to find conversation about religion and faith embarrassing and 'private', and are distressed and even feel harassed by non-English colleagues naturally and openly discussing these matters. The new legislation about religious discrimination has forced such 'private' issues out into the public arena, and the cultural implications of this have yet to be seen.[5] This is a key training opportunity for spiritual bereavement caregivers to support and develop staff. Rabbi Julia Neuberger has argued that world religions other than Christianity are better at long-term bereavement care, whereas the Christian (particularly the priest) practises theologically pastoral care before death, at death and immediately post-death, although she recognizes that comparisons are not that simple.[6]

For the Christian minister, although not necessarily a Christian counsellor or therapist, pastoral care and liturgical action are completely intertwined at all stages of the bereavement journey. The minister must always attend to the dying and to the dead on behalf of the living, and care for the suffering – in this instance, the grieving relatives and friends. The importance of religious observance such as prayer and sacramental ministry (e.g. Holy Communion and anointing) means that a secular caregiver, such as a nurse, or even a religious leader of another faith, would be entirely inappropriate to fulfil the role.

Third, working with the dying, caring for the bereaved, and relating spiritual, religious and, to a lesser extent, cultural care, normally has long-term effects on the caregiver in a way that, for example, dispensing the correct palliative care drugs or ensuring appropriate nutrition does not. Staff may not feel ready to allow this access to their 'private' world. Some staff members may prefer tasks which give easily quantifiable targets;[7] it is simpler to argue that good bereavement care has been achieved, for example, if all deceased patients had clean clothes when leaving the ward, the correct medication was documented, and the bereavement certificate handed over to the correct next-of-kin within two days. Who is able to decide how satisfactory has been long-term pre- and post-bereavement care, or how well has the Church performed its ministry of caring for the bereaved? Which evidence-based measures can be used to quantify such qualitative data?[8] The role of the hospital chaplain is often to pick up the pieces of scarred individuals who, often after a particularly stressful bereavement experience, have left the Church and never returned. Nearing death, there can be a huge vacuum of need, which only a return to a loving God can ultimately fulfil.

Practical aspects of metropolitan funerals

Clergy in London learn the location of burial grounds, cemeteries and crematoria like some sort of ghoulish 'knowledge'. Robed and anxious men and women of the cloth criss-cross the capital to its far-flung corners, dodging congestion charges, road closures and gridlock. Hospital chaplains conduct contract funerals (where there are no next-of-kin or none willing to organize a funeral), often in the borough where the deceased lived as it is cheaper. The funerals typically take place between 8 am and 9.45 am – cheaper, but this means travelling in the rush hour, although, as the central London burial grounds were closed by the government's burial laws of the 1850s,[9] one normally cuts across or against the traffic, or is squashed into the Tube. Details such as address, next-of-kin, religion, even the name may be unknown, leaving the minister with a sense of spiritual unease and theological nakedness. The funeral congregation can be stripped down to the chaplain alone, with the deceased in the cheapest coffin, sometimes an undertaker or verger, or a case worker or a drug or alcohol counsellor – at least with the last there is some knowledge to construct the story of the person who has died – sometimes a friend or two, occasionally family members. Generally, circumstances surrounding the deceased person's conception, birth, childhood and life are unknown. I hope the person had received some human love in the past, I believe this person *is* beloved of God and that the original spark of godliness can be seen by the Divine. Why does a person die alone? Stories of abusive behaviour, mental health or substance issues, personal hygiene, age, destruction of life trails, murders, suicides, John Doe's – all these are sad endings, the forgotten metropolitan souls for whom streets proved far from paved with gold, more likely excrement and vomit. Some funerals I have led include:

- A *Big Issue* seller, homeless after having a breakdown, but with a strong poetic streak. Many fellow sellers coming to share their writings, readings and thoughts. Extremely moving.
- An alcoholic, where a minibus arrived from the last shelter in which the deceased person had stayed. Two support workers, people in various states of intoxication, with bottles, cans and furious, with furious smoking taking place outside around the coffin, under which two women collapse. We wait until workers feel all are able to sit for most of the service – toilet breaks, smoking breaks and drinking breaks elongate proceedings.
- A suicide, where the person has tried to follow alternative spiritualities and become lost and confused. Trying to help a mainstream Christian family feeling abandoned and shunned by one they once loved, and working to achieve a service which links with emotional need, is appropriate for the deceased and others from the new spirituality, and allows the priest to retain integrity.

- A drug-fuelled murder victim, with children, support workers and police the only mourners – hearing the children ask 'Why?', and praying for their future, and thanking God for caring professionals going beyond basic guidelines.

Hospital-led funerals do not have the local sources of support or follow-up; they are often for transient people who have come adrift from all forms of spiritual support. Where there is no next-of-kin, the resident borough will pay for a local funeral if there is no estate. Usually the hospital will organize, and money is collected afterwards, although with financial and geographical complications this may take months. It is a final act of Christian love for a person whom 'normal church' failed to reach. Usually the person lived frugally and alone, with few friends and fewer family, and the chaplain, at the last, requests God's forgiveness, gives the blessing of peace, and traditional prayers and sacred readings suffice.

Baby and child funerals

For most clergy, the saddest funerals are those of a baby or a child,[10] most poignant when there are no mourners. I have been involved with the following situations:

- An unmarried mother, who has had difficulty having a live pregnancy, has come to England seeking help – the child has been born dead, so does not have a birth certificate (pre-24-week gestation). The mother, alone in London, with a fluid address, returns home, signing a form to say she wants a hospital contract funeral. The mother may never be seen again. The child has no name.
- Tiny bodies which remain after miscarriages and medical terminations. All mothers are asked if they wish to organize a funeral, or if they would like the hospital to make arrangements and provide a chaplain (Christian or other if requested) to officiate. Often mothers or parents choose not to attend – it may be difficult, may make the dead baby and the event 'too real'. Sometimes the only way to cope with the reality of an abortion/termination is to dehumanize the child in your mind, or maybe the guilt is too strong, and attending would seem hypocritical. Yet, up to 30 years later, mothers can come back to the hospital to ask what happened to their baby.
- Mothers who are very ill in hospital after their baby's death do not

wish to wait any longer and prefer to let the funeral take place without her being present. The father may attend, or simply ask that the funeral take place without him.

- It may go against the parents' culture to attend a child's funeral (some Nigerian families practise this custom), and it is not uncommon for other African parents not to attend a baby's or young child's funeral. Parents say, 'A child is not supposed to die before the parents.' For older children, the community may organize and attend the funeral on the parents' behalf.

- The death of a child may be seen as spiritually affecting the future fertility of the parents, so they do not wish to view or to touch the body. Maybe a man or a leading male of the community will make all the arrangements and the parents are not even told where the child is laid. I have seen this in several Nigerian and other African families.

- The death of the child is sometimes blamed spiritually on the mother, that is the child's profound disability and subsequent palliative condition is seen as a direct result of sin in the mother; hence the mother is banned from all worship and services (including the funeral) until the final rites are completed after the death of the child. Only then will the mother be spiritually cleansed and rejoined to her worshipping and cultural community. I have seen this in several independent African-led churches.

- Occasionally, families choose to have no funeral service, but it is rare. In these cases, the child is usually cremated without words being said, and without naming the child before God. Other families may request a chaplain or religious leader from a particular faith community, or a celebrant from the British Humanist Association. As far as possible, such choices should always be given a positive response.

There are community shockwaves after the death of a child. In London, particularly among the migrant communities, the death may well be the first in the UK that the church group has ever faced. Parents have struggled to come to this country, to give their children better lives, and yet the child has died. In the UK, they find that the death process is very slow – but families from overseas are generally used to quick funerals.

- A slow, gentle, normal British response to a baby death and funeral could see the bereaved mother arranging a flight home to see her own family – maybe booking for a week after the death, and being shocked that the funeral is arranged for two weeks after the death. She misses the funeral as she has arranged flights, time off work, maybe her mum is waiting for her with a ceremony at home. She is very angry that in London the funeral is not the next day.

Culture, money, death and funerals

Death in the UK can be very expensive. Ghana is one of few countries where death costs more, hence Ghanaian families can be quite relieved by the level of British funeral costs. Migrant families often have to share funeral expenses, and they simply cannot believe the thousands of pounds it all costs. I was with a family who wanted 'the works' – a big elaborate coffin, a burial plot, horses, several cars, a band. The cost would have been over £10,000, and the family were poor – they were so ashamed they couldn't afford it. The English paperwork seems to take longer than almost every other country in the world, whereas in Scotland a funeral can take place almost immediately, and before the death certificate is formally issued. In Ireland, funerals are organized in a few days. In London, the process usually takes ten days to a fortnight, and over a month is not unusual.

Twice, after taking a cremation service for Eastern European families (they had signed forms requesting cremation) I have been met with bewildered relatives waiting for the burial after the service. They thought 'cremation' was an English word for funeral. They could not believe that something as terrible as cremation could really exist. Since retelling these stories to hospital staff, I have met other migrant health-care staff who are similarly unaware.

A relatively new issue concerns those families who are mixed cultur-ally and religiously. Sometimes the first time this new 'family' has ever met is at the deathbed, and that is the only place for negotiations with regard to rites, rituals and the way to say goodbye. I was called to the bedside of a dying Catholic woman, married to a Muslim. She was European, he was Arabic, and they didn't know what to do, so they asked for a Church of England chaplain, because they were in England, and they thought it was somewhere in the middle! Especially when there are language difficulties, liturgical gestures (such as touch, making the sign of cross) are often appreciated, yet one has to act both with integ-rity according to that office to which we are called, and be acutely aware of the sensitivities that surround death and death rites. At particular times, different parts of the Christian Church have unique gifts; I think Anglican theology lends itself to these deeply sensitive yet divisive occa-sions. It has an ecclesiology which brings Church, state and community together in a ritual action and in the person and authority of the priest, and offers a final rite of peace.

For those communities who have been settled in the UK for a considerable time, such as peoples from the Caribbean islands, funerals have developed into a hybrid of 'back home' and 'over here'. Both African and Caribbean funerals can be loud and noisy occasions, unlike the quiet, short affairs of white English funerals with their usually small number of mourners. By contrast, West Indian funerals tend to have very long services, lots of music, instruments and bands leading processions. Many people attend. Caribbean Anglicans tend to be very 'high', so there may be a full Requiem Mass, after a night's vigil with the coffin in the church, followed by prayers and music at the cemetery.

For a Pentecostal service, people will take the day off work; there may a full Bible sermon and testimonials witnessing to the life of the departed, followed by the procession to the cemetery. Sometimes (due to cost) people are cremated, and their ashes taken back to the land of birth. There may be chanting and spontaneous prayer; it is not unusual for a release of white doves in the cemetery as a symbol of the release of the Holy Spirit. The coffin may be on a horse-drawn hearse followed by a hundred cars (the more people attending, the more important the person who died). The funeral procession through the cemetery or crematorium may follow a jazz band, and there will be loud singing all the way.

At a burial, for many Afro-Caribbean funerals, the coffin is laid in the grave; men – family and friends – will then fill in the grave, while women sing and scatter earth on top. Then the long procession will go to a reception, often in the church hall, where the whole community gathers to share food, maybe remaining long into the evening. People bring food or drink for the reception. Attendance is seen as a mark of respect for the family, whether or not the deceased was personally known. Clergy and undertakers alike will book out the whole day. When the deceased or bereaved attend a 'white' church, there is often puzzlement by community members as to why funerals are so short and formal. I have heard whispered arguments between the bereaved and well-meaning friends: 'Why aren't you burying [him] our way?' 'Because we live here now, and she is our minister and it is what he wanted.' 'But it ain't right!' 'Yes it is, this is our home now, and we are doing it the white way.'

Chinese families can be suspicious of Christian clergy doing the 'wrong' thing, wearing wrong colours, and not allowing the spirit of the deceased time to leave. Usually white is worn, with some red if the person was old. There are lots of flowers and maybe banners; the hearse may be covered in flowers and symbols of life. Families may wish to bow nine times, and children may crawl before the coffin to show respect, and usually a photograph of the deceased is carried. Many prayers are said at the grave by mourners.

Conclusion

With the increasing complexity of inner-city life, the rise in the number of immigrants (most of whom come from non-secular countries), and the increasing secularization of the UK, the role of the generic chaplain and the need for aware Christian spiritual caregivers in the multicultural city are more important than ever. The range of the role is increasing, as the need for extreme sensitivity, the ability to empathize with complex distress and an understanding of a variety of religious expression and faith-based needs are simply not seen in any other profession. The spiritual caregiver of all faiths and none, the Christian clergy and ministers called to this work need to have understood the life-and-death issues that surround dying people and those who love them and care for them, feeling secure in their own faith and calling. There is an even greater need for the Churches to be aware of the long-term needs of the bereaved, to make times and occasions to remember the departed. Bereaved people need to be acknowledged, with space in which to grieve and a theology of death and resurrection that will not leave them bereft of hope. The Christian Church has a unique message of hope and eternal life, and it needs to be made known. Chaplains have a unique role in ministering to those who die forgotten in the hospital. The Church makes sense of life and death in the community. Church leaders need to remain true to the integrity of their own calling. It is a tough calling, but, by God's grace, a profoundly joyous one.

Notes

1 Jane Hopkinson, Christine Hallett and Karen Luker, 'Care for Dying People in Hospital', *Journal of Advanced Nursing*, Vol. 44, No. 5, December 2003, pp. 525–33. This is a study of newly qualified nurses and dying patients, around six 'essences': nurses' personal ideals of care for dying patients; their actual experiences; 'the unknown' with difficult judgements and unanswerable questions; a sense of isolation from others; the tensions that arise between their ideals and their actual experiences; and anti-tensions, the stratagems that enable them to achieve degrees of personal comfort.

John Costello, 'Dying Well: Nurses' Experiences of "Good and Bad" Deaths in Hospital', *Journal of Advanced Nursing*, Vol. 54, No. 5, June 2006, pp. 594–601. This study highlights significant variation in hospitals in the care of dying patients, and the fact that management of death is a major source of conflict for nurses. The findings challenge practitioners to prioritize patients' needs above the organization.

2 These include, e.g., (a) NICE (National Institute for Clinical Excellence), *Improving Support and Palliative Care*, 'When a Patient Dies', advice on developing bereavement services in the NHS, DH, 2005, where it states (p. 4): 'NHS Trusts may wish to consider how best to provide spiritual care as an integral part of the overall bereavement care they provide'; (b) National Service Framework for Older People, DH, 2001, which recognizes the needs of family, friends and carers to be provided for, including relieving distress and meeting spiritual needs and offering bereavement counselling; (c) Marie Curie, *Spiritual and Religious Care Competences for Specialist Palliative Care, and Competencies Assessment Tool and Self-assessment Tool*, London: Marie Curie Cancer Care, 2004.

3 Liverpool Care Pathway for the Dying, Marie Curie Institute, Liverpool. Competencies are based upon four levels of spiritual/religious/cultural awareness and knowledge, and are a useful tool for teaching staff who come into contact with the dying and bereaved. The competencies include an assessment tool, based upon a healthcare setting, where staff are line managed and have a regular performance appraisal. It is assumed that staff will be able to develop a rapport with the dying/bereaved, whose particular spiritual or cultural needs will be recognized and supported. There is an assumption that senior staff will have an awareness of their own spiritual needs and be able to articulate their spirituality to some degree, and demonstrate their ability to recognize and respond to such needs in their patients or their bereaved relatives. Tools such as written reflective accounts are encouraged where staff have a managing role for patient or client care, which demonstrates competency. The competencies are useful within the healthcare setting in particular, because they speak the same language as in other areas where work can be measurable and targets set for compliance.

4 Clinical indicators are counted ward by ward, using SMART objectives. SMART stands for: specific, measurable, agreed upon, realistic, time-based. The measures used by the Department of Health to assess the effectiveness of a hospital do not include spiritual care (Rosie Winterton, 'The Department does not collect data on NHS chaplaincy', answer given 9 October 2006).
See Daniel P. Sulmasy, 'A Biopsychosocial-Spiritual Model for the Care of Patients at the End of Life', *The Gerontologist*, Vol. 42, Spec. No. 3, October 2002, pp. 24–33, 84. According to Sulmasy, 'Transcendence itself, by definition, cannot be measured. However, one can measure patients' religiosity, spiritual/religious coping, spiritual well-being, and spiritual needs. A research agenda in this area would include (a) improving measurements of spiritual states; (b) better defining who is best to address these issues with patients; (c) studying the interactions between the measurable dimensions of spirituality and more traditional health measures; (d) designing and measuring the effectiveness of spiritual interventions; (e) assessing the spiritual significance of patient-professional relationships; (f) refining and testing tools for taking spiritual histories; (g) assessing the impact of the health professional's own spirituality on end-of-life care; (h) devel-

oping measurement tools for assessing the religious coping, spiritual well-being, and spiritual needs of those who mourn the dead; and (i) encouraging scholarship in the humanities about these issues.'

5 *Religion or Belief and the Workplace: Putting the Employment Equality (Religion or Belief) Regulations 2003 into Practice*, London: ACAS, 2005.

6 Rabbi Julia Neuberger, 'And Then We Die', published sermon, the Memorial Church, Harvard, 7 May 2006.

7 See note 3.

8 See note 3.

9 See Jupp and Kellaher, this volume.

10 See Dent, this volume.

Characteristics of Scottish Funerals

DEREK MURRAY

Introduction: the Scottish ethos, and changing times

In Inverurie, a rapidly growing market town in Aberdeenshire of around 12,000 people, there are two cemeteries, owned, as most cemeteries are now, by the local authority. The main burial ground, around the sites of the medieval castle and kirk, has graves from early times until the 1990s. At that time it was pronounced full except for those whose families had lairs, which are plots of land containing a number of graves. A new cemetery was opened around 1995, and the contrasts between these burial grounds are instructive. In the large, older cemetery there are many granite gravestones with plain inscriptions containing names and dates and occasionally a scripture text. On the stones in the new cemetery there is only one that I can find that has a text cut on it. There are several with sentimental verses, and new graves are decorated with flowers – growing, cut or artificial – and with toys, fluffy animals and lights which glow in the evenings, giving the place, new though it is, a rather eerie air. There is also a wall with plaques remembering those who have been cremated.

Especially in country districts, old habits die hard in Scotland, but changes from the plain old Presbyterian style are certainly happening.[1] Movement of population means that fewer die in the parish where they were born, and incomers from other parts of the United Kingdom and from elsewhere have ensured that new customs, influenced by celebrity culture, television serials and other cultures, have influenced even quite remote districts. There are regional variations between city and rural areas and in the various regions of the country, so that no short survey can do justice to the localism of a small country.[2]

Until the Reformation there seems to have been little if any variation between Scottish and other British customs surrounding death and the funeral.[3] The ceremonies of the Church ensured a sense of community between the living and the dead, and sought for the dead the end of purgatorial sufferings and the bliss of heaven. The Reformation, especially in the Calvinist form, which was established in Scotland in 1560, moved the focus of the funeral from the benefit of the dead to the exhortation of the living, and to avoid superstition, drastically simplified the ritual. At the graveside no words were to be spoken.

The *Buke of Discipline* (1561) is quite explicit:

> ... buriall in all aiges hath been holden in estimatioun, to signifie that the same body that was committed to the earth should not utterly perishe, but should ryse agane. And the same we wold have keapt within this realme, provided that superstitioun, idolatrie and whatsoever hath proceaded of a fals opinioun, and for advantage saik, may be avoyded: as singing of Messe, Placebo, and dirige, and all other prayeris over and for the dead, are not onlie superfluous and vane, but also ar idolatrie and do repugne to the plane Scriptures of God . . . And thairfoir, we think most expedient that the Dead be convoyed to the place of buriall with some honest cumpany of the Churche, without eather singing or reading.

Sermons were being preached daily, and in them the bereaved should be able to find comfort. Churches were not to be used for burial, but 'some other secreat and convenient place, lying in the most free air be appointed for that use, the which place aught to be weill walled and fensed about, and keaped for that use onlie'.[4]

In 1638 the General Assembly forbade funeral sermons. The Westminster Directory of 1644, based on Travers' work of 1586, gave very similar instructions, while allowing civic honours to those to whom they were due. 'For long no more (was) done than to place the body in the grave and cover it with earth, as is still the custom among the Sandemanians.'[5] So the norm was a silent burial, in a graveyard which usually surrounded the church, the only concessions being for the nobility and gentry, who sometimes were allowed to use areas of the old church for a burial aisle.[6] Until the nineteenth century the Church of Scotland derived income from burial dues, charged on a carefully calculated scale, but now churchyards are the responsibility of local authorities, and the Church no longer benefits financially from burials.

Historic customs, such as covering the coffin with a mortcloth, appear to have died out, and very few of these artefacts survive.[7] In the nineteenth century there was an outbreak of bodysnatching (the story of

Burke and Hare is the best known example) and many churches acquired some form of mortsafe – a grill to lay over the grave – or a heavy stone to place on top of the coffin. Watchtowers and morthouses are still to be found. One at Kemnay, Aberdeenshire, is described as 'built 1831: impregnable: leadlined and semisubterranean with granite ashlar front and iron door'.[8] In Inverurie the elaborate mortsafe tackle for lifting the safe is now housed in the museum.[9]

Because there was a theological and social shift towards simplicity and the avoidance of even the appearance of prayer for the dead, funerals were conducted not from the church but from the home, and this domestic aspect, while modified by the introduction of cremation, has persisted, and may be one reason for the reluctance of Scots to adopt cremation. In the Free Church of Scotland, the group which remained outside the union of 1900 and which has its main strength in the Highlands and Western Islands, a relatively simple service continues, with prayer at the graveside. Cremation is reluctantly permitted, but many older and stricter folk prefer burial. There was no crematorium in the Highlands until 1995, when conservative Christian objections were overcome and a facility was opened in Inverness.

The Free Presbyterian Church of Scotland, formed by seceders from the Free Church in 1893, still holds to the Directory. Cremation is strictly forbidden.

> The funeral service consists of worship on the day of the burial which may be in the church or the home of the family. The worship begins with prayer, asking God's blessing on the Word of God to be read and upon all persons present. Then there is the singing of a psalm, the reading of a chapter from the Word of God, and the worship is concluded with prayer. At the graveside an address by the minister is given appropriate to the occasion and in particular commending Jesus Christ as the only preparation against death. During the burial of a minister a tribute may be given in the church.[10]

Scottish customs

Once, in the late 1960s in Kirkcaldy, I was asked to perform a kisting service. I was taken to a cottage on the outskirts of the town by the undertaker, and discovered the open coffin in the living room, surrounded by the family. After I offered suitable prayers, the coffin lid was put in place and screwed down. The undertaker remarked that older ministers were happy to do kistings as they got an extra fee! The origin of this service is said to be the enforcement of the *Act anent Burying in Scots Linen*, which was passed in 1686 by the Scots Parliament as a commercial protection for native products.[11] The minister attended only in an administrative capacity, to ensure that the linen was Scottish, but it became natural to ask a blessing on the refreshments provided, and this is one of the factors that allowed burial services back into Scottish practice. This practice has probably died out now.

Until recent rapid changes in the cities, and still in some country areas, the funeral proceeded in a fairly predictable way.[12] A death notice was inserted in the local newspaper, especially if it appeared daily. Sometimes notices were put in the undertaker's window and displayed in other shops. Ringing of the mort- or passing-bell and personal invitations to the funeral seem to have died out in the early twentieth century. The family and friends and neighbours gathered in the home of the deceased. Dress was uniformly black. The undertaker was in attendance, and if the coffin was not already in the house it was brought in before the service and placed in a prominent place in the best room. The minister arrived and conducted a brief service of scripture readings and prayers. Usually at this point there was no address. Then the men of the company made their way to the cemetery, and the women stayed at home to prepare the refreshments. Scotland, it should be noted, was a patriarchal society and women began attending burials and holding cords only recently, possibly after the church-like service in the crematorium made it respectable for them to be present. When everyone had gathered, the coffin was laid on trestles on the open grave. Cords attached to the coffin were given to men who had already been approached and given a card with a distinguishing number. The coffin was then lowered into the grave, the minister read again from the scriptures and prayed. As he pronounced the words of committal, 'earth to earth, ashes to ashes, and dust to dust, in sure and certain hope of the resurrection to eternal life through Jesus Christ our Lord', either the gravedigger or a member of the family threw three handfuls of earth onto the coffin. A covering of fabric was then laid on the grave and the funeral wreaths laid on top of it. The grave was then filled by the gravediggers, and the family lined up and were greeted by the other mourners.

Many funerals still follow this pattern, but certain changes are noteworthy. Until fairly recently church services with the coffin present were almost confined to Roman Catholic and Episcopalian Churches and were looked on with suspicion by many Protestants, but holding a service in the family church either before or after the cremation has become much more acceptable recently. If the home was not suitable for a service, most undertakers provided a funeral parlour, furnished with pews and an organ, where a service could be conducted. As cremation became the norm, at least in the cities, the service could take place completely in the crematorium chapel, where the mourners wait outside until the coffin is carried in silently, preceded by the minister. Then the family enters, followed by the other mourners. Even when the service is advertised to be at the crematorium, many families still request a service in the house attended by family and neighbours, so demonstrating the continuing domestic character of the Scottish funeral. After the service a post-funeral meal is usually provided, at a local hotel or in the family home, where relatives who have come from a distance can be entertained and reminiscences shared. This is the remnant of the eating and drinking that characterized older Scottish funerals, which often put bereaved families to great expense.

There are also grand funerals for notable citizens held in churches such as St Giles, Edinburgh or Glasgow Cathedral,[13] and at ministerial funerals the local Presbytery is present. Freemasons have their own rituals. But most services follow the pattern described above.

The growth of a funeral liturgy

While a service crept into Scottish practice at the 'kisting', prayers at burials entered by way of an extended grace at the meal which followed. This was offered by the minister or, in the minister's absence, by an elder. In the mid-nineteenth century there was a general movement, at least in the Lowlands, towards a more liturgical form of church service, and this influenced funeral practice. In 1867 the Church Service Society issued *Euchologion or Book of Services* and this innovative book included funeral services for the church and graveside. In the introduction it is stated, 'the gradual and general resumption of prayer at funerals has long proclaimed the universal conviction that no good reason for omitting on such occasions the devotional observances solemnizing and comforting to the living can be found in the fact of their having once been regarded as beneficial to the dead'.[14] It was as late as 1897 that the Church of Scotland sanctioned officially services at the burial of the dead and in 1928, just before the Union of the Churches, the United Free Church issued a Book of Common Order including services for cremations. The most recent Book of Common Order (1994) of the Church of Scotland has a comprehensive range of funeral services, with additional prayers and readings including 'Go forth, O Christian Soul'. There are orders for the burial or scattering of ashes and for the dedication of a churchyard or burial ground. Much more attention has been paid to the burial of stillborn babies and miscarried foetuses in the past ten years.[15]

The prevalence of cremation in cities and large towns has had a profound effect on funeral practice. Services, until recently confined to 20 minutes, have now in many places been slightly extended as more time has been given to each 'slot', and unseemly queues are rarer. As the service is conducted in a churchlike atmosphere, it has become more like a service of worship, at least when a minister is the sole conductor. Sometimes, especially among evangelicals, there is a sermon, possibly directed to non-churchgoers in the congregation, but more usually there is a word of remembrance of the deceased. Influenced perhaps by films and TV serials, the practice of a relative or friend delivering the eulogy has grown, as has the replacement of organ music with favourite songs for entrance and exit, and the presence of a bagpiper to play the family in is not uncommon. Wreaths and more complicated flower arrangements are laid outside the chapel for admiration and examination, the family stand at the door of the chapel and greet the mourners, and then proceed to the post-funeral meal. Ashes may later be collected and buried at a small ceremony in a family grave.[16]

Although anyone may lawfully conduct a funeral, there is still, even among those who have little connection with the Church, an expectation that an ordained minister will conduct the service and that at least one hymn will be sung. The metrical version of the twenty-third Psalm, 'The Lord's My Shepherd', sung to Crimond, is an almost inevitable choice. If there is a second hymn, 'Abide with me', 'The old rugged cross', and 'All things bright and beautiful' are favourites. If the deceased and family are churchgoers, then a more imaginative selection can be made. Ministers sometimes face a dilemma when what they regard as an unsuitable choice is insisted upon. Whose wishes are paramount? Some would let the family be the arbiters, others insist on the dignity of their calling. Usually a compromise can be reached.[17]

If the family belong to a church then the minister of that church is almost always invited to take the service. If there is no connection, then the minister of the parish may expect to be asked to conduct the funeral, and it is part of a parish minister's duty to do so in most cases. Alternatively, a hospital chaplain may be involved.[18] In some parishes, especially where there are many elderly and vulnerable folk, readers, deacons and elders are being trained as funeral officiants, and undertakers usually have contacts with a retired minister on whom they can call. Such variety has implications for bereavement care, both in preparation and in follow-up after the funeral.

For those wishing a non-religious funeral, the British Humanist Assocation, in co-operation – at least in Edinburgh – with the Unitarian Church, offers a suitable alternative to a religious service.[19] Acknowledgement notices in newspapers often include thanks to the officiant, and quite recently have begun to give details of the amount of the collection at the crematorium doors for the charity of the family's choice. Funeral fashions appear to spread rapidly and are controlled not by church practice, or by the advice of funeral directors, but by the changing nature of society and the decline of overt religious practice. *The Naming of the Dead* by the Edinburgh crime writer Ian Rankin begins with a description of a typically bleak family funeral. 'In place of a closing hymn there was music. The Who's "Love Reign O'er Me."' The only warm part of Rankin's description is that the minister reminds the mourners of their invitation to refreshments in a local hotel.[20]

Until recently, blinds were drawn on the day of the funeral, not only in the deceased's house but also in those of immediate neighbours. Men would lift their hats or caps as the cortege passed, and this still happens even in cities. Some funeral directors still keep a horse-drawn hearse for families who request it, and the practice of the funeral director walking from the house for a few hundred yards, top hat in hand, in front of the motor hearse appears to have been reintroduced recently. The funeral director also leads the cortege along the driveway of the crematorium, or on the road within the cemetery.

A variety of Churches

The majority of Scots would claim some kind of allegiance to the national Church, even if only at the time of a death in the family. But there are large numbers of Roman Catholics, both in areas (mainly in the Western Islands and West Highlands, and parts of Speyside) where the Reformation was relatively ineffective and in the industrial lowlands. In seventeenth-century Roman Catholic funerals, a crucifix was placed on the coffins. Action was taken by the magistrates in Aberdeen against men who painted crucifixes, and some Catholics were buried in abandoned medieval chapels. 'When a (certain) noble lady died Gilbert Blakhal blessed earth to put on each side of her in the coffin and thus did privately bury her in her chest with Catholick ceremonies' before the public funeral took place.[21]

In current Roman Catholic practice, the coffin may be received in the church on the evening before the funeral (although this custom has recently become less common). After Requiem Mass, at which the homily emphasizes faith in the resurrection and when a family member may give a eulogy, the coffin is taken for burial or, increasingly, since permission was granted in 1963, for cremation. There is usually a detachable crucifix in the crematorium chapel. In the cities there are undertakers who deal mainly with Catholic clients and at least one Catholic cemetery in each. Many older Roman Catholic churches also have their own cemeteries.

This is also true of older Episcopalian Churches. After the settlement of 1690 when Presbyterianism was established, the Scottish Episcopal Church remained strong in Aberdeenshire, Edinburgh and elsewhere, and has grown significantly since the lifting of penal sanctions in the late eighteenth century.

> The distinctive feature of the Episcopalian funerals in the north-east was the 'chestings'[22] on the evening before the funeral, in the presence of a few women. A lighted candle was placed beside the corpse and a plate of salt was placed on the breast. This evening service (usually from the Book of Common Prayer) was distinctive because the Presbyterians had no service at a funeral, and their ministers did not attend funerals. The saying of prayers at the graveside was unknown (hence the prayers the night before), and its introduction by Episcopalians caused a great stir in country areas.[23]

Gradually funeral services in the church became the norm, and ceremonies such as aspersing the coffin are used in 'high' churches.

In the seventeenth century the Society of Friends attained some strength and notoriety in Scotland, especially in the north-east. They wanted no part of the established church and in Aberdeen in 1671 they challenged accepted custom by rejecting the idea of consecrated ground for burial and opened their own burial space. The affronted authorities exhumed the body – of a child – and reburied it in a churchyard. The walls of the Quaker graveyard were pulled down and rebuilt six times in the next five years. Quakers were seen to be robbing the kirk of burial dues as well as separating themselves from the Burgh Corporation. There is a Quaker burial ground lovingly maintained at Kinmuck, near Inverurie, and the Aberdeen meeting has a continuous history from 1663.[24]

The small Jewish community in Scotland had its own cemeteries. There is a tiny one in Edinburgh, and in 1831 a plot in the Glasgow Necropolis, big enough for 51 interments, was purchased for 100 guineas. At this time there were 47 Jews in Glasgow.[25] Later, areas of public cemeteries have been used, and the stones are notable for standing close together. Other ethnic communities, growing in number in recent years, especially in the lowlands, continue their own burial practices, although a plan for a crematorium at the Samye Ling Tibetan Monastery in Dumfriesshire aroused great local opposition in the 1980s. The beliefs of the Chinese communities remain largely private, although the practice of burning paper money at the graveside has been observed in Edinburgh.[26]

At a time when many young people were dying of HIV/AIDS some creative liturgies were evolved, using music, art and artefacts. The release of doves, mourners wearing bright clothes and an almost festal air transformed the image of the dour Scottish funeral. One firm of funeral directors, asked to dress their attendants as clowns, demurred on the grounds that this would lower the standard of dignity for which they were justly acclaimed. One result is the insertion in death notices of injunctions for those attending not to wear dark clothes. In country areas and in urban housing schemes, however, black clothes are still the norm.

There are several woodland cemeteries for ecological burials, and these are increasingly being used. This contrasts with the increasing elaboration mentioned above. Gravestones with photographs of the deceased, pictures of cars or ships, and many surrounding ornaments have displaced stone angels, broken columns and other more traditional funerary architecture. The great Glasgow Necropolis above the cathedral is a monument to the prosperity of Glasgow merchants in the nineteenth century and is fittingly crowned with a statue of the Reformer John Knox.[27] Mortuary chapels in cemeteries where services could be held before burials are extremely rare. The only one known to the author is in the Western Cemetery in Arbroath (1875–1880), with spiky exterior and suffocatingly massive interior.[28]

Roadside and mountaintop shrines have recently become widespread. Bunches of flowers wrapped in cellophane, school scarves, football insignia and occasionally lanterns mark the spot where someone, often a young person, has died in a car or climbing accident. Most remain for a few weeks, but some are carefully maintained for much longer, and memorials on such peaks as Ben Nevis have led to local controversy. Memorial plaques or seats in public gardens are probably more useful, although the Royal Botanical Garden in Edinburgh has put a temporary stop to the practice, pending review, and recently signs of remembrance such as bunches of flowers and teddy bears which have been placed in public parks in South Lanarkshire are being removed because of complaints by other park users.[29] Perhaps, as overt religious practice recedes, new ways of remembering the dead will take its place. Instead of a service of remembrance or a gravestone with a biblical text, there is a shrine to visit – and to provide a warning.

As in the rest of the United Kingdom, funeral practices in Scotland are changing quite rapidly, influenced by the movement of population – which results in a dilution of local customs – and by the media. Even in country places, where there is space in churchyards, cremation is becoming more common as families move in who have no roots in the area. Clergy are still called upon for the great majority of funerals, and the personalization of services is increasingly expected, with the deceased rather than the mourners taking centre stage. The elaborate hospitality before and after the burial that characterized older Scottish funerals has declined, but the proper conduct of a crematorium or graveside service remains a touchstone of ministerial competence and humanity.

Notes

1 The best introduction to Scottish funeral customs is Anne Gordon, *Death is for the Living*, Edinburgh: Paul Harris, 1984. See also Anne Gordon, *Candie for the Foundling*, Bishop Auckland: Pentland Press, 1992; and Margaret Bennett, *Scottish Customs: From the Cradle to the Grave*, 2nd edn, Edinburgh: Birlinn, 2004. For an excellent short guide to archaeological issues with graveyards, see Betty Willsher, *Understanding Scottish Graveyards* 2nd edn, Edinburgh: Canongate Press, 1995.

2 For a good account of the localities of Scotland, see Robin Smith, *The Making of Scotland: A Comprehensive Guide to the Growth of Scotland's Cities, Towns and Villages*, Edinburgh: Canongate, 2001.

3 Gordon Donaldson, 'Reformation to Covenant' in Duncan B. Forrester and Douglas M. Murray (eds), *Studies in the History of Worship in Scotland*, Edinburgh: T&T Clark, 1984, pp. 33–51.

4 John Knox, *Works*, vol. 2, ed. David Laing, Edinburgh: Wodrow Society, 1868, pp. 249–51.

5 A. L. Drummond and J. Bulloch, *The Church in Victorian Scotland 1843–1874*, Edinburgh: The St Andrew Press, 1975, p. 195. Since the publication of this book the last Glasite or Sandemanian Meeting has closed, in 1999, and so this primitive Presbyterian custom is probably no longer observed, even by Free Presbyterians.

6 Andrew Spicer, 'Defyle not Christ's Kirk with your Carrion' in Bruce Gordon and Peter Marshall (eds), *The Place of the Dead: Death and Remem-*

brance in Late Medieval and Early Modern Europe, Cambridge: Cambridge University Press, 2000, pp. 149–69.

7 There is much detail on these matters in the writings of Anne Gordon, *Death Is for the Living, Candie for the Foundling* and *Death and Associated Customs* Part 1:7 *The Individual and Community Life: A Compendium of Scottish Ethnology,* Edinburgh: John Donald, 2005.

8 Ian Shepherd, *Gordon: An Illustrated Architectural Guide,* Edinburgh: The Rutland Press, 1994, p. 137.

9 Shepherd, *Gordon,* p. 123.

10 Personal communication from the Revd D. A. Ross.

11 *Acts of the Parliament of Scotland,* VIII 1686, 598, quoted in Anne Gordon, *Death and Associated Customs,* p. 104.

12 Legal note: whereas in most circumstances in England and Wales a certificate for burial or cremation must be obtained from the Registrar before burial or cremation, in Scotland a body may be buried (but normally not cremated) before the death is registered. See *Whitaker's Scottish Almanac,* London: Whitakers, 2003, p. 157.

13 The Funeral of the Duke of Buccleuch on 11 September 2007 drew 2,500 mourners to the ruins of Melrose Abbey. See *The Scotsman,* 12 September 2007.

14 Henry R. Sefton, 'Occasions in the Reformed Church' in Colin MacLean and Kenneth Veitch (eds), *Scottish Life and Society: A Compendium of Scottish Ethnology,* vol. 12, Edinburgh: John Donald, 2006, pp. 469–8.

15 Information from local joiner-undertaker in Aberdeenshire. See chapters by Dent, Cobb and Rogers, this volume.

16 See Kellaher, this volume.

17 See Parsons, this volume.

18 See Cobb and Hilborn, this volume.

19 See Jupp, chapter 2, this volume.

20 Ian Rankin, *The Naming of the Dead,* London: Orion, 2006, p. 5.

21 Mark Dilworth OSB, 'Roman Catholic Worship' in Forrester and Murray (eds), *Studies in the History of Worship in Scotland,* p. 119. For a vivid description of a funeral of a member of an old Catholic family in the late eighteenth century, see Sir Walter Scott, *The Antiquary* (first published 1816), London: Nelson's Classics Edition, n.d., pp. 295ff.

22 Allan Maclean, 'Episcopalianism' in MacLean and Veitch, *Religion,* pp. 191–234. 'Chesting' is an alternative form of 'kisting'.

23 Maclean , 'Episcopalianism', p. 204.

24 Michael Lynch and Gordon DeBrisay, with Murray Pittock, 'The Faith of the People' in E. P. Denison, D. Ditchburn and M. Lynch (eds), *Aberdeen before 1800: A New History,* East Linton: Tuckwell Press, 2002, p. 305.

25 K. Collins, 'The Jews in Scotland', in MacLean and Veitch, *Scottish Life and Society,* pp. 256–80.

26 Personal observation.

27 Ronnie Scott, *Death by Design,* Edinburgh: Black and White, 2005, gives a full description of this extraordinary place.

28 M. Glendinning, R. MacInnes and A. MacKechnie (eds), A *History of Scottish Architecture,* Edinburgh: Edinburgh University Press, 1997, p. 281.

29 BBC Radio 4, *You and Yours,* 22 August 2007.

22

Funeral Ministry in Wales

KEITH DENISON

Introduction

It may be thought that the title of this chapter is an oxymoron: that funeral ministry in Wales is, or should be, no different from funeral ministry in England, except, perhaps, in the Welsh-speaking heartlands of north-west and south-west Wales. Language is, of course, one distinguishing characteristic (though not, as we shall see, one that applies only to those areas already mentioned); but it is by no means the only one. This chapter will, therefore, attempt to identify some of the key areas of both similarity and dissimilarity between the two countries which influence the exercise of funeral ministry.[1]

Welsh church disestablishment and church burial grounds

Attention must first turn to the fact that, whereas the Church of England remains the Church by law established in England itself, the (then) four Welsh Dioceses of the Church of England in Wales were disestablished and disendowed under the terms of the Welsh Church Act of 1914. Because of the outbreak of World War One, implementation of this Act, along with other domestic legislation, was deferred by the Suspensory Act 1914; and its provisions were subsequently significantly modified by an Amending Act, the Welsh Church Temporalities Act 1919. It was not until 31 March 1920 that the Welsh Church Act finally came into force, and the Church in Wales was then effectively constituted as an autonomous Province of the Anglican Communion, with its own archbishop (elected from among the diocesan bishops), its own form of synodical government (the Governing Body of the Church in Wales), and its own Constitution. Soon afterwards, two new Dioceses – Monmouth (1921) and Swansea and Brecon (1923) – were created out of the ancient Sees of Llandaff and St David's respectively.[2]

The Welsh Church Act provided that only those burial grounds which derived from private donation, and those which were already closed to new burials, should pass to the Representative Body of the Church in Wales. This body had been established to hold such church property as had not otherwise been alienated from the new Province under the terms of the Act. All other church burial grounds were to be vested in the relevant local authorities – although the Amending Act of 1919 provided that local authorities could decline to accept such burial grounds unless the Home Secretary should direct otherwise.

Welsh Nonconformists had attached great importance to this proposed transfer. They had long resented Anglican control over what were, in many places, the only available burial grounds. Since the seventeenth century, some of the older Nonconformist denominations, notably the *Annibynwyr* (Welsh Independents), Baptists and the Society of Friends, had been providing a few burial grounds. As Murray notes of the parallel development in Scotland,[3] these were provided because of the principled rejection of the very notion of consecrated ground. But they were few and far between. Hence, alienating the graveyard from the control of the church authorities had long been viewed as one of the great prizes to be gained by Nonconformists in Wales from the disestablishment and disendowment of the Church of England in Wales.

In practice, however, most local authorities were reluctant to take advantage of this provision. By 1934, of the 919 burial grounds which had passed to the hands of the Welsh Church Commissioners for them to transfer to the care of local authorities, only 149 transfers had actually been effected. One likely reason is that so many additions to the ancient burial grounds had been made by private benefaction that the local authorities would have found themselves holding disconnected parcels of land. In other cases, especially in the more rural parishes, burial grounds and their upkeep would have been disproportionately expensive for the ratepayers, because of the rare occurrence of funerals and the concomitant absence of an income stream to help offset the costs.

After several abortive attempts to address these anomalies, the Welsh Church (Burial Grounds) Act 1945 empowered the Commissioners to transfer to the Representative Body those burial grounds which local authorities had declined to accept. This transfer was effected in the following year. The 1945 Act virtually re-enacted those conditions which had pertained to the use of burial grounds prior to disestablishment. All persons residing in the parish, and those dying in the parish, have a legal right to burial in their parish burial ground; and no discrimination may ordinarily be made between the burial of a member of the Church in Wales, and that of any other person. Roman Catholic clergy, Nonconformist ministers and secular celebrants have the legal right to officiate at the graveside without the presence of the Anglican parish priest, though not, of course, to use the parish church itself for a service. In such cases, churchyard fees must still be paid to the Churchyard Maintenance Fund. In practice, where other ministers or clergy officiate at the graveside, the Anglican parish priest is usually invited to attend and assist.

One unforeseen consequence of this particular historical development in Wales is that, whereas in England local authorities can be required by law to take responsibility for closed churchyards, no such provision applies in Wales. The maintenance of closed churchyards is expensive, and they may also pose significant health and safety risks. The Representative Body of the Church in Wales has tried repeatedly to secure an amendment to the law to achieve parity with the Church of England in this regard, but local authorities are understandably reluctant, and success therefore remains elusive.

Under the rules made by the Representative Body of the Church in Wales pursuant to section 4(2) of the 1945 Act,[4] the time for a funeral must be arranged with the incumbent, and adequate notice must be given. No interment may take place at the same time as a scheduled service in the adjoining church building, or on a Sunday, Good Friday or Christmas Day 'except in cases of emergency certified as such by a coroner or a registered medical practitioner' (Rules 5 and 6). The associated Churchyard Regulations provide that 'the Incumbent shall be responsible for the general supervision of all churchyards in the parish and for the allocation of grave spaces'. The incumbent's consent is also required before any gravestone or memorial tablet can be admitted into the churchyard, and to the wording of any inscription; and the prescribed fees for these must be paid.

Regulations are precise about the maximum permitted size of any headstone, slab or ledger stone, and about the siting of graves in relation to the fabric of the church and to the churchyard boundary. However, although they prescribe 'a simple and appropriate inscription', or 'an appropriate motif', they give no guidance as to what these expressions might or might not cover. There is, therefore, ample scope for disagreement between the incumbent and the families or executors of the deceased on such issues, though pastoral sensitivity ensures that a compromise acceptable to both parties can generally be reached. However, should the incumbent decline to approve a gravestone or an inscription, application may be made to the archdeacon, who may override the incumbent's discretion. Alternatively, Faculty procedure may be invoked, which in principle could override any or all of the limitations laid down by the regulations; but this is a rare occurrence.

The 1945 Act also gave the Home Secretary (subsequently the Secretary of State for Wales, and now, under devolved arrangements, the National Assembly of Wales) the power to determine fees for burials in churchyards, and for headstones and memorials. These fees remain somewhat lower than corresponding fees in England, though the disparity is not as great as it once was. The Church in Wales might be disestablished, but it remains subject to the control of the state in significant respects!

A universal ministry?

As already noted, despite disestablishment, all parishioners in Wales, as in England, retain the legal right to burial in their parish churchyard, where this exists, and where there remain available grave spaces. In parallel with this right on the part of their parishioners, incumbents have a corresponding duty to provide a ministry to all the bereaved families within their parishes. This underlines the important truth that whether the Church was established by law or not, its clergy were still instituted and inducted into the cure of souls of all who lived within their parish boundaries, and so had a pastoral responsibility towards them, whether they themselves wished to be ministered to or not.

In practice, of course, there were, and are, severe limits to such a universal ministry. Partly these concern the physical capacity of the clergy to minister effectively in large and populous parishes – some urban parishes contain in excess of 20,000 people, and some rural parishes cover a vast geographical area; partly they relate to the declining numbers of stipendiary clergy, with a planned reduction from 650 to 450 (by 'natural wastage') over the next few years, and with those clerics who remain having to undertake responsibility for ministry to ever larger groupings of parishes. To some extent, these burdens will be mitigated by an increasing reliance on the ministry of non-stipendiary clerics, and by a move towards using licensed Readers to exercise a funeral ministry. Each diocese is responsible for providing appropriate training to equip non-stipendiary ministers and Readers for this, but the quality of such training remains variable.

More generally, limits are imposed by the would-be recipients of such a ministry. Ever since, ironically, it achieved its long-desired objective of the disestablishment and disendowment of what it had dismissively termed 'the alien Church' or 'the English Church', historic Welsh Nonconformity has been in long-term decline, mirroring the general decline in formal religious allegiance across the United Kingdom as a whole. In much of Wales, it is now only the Church in Wales which retains a ministerial presence – or, indeed, any physical presence at all. Even so, over large areas of the country, a residual attachment to 'the chapel' remains, and inevitably re-surfaces at times of bereavement; while in urban areas, 'Free Churches' (really a misnomer in Wales, of course, where all Churches are disestablished!) are still strong in some areas. In addition, Pentecostal and other newer ('New Life' and similar) churches are having a growing presence, especially in the cities and larger towns, at the expense both of the Church in Wales and of historic Nonconformity. It remains rare, however, for there to be anything approaching interchangeability of ministries in response to the pastoral demands of funeral ministry, though canon law in the Church in Wales does allow for this.

As yet, other world faiths have a limited presence in Wales. Numbers of practising Jews, Sikhs, Hindus and Buddhists are small, and their places of worship few and far between. Growing immigrant communities from Pakistan, Bangladesh, Somalia and the Middle East have led to a significant Muslim presence in the cities and a few other areas, but these still account for only between five and eight per cent of the population even in these localities.

A much greater challenge is the increasing secularization of Wales. Both the historic and the newer Churches have to face the reality that though there may be a residual attachment to Christianity by a majority of the population, church membership, however that may be defined, means little to most people in today's Wales. Although most funerals are still conducted by clergy and ministers of the historic Christian denominations, the number of those conducted by secular celebrants, Humanists or members of the Institute of Civil Funerals, or where there is no celebrant at all, are growing and seem likely to grow further. There is little evidence as yet that clergy and ministers, or their bishops or other church leaders, are taking this challenge as seriously as they should, or that ministerial training is an adequate preparation for funeral ministry in such a changing society. This could well prove to be a serious miscalculation, with both financial and pastoral consequences, as Derek Murray also notes in his chapter on the characteristics of Scottish funerals (pp. 228–9).

Christian funerals in Wales today

All Christian Churches, whether they have a strong liturgical tradition or not, in practice have a clear and common format for funeral services. This comprises hymns, Bible readings, homily and/or eulogy, and prayers, followed by commendation and committal of the deceased. For Roman Catholics and Anglicans, there may also be a funeral Eucharist. But in Wales as elsewhere, there is increasing pressure to personalize funerals, including the introduction of articles and artefacts with a particular relevance to the deceased; tributes by family members, friends and colleagues; the use of secular readings alongside the scriptural readings; and the playing of secular (usually, though not always, recorded) music before and/or after the funeral. That last subject is covered in some depth by Brian Parsons.[5] He quotes Tony Walter as pointing out that 'When all else fails, there is music, for it can speak the unspeakable' though, as he adds later in that chapter, this undoubtedly 'brings challenges' for funeral celebrants as for others professionally involved in the process of disposal. Some clergy are happy to adapt, and may indeed enthusiastically embrace the concept of personalization. Others are less willing to accommodate themselves to what they perceive as the secularization of what is, or should be, an essentially sacred event.

The tension becomes particularly apparent, for example, at the funeral of a young person, or of a committed rugby player or supporter. The risk of alienating a whole generation within the community is quite real where the funeral celebrant refuses to accede to the bereaved family's wishes. There remains in Wales a strong sense of community which especially manifests itself at a funeral, as Hugh James notes in *A Fitting End*[6] which the editor of this volume commends in his introduction. A Welsh funeral is very much a community event, where solidarity is shown with the deceased and the bereaved. The community may no longer be a geographical community, though very often it still is – there is a strong sense of place in Wales.

For example, in Newport's docks parish, St Stephen's, Pillgwenlly, where I am often asked to assist, funerals regularly attract several hundred mourners who once worked at the docks or lived in the parish and who have long since moved away; they return faithfully for the funeral of a deceased former colleague or neighbour. Equally, the funeral of a Welsh farmer will be attended by others in the farming community from far and wide. In such cases the community is tightly knit, and there is a particular burden on the funeral celebrant: get it wrong, and a whole community will be offended, and may well look elsewhere for funeral ministry and for wider pastoral care and any sense of religious identity.

At the same time, the officiant has to take great care to retain both personal integrity and faithfulness to the Christian tradition. It must never be a case of 'anything goes'. For example, there might be no self-evidently inherent problem about agreeing to the siting of a rugby scarf or cap, or a teddy bear or some other soft toy, on or near the coffin during the funeral service in church; but, clearly, there are articles which would be wholly inappropriate (for example, a swastika flag) and the funeral celebrant must exercise due diligence. Again, much music requested may be wholly unexceptionable, but some will be highly questionable, and the right of veto may need to be exercised. Above all, anything must be eschewed which detracts from the central function of a Christian funeral: to give thanks to God for a life which has been given by him; to commend the departed into God's keeping in the light of the Christian doctrine of the resurrection of the dead; and to express sympathy and solidarity with the bereaved. Inevitably, lines will sometimes be crossed, but these lines exist and should be recognized and respected. It is the duty of those exercising funeral ministry to clarify where those lines are, and, in particular, to ensure that funeral directors fully understand them and will co-operate with the funeral celebrant in avoiding confusion about those boundaries on the part of the bereaved.

Having said that funerals are a focal point for community meeting, this is not necessarily so in all cases. In Wales as elsewhere, older community loyalties are gradually dissolving, as Hugh James has noted in *A Fitting End*. This presents particular difficulties for the exercise of funeral ministry. The priest or other minister may well find it difficult to meet the immediate family before the day of the funeral, because they are geographically dispersed and only come together for the funeral itself. Added to that are the complications arising from family breakdown; in some cases, conflicting directions come from different groupings within the family. Again, people increasingly belong to a variety of non-geographical communities, which, although they may come together at a funeral, find that they have nothing in common except knowledge of the deceased – and that knowledge only partial. The officiant in such cases has a difficult balancing act, and might find it hard indeed to satisfy the expectations of all the interested parties.

In all of this, it is necessary to add that custom and practice vary across the diverse communities that co-exist and overlap in Wales, as they do elsewhere. Hugh James has drawn attention to a range of local peculiarities in Wales, such as the differentiation in parts of west Wales between public, private and strictly private funerals; the practice of the 'following', where a deceased's family might attend the main Sunday service at the church or chapel where the funeral had taken place, remaining seated throughout; the custom in some former mining valley communities in south Wales of 'men only' funerals, where the women stay at home to prepare the refreshments; and the strongly entrenched practice of dressing graves with a profusion of colourful flowers on Palm Sunday (*Sul y Blodau* or Flowering Sunday), though I would add here that this is not confined, as James suggests, to Welsh-speaking areas, but is as enthusiastically practised in parishes along the English border, both north and south.

Cremation in Wales

In the history of funeral practice in the United Kingdom, the nineteenth-century pioneer, Dr Price of Pontypridd, has a special place as the father of the modern cremation movement, as Hilary Grainger has noted.[7] Even so, the progress of cremation as against burial in Wales was rather slower than over the English side of the border, partly because of the rurality of much of Wales and the significant distances entailed in travelling to crematoria, but largely, I suspect, more positively, because of continuing attachment to the local burial ground as the focus for family and community memory. More people are now cremated than buried, but it remains a smaller proportion in Wales than in England.

In *The Book of Common Prayer of the Church in Wales, Volume II,*[8] a rubric indicates that where cremated remains are to be buried in consecrated ground, cremation may take place without a formal service. This allows the major liturgical celebration, especially the Eucharist, to take place immediately before the burial of ashes. But disposal must be by burial, not scattering; the prayer book contains the unambiguous prohibition on the participation of the clergy of the Church in Wales in the scattering of ashes, nor may they allow scattering in the churchyard.[9] This is reinforced by the Churchyard Regulations, breach of which would be actionable in the Courts of the Church in Wales. The prohibition of scattering reminds us that the integrity of the body has a doctrinal significance for Christians, a subject covered extensively by Douglas Davies above.[10] And, as Kevin McGinnell notes,[11] 'the act of burial becomes deeply symbolic' – whether the burial be of an intact corpse or of that corpse's cremated remains. The credal affirmation of belief in the resurrection of the body could be seen to be undermined by the practice of scattering. Insistence on burial of the remains upholds the principle that the body should be returned to the earth ('earth to earth, ashes to ashes, dust to dust'). Even following cremation, therefore, the primary significance of burial is retained, and there is a strong presumption in Welsh Faculty jurisdiction against any subsequent removal of cremated remains. Their place of burial is seen as their final resting place, and that remains the case even if the grave space is subsequently reused.

In this matter, as in so much else, the Church in Wales' position mirrors that of the Roman Catholic Church. For Nonconformist and secular funeral celebrants there are no such restrictions. With funerals conducted by them, cremated remains may be scattered or strewed rather than buried, and often they will be divided into portions, and left at places which were significant in the life of the deceased, such as favourite walks, mountaintops, riverbanks, or sporting venues. However, disposal of cremated remains in this fashion is more likely to be a family-only affair, with no involvement by the person who officiated at the funeral.

A bilingual Wales

The reality of today's Wales is that it is now officially and in practice a bilingual country. The number of Welsh language speakers is growing steadily as a result both of Welsh Assembly Government policy and of a growing awareness, especially among the professional middle classes, of the advantages of bilingualism, for example in securing employment in government or the media. So the irony is that, despite increasing erosion of the Welsh-speaking heartlands of north and west Wales caused by English in-migration, the numbers of Welsh speakers in the traditionally Anglicized areas of south-east Wales are growing steadily. Even in Monmouthshire, there are now two Welsh-medium primary schools, and Cardiff, the Welsh capital, has ten such schools, with demand growing year on year.

All this means, of course, that anyone exercising a funeral ministry almost anywhere in Wales will, sooner or later, encounter the need to conduct a funeral wholly or partly through the medium of Welsh. The Church in Wales, like most other Christian denominations, has officially embraced a bilingual policy, and the bereaved are entitled to a ministry which respects their linguistic identity. As Hugh James[12] points out, linguistic differences may overlay cultural differences, and it is not always simply a matter of using the appropriate language. Any Anglican priest or Methodist minister moving from England to Wales needs to be aware of this linguistic and cultural context – and to remember that Welsh is a core National Curriculum subject in all maintained schools in Wales (a particularly relevant consideration if they have children who are, or will be, of statutory school age).

Wales is different from England in many respects. But it is perhaps her distinctive language which is one of her most defining characteristics. Funeral ministry in Wales is by no means the same as funeral ministry in England, Scotland or Ireland.

Notes

1 See also K. M. Denison, 'The Theology and Liturgy of Funerals: A View from the Church in Wales', *Mortality*, Vol. 4, No. 1, 1999, pp. 63–74.

2 The major historical and legal sources for this chapter are: P. M. H. Bell, *Disestablishment in Ireland and Wales*, London: SPCK, 1969; *The Constitution of the Church in Wales*, Cardiff: The Governing Body of the Church in Wales, n.d.; and D. Walker (ed.), *A History of the Church in Wales*, Penarth: Church in Wales Publications, 1976.

3 See Murray, this volume.

4 *The Constitution of the Church in Wales.*

5 See Parsons, this volume.

6 H. James, *A Fitting End: Making the Most of a Funeral*, Norwich: The Canterbury Press, 2004.

7 See Grainger, this volume.

8 *The Book of Common Prayer for use in the Church in Wales Vols I and II*, Penarth: Church in Wales Publications, 1984, p. 797.

9 For a fuller discussion, see Denison, 'The Theology and Liturgy of Funerals', pp. 71–2.

10 See Davies, this volume.

11 See McGinnell, this volume.

12 James, *A Fitting End*.

23

Funerals in Northern Ireland

GODFREY BROWN

Introduction

For a lifetime Northern Ireland has hit the headlines for all the wrong reasons. The Province is made up of the six north-eastern counties which remained part of the United Kingdom after the rest of the island opted for independence in 1922. From the outset it has been a divided society with deeply held cultural, religious and political convictions. Northern Ireland's slender majority and sizeable minority have each feared the dominance of the other, and these fears and animosities have erupted from time to time into violence. In 1969 there broke out a period of bitter conflict known euphemistically as 'The Troubles', waged with brutal determination by various paramilitary groups. Thankfully the Troubles have now ended, and politicians from both extremes of the political spectrum have come together and are now trying to make the political settlement work. The vast majority of the people want their politicians to work together to establish a peaceful and prosperous society for all.

Paradoxically, alongside this deep division at the heart of society there has also been a strong tradition of local neighbourliness and mutual help that was especially evident in rural areas, but was also present in varying degrees in many parts of the community. This apparent contradiction is reflected in the funeral customs that go back over many generations. Catholics and Protestants in many places were good neighbours. They worked together and shared each other's joys and sorrows. They attended one another's wakes, and walked in procession in one another's funeral corteges. When they reached the church, however, they tended to stand outside, not wishing to take part in one another's religious ceremonies. This attitude had begun to break down in the years following World War Two, and has now almost totally disappeared.

Roman Catholic funerals

Roman Catholic funerals have always been conducted according to the rites of that Church. The long-established pattern remains: of prayers at the home, the taking of the body from the home to the church on the night before the funeral, the funeral Mass and prayers at the graveside. The Second Vatican Council has opened the door for greater flexibility regarding the funeral rites. The service is now in English, or in certain areas in Irish, and increasingly includes a homily in which, in the manner of the Protestant Churches, the priest will speak of the deceased and pay tribute to his or her qualities and character. From time to time family members and others may be invited to read or speak, or a simple tribute may be given by a friend at the grave. Where appropriate, some modern worship music may be included. As with all denominations in Northern Ireland, funerals tend to be held on the third day after the death, with a wake the night before, though that practice is weakening. The body is often visited by family and friends. The body is often at home throughout the pre-funeral period, but there is an increasing use of funeral parlours. The Roman Catholic Church now permits cremation. This will normally take place before the funeral Mass, at which the ashes will be present, prior to burial in the graveyard.

The Church of Ireland

The Church of Ireland (Anglican) was the established Church throughout Ireland until 1870. Its funeral services have always been those of the *Book of Common Prayer*. More recently this has been supplemented by *The Alternative Prayer Book* (1980) and now by the *Book of Common Prayer* (2004). Services are most frequently conducted in the home, in church or at the graveyard. Services in church may include some modern sacred music and family participation in the readings, but more secular elements will only be likely in a funeral parlour or at the crematorium. For generations the graveyard of the parish church was the burial ground for everyone in the community. In course of time, Catholics, Presbyterians and others acquired their own graveyards, while in the larger towns civic cemeteries were opened, sometimes with separate areas for Protestant and Catholic use.

The Presbyterian Church in Ireland

The largest Protestant denomination in Northern Ireland is the Presbyterian Church in Ireland. Its culture and ethos is strongly Ulster-Scot, and its worship is rooted in the Reformed tradition of the Church of Scotland. Many parallels may be drawn with Murray's account of the Scottish situation. The Scottish *Book of Common Order* (1564) followed closely *The Form of Prayers* (1556) of the English congregation in Geneva in discouraging formal ceremonies at the graveside, but allowing for the possibility of the minister exhorting the people after the burial about death and resurrection, probably in the church if it were nearby.[1] The *Westminster Directory for Public Worship* discouraged the practice of funeral services, and it would seem that in Scotland in the second half of the seventeenth century neither Episcopalian nor Presbyterian generally conducted them. In Dublin, the Revd Thomas Steward of Cook Street, writing to his mother on 26 April 1708, complained, 'Funeral sermons are quite out of fashion here. I never preached one since I came, so that I get nothing in that way.'[2]

Changing Presbyterian styles

It would appear, however, that customs were changing in Ireland by the early eighteenth century. In the fashionable Dublin congregation of Wood Street, its minister, the Revd Joseph Boyse, justified both prayer and preaching at funerals and the expression of a general hope of the resurrection of all good men,[3] and several examples of funeral sermons are included in his published works.[4] Nor was the custom restricted to Dublin, with its more English ethos. Memorial sermons were also preached in the north of Ireland, though more likely some days after the funeral was over.[5] Later in the century it was the custom for some congregations to own and rent out palls for the covering of coffins at funerals and black cloaks for the chief mourners.[6]

A recent study of Ulster Presbyterian belief and practice in the period 1770 to 1840 has shown how the influences both of romanticism and evangelicalism affected funeral practices. The popular expression of 'grief' in the customs surrounding wakes and the folk beliefs and superstitions associated with dying were a matter of considerable concern to church people of all denominations. For Presbyterians, however, the absence of clear guidelines as to how funerals were to be conducted meant it was not easy for them to reform such abuses.[7]

As the nineteenth century progressed, the general pattern of funeral services became more accepted. Only rarely were services held in church. The pattern was one of readings, exhortation and prayer, and perhaps the singing of a metrical psalm in the home and at the graveside. Preaching often tended to be evangelistic in its aim, exhorting the living to prepare for their own departure by repentance for sin and turning in faith to Christ. It was not until 1912, however, that the General Assembly approved the idea of producing a directory for public worship, and it was only in 1923, after much criticism and many difficulties, that *The Book of Public Worship* first appeared. In it was an order for a funeral service. A revised edition appeared in 1931, and a further revision in 1942 was the first to be published with the authority of the General Assembly. In less than a decade this book was out of print, and increasingly the seminal *Book of Common Order* of the Church of Scotland (1940) came to be used by a new generation of ministers. The influence of Professor John M. Barkley upon a generation of students, and the publication under his editorship of a new edition of *The Book of Public Worship* (1965), the most recent book to have the authority of the General Assembly, provided a form of service almost identical to that of the Church of Scotland as the norm for the conduct of Presbyterian funeral services. Later experimental revision in 1985 did little to alter its basic structure. Interestingly, it did provide a 'Service in the Church before a Funeral' for those few localities where the Catholic custom of bringing the body to church on the evening before the funeral had been adopted. Since the publication of the Church of Scotland *Book of Common Order* (1994) with its rich provision of scripture and prayer resources, Irish Presbyterians have made increasing use of it.

Most of the other Christian denominations have service books of their own, though in practice their funeral services have many things in common and tend to follow the customs and traditions that are prevalent in the areas where they find themselves.

Contemporary funerals

In the cities and larger towns some of the former traditions are no longer carried out. The demands of traffic and the introduction of stricter timing at cemeteries and the crematorium leave little room for walking and shouldering the coffin as of old. In many parts of the country, however, it is still the tradition for large numbers of people to attend the funeral, waiting outside the house while the service is conducted and then carrying the coffin and walking often a considerable distance to the church or churchyard. In at least one part of Co. Down it remains the custom for the body to remain uncoffined until immediately before the funeral service, a custom reminiscent of the 'kisting' custom in parts of Scotland.

Cremation practices

The practice of cremation is a relatively recent one in Northern Ireland. The one and only crematorium is situated just outside Belfast. It was opened in 1961 and has attracted a growing percentage of funerals, and especially from the greater Belfast area. It provides a well-appointed chapel capable of taking 100 worshippers and with other helpful facilities. Many families dispose of the ashes of their loved one there, perhaps arranging for a memorial tree to mark the spot. Others prefer to inter them in a family grave. Some churches offer a small area of their graveyard specially arranged for the burial of ashes. Other families prefer to scatter ashes at some favourite beauty spot, or arrange for their disposal at sea. It is estimated that in Northern Ireland almost 70 per cent of the population still prefer burial to cremation, almost the reverse of the situation in most other parts of the United Kingdom. In the greater Belfast area there is now an acute shortage of burial space, and obtaining a grave has become both difficult and costly.

Funeral ministry in 'The Troubles'

'The Troubles' brought about a new kind of quasi-public funeral, with families and communities compelled to bury their dead, often after some terrible atrocity, in the full glare of media publicity.

The present writer, both in his role as a parish minister and also during his time as Moderator of the General Assembly, found himself involved in funerals of this kind. It was the practice of the main Churches in Northern Ireland to be represented at all such funerals by the appropriate church leader, bishop, moderator or president. It was a demanding task, especially as one feared being an intruder in the intense pain and tragedy of widows and orphans at such a time. The value of such a ministry however was undoubted. The local minister was often himself under deep emotional stress, sharing in the grief of people whom he knew well and wanting to concentrate on his pastoral role to them and to the wider community.

It was the church leader's task to minister to the minister, and to remove from the local minister the burden of coping with the media, and of saying the more public and 'political' things that needed to be said on such occasions from a Christian perspective. Particularly impressive were the many police funerals, always attended by the magnificent Royal Ulster Constabulary silver band. In addition to family grief, the grief of colleagues in full uniform was often palpable. The dignity and pageantry of such occasions was never intended to mask the horror of what had taken place.

Secular funerals

Northern Ireland for long remained the most churchgoing part of the United Kingdom, and probably still remains so to this day. Nevertheless, it is a fact that a great many people have given up on church, and no longer regularly attend. Growing secularization has affected people's attitudes to dying and to the way in which funerals are conducted. A few may opt for a totally secular funeral, with some favourite music, some words of tribute from a family member or a friend, a poem or some reading such as those on offer from the British Humanist Association. Many more still seek the services of the Churches, either requesting the help of the local minister or priest or using the services of an officiant whom they know. Many funeral directors have a pool of retired ministers to whom they turn to take a service as required. For the churches themselves, such funerals provide an area of encounter with people who may have drifted from church and are an opportunity to minister to them sensitively, listening to their requests and trying so far as possible to help them find appropriate ways of expressing their sorrow and love, and of encountering the love of God in Christ. Some clergy feel completely unable to cope with demands that upset their normal way of doing things, and some of the things they are asked to do are clearly unhelpful and inappropriate. Careful thinking is needed to decide what are the essentials in a funeral service and what are those areas where a more flexible approach may helpfully open doors of opportunity.

Lay participation

Increasingly today funerals are being held in church, or in one of the many 'funeral churches' provided by funeral directors.[8] It has also become common for family members to take some part in the service –

a Bible reading, a poem, or a song, or even a full-scale tribute to their loved one. Sometimes at the grave, flowers will be dropped on top of the coffin by the family. In place of the numerous wreaths that were given at funerals in a previous generation, many families will now request donations in lieu of flowers for a favourite charity, or a local church, or some other worthwhile project. It will often fall to the undertaker, or to the local minister, to receive such donations and pass them on to the appropriate beneficiary, as well as provide the family with a list of those who have given.

Another custom of recent times has been the erection of local shrines at the roadside to mark the spot where someone died as a result of a murder or a road accident. What began as a pile of flowers spontaneously placed there will often result in a small monument bedecked with flowers, and sometimes with little regard for planning regulations or the wishes of local residents. At a time when the design of graves and the layout of cemeteries are being more regulated, such local shrines are seen as a right and are expressions of the postmodern spirit of individualism.

Celebrity funerals

The funeral of Princess Diana in 1997 was a new phenomenon in the expression of public grief. Northern Ireland has had its own share of such public outpourings of community adulation and sorrow. One such was the death of Joey Dunlop, a local motorcycle road racing hero, who was killed in Estonia on 2 July 2000. His body was brought home to his native town of Ballymoney in Co. Antrim and buried at Garryduff Presbyterian Church. It was a state funeral in everything but name, and was attended by government ministers from Belfast, London and Dublin. It is estimated that 50,000 people accompanied his coffin up the road from where he had lived to the church. The local custom of a family service in the home, followed by a walk from there to the church, was faithfully observed. The service itself was in many ways a traditional service, conducted by the Revd John Gilkinson, the family's minister, and the Revd John Kirkpatrick, his former minister and a fellow motorbike fan. Traditional Christian hymns were sung. Additional elements included a tribute from Bob McMillan, General Manager of Honda Racing UK, who had worked closely with him, and a poem to 'Daddy' composed and read by his daughter Donna.[9]

The other such occasion was quite different in character. It was the funeral of George Best, the legendary football star who died on 25 November 2005. His was in every sense a state funeral! It was held not in a church but in the great hall of the Parliament Buildings at Stormont in Belfast. At the family home there was a service. The journey from his home through the main thoroughfares of the city and up the long processional drive to Stormont was attended by enormous crowds. It was estimated that between 75,000 and 100,000 were there. Constantly flowers and football shirts were thrown onto the hearse. The service itself was attended by some of the biggest names in football. The 300 invited guests included the Secretary of State for Northern Ireland, the Chief Constable and leading figures from every section of the community. A small part in the service was taken by a church pastor, but the ceremony was essentially secular in character. It included a poem from a woman in Belfast read by his son, Callum, and contributions from his sister Barbara and from his surgeon, Professor Roger Williams. School choirs, Belfast singers Brian Kennedy and Peter Cory and others took part. Everything was done to perfection, and was relayed on large screens to the crowds outside, as well as being broadcast live on television. Later the funeral procession set off to the family grave where George Best was buried with his mother.

Such services remind us of the fact that people need to find ways appropriate to them to express their sense of shock and grief when overtaken by tragedy and sorrow. Christians will turn to God, and seek the help and comfort of worship and the promises of scriptures to find the strength they need. Those of different faiths will seek the comfort their religion offers. Clearly, we must seek to help those without faith to find what inner strength and peace they may in their hour of need.

Christian funeral ministry today

The Christian conviction is that the true hope of the human spirit is to be found in Christ, in his words of promise, and especially in his death on Calvary and his resurrection victory over death. We long to share this hope sensitively and sincerely as we are given opportunity to do so. This includes respecting the wishes of those who do not want a Christian funeral. It may also mean finding a way of comforting those Christians within a family circle who may feel excluded by the choice of a secular ceremony.

In a growingly secular society, the challenge of pastoral care becomes increasingly complex, and depends on the willingness of those concerned to receive ministry. The essence of good ministry in the time of death and through the trauma of bereavement is to keep close to those to whom we minister, while taking care not to be overly intrusive.

People nearing death need to be helped to talk through their situation and to reflect upon their life journey, sharing their hopes and fears and finding ways to cope with practical concerns and the unfinished business that often weighs upon them when they know that time is short. Good pastoral care will want to help them on a spiritual journey, discovering the unconditional love of God, and assuring them of his grace and forgiveness, no matter how estranged from God they may feel themselves to be.

The minister will also be involved with the family in the planning of the funeral and, not least, of the funeral address. It has long been the present writer's custom to reproduce copies of this in an attractive format, and to take them to the home soon after the funeral for family members to read and reflect upon, and to pass on to others. It is important to remain in touch with the bereaved in the months ahead, provided they are open to such visits. The long tradition of close pastoral relationships in all the Christian denominations in Northern Ireland makes it natural to do this, and to extend it to others who have lost connection with a local congregation. In Northern Ireland society, there are many families who still remain open to the sensitive care of the Church at such a time.

At the height of the Troubles, politicians and preachers were often heard to say that there was no such thing as 'Catholic tears' and 'Protestant tears'. Death and bereavement are experiences that transcend human differences. They are deeply human events that bring us face to face with the ultimate mysteries. As such, they present all who take funeral services with their most testing challenge, and one of their most valuable opportunities.

Notes

1 J. M. Barkley, 'Reformed', pp. 128–31 of entry on 'Burial' in J. G. Davies (ed.), *A New Dictionary of Liturgy and Worship*, London: SCM Press, 1986.

2 Cited in T. Witherow, *Historical and Literary Memorials, Vol I*, London and Belfast: Wm Mullan and Sons, 1979, p. 175.

3 Cited in R. Craghead, *An Answer to the Bishop of Derry's Second Admonition*, 1697, p. 134.

4 See, for example, the *Works of the Revd Joseph Boyse*, cited in T. Witherow,

Historical and Literary Memorials, Vol. I, p. 80.

5 For example, the Revd Samuel Haliday of First Belfast preached on *The Death of Mr Michael Bruce at Holywood 7th December 1735,* cited in Witherow, *Historical and Literary Memorials, Vol. I,* p. 266.

6 A. H. Dill and others, *A Short History of the Presbyterian Churches of Ballymoney, Co. Antrim,* Bradford and London: Percy Lund, Humphries and Co., Ltd, 1898, p. 25. This refers to the period 1730–1759. Similar articles are mentioned in connection with First and Second Belfast congregations.

7 Andrew R. Holmes, *The Shaping of Ulster Presbyterian Belief and Practice, 1770–1840,* Oxford: Oxford University Press, 2006, pp. 230–57.

8 A funeral church is where funeral directors provide a chapel on their own premises. This custom has come in quietly over the last 20 years and is very frequent now. Small funerals are often held in the rest room attached to the hospital mortuary.

9 A moving account of the funeral is given in Mac McDiarmid, *Joey Dunlop, His Authorised Biography,* Yeovil: Haynes Publishing, 2001, pp. 174–5.

Recommended Reading

Chapter 2: The Context of Christian Funeral Ministry Today

A. Billings, *Dying and Grieving: A Guide to Pastoral Ministry*, London: Hodder, 2002.

T. Cocke (ed.), *The Churchyards Handbook*, 4th edn, London: Church House Publishing, 2001.

D. Francis, L. Kellaher and G. Nyophytou, *The Secret Cemetery*, Oxford: Berg, 2005.

R. A. Horton, *Using Common Worship Funerals: A Practical Guide to the New Services*, London: Church House Publishing, 2000.

H. James, *A Fitting End: Making the Most of a Funeral*, Norwich: Canterbury Press, 2004.

Ministry of Justice, *Burial Law and Policy in the 21st Century*, London: Ministry of Justice, 2005.

P. C. Jupp, *From Dust to Ashes: The Development of Cremation in Britain*, Basingstoke: Macmillan Palgrave, 2006.

National Association of Funeral Directors, *Manual of Funeral Directing*, revised edn, Solihull: the National Association of Funeral Directors, 2007.

P. P. J. Sheppy, *Death Liturgy and Ritual, Volume 1: A Pastoral and Liturgical Theology*, Aldershot: Ashgate, 2003.

J. Thewlis, 'The difficult funeral', *Theology*, January 1997, pp. 2–9

T. Walter (ed.), *The Mourning for Diana*, Oxford: Berg, 1999.

J. W. Wilson, *Funerals without God*, 6th edn, London: British Humanist Association, 2006.

C. Worsley, 'From Death to Life: Pastoral Integrity and Funerals', *Theology*, May/June 1999, Vol. CII, No. 807, pp.202–9.

Chapter 3: Dealing with Disasters

A. Eyre, V. Brunsden and J. Murphy, *Humanitarian Assistance in the UK: Current Capability and the Development of Best Practice*, Independent report commissioned by the Department for Culture Media and Sport, Contract Number: D3/621, October 2007. <http://www.ukresilience.info/upload/assets/www.ukresilience.info/ha_capability0710.pdf>

A. Eyre, 'More Than PTSD: Proactive Responses Among Disaster Survivors', *The Australasian Journal of Disaster and Trauma Studies*, Vol. 1998, 2 September 1998, Massey University <http://www.massey.ac.nz/~trauma/issues/1998-2/eyre.htm>

M. Gibson, *Order from Chaos: Responding to Traumatic Events*, 3rd edn, Bristol: BASW/Policy Press, 2006.

HM Government, *Emergency Preparedness*: Guidance on Part I of the Civil Contingencies Act 2004, its associated Regulations and non-statutory arrangements, Crown Copyright, 2005. <http://www.ukresilience.info/upload/assets/www.ukresilience.info/emergprepfinal.pdf>

HM Government, *Emergency Response and Recovery*: Non-statutory guidance to complement Emergency Preparedness, Crown Copyright, 2005. <http://www.ukresilience.info/upload/assets/www.ukresilience.info/emergresponse.pdf>

Chapter 4: Before and After the Death of a Child

G. Christ, *Healing Children's Grief: Surviving a Parent's Death from Cancer*, Oxford: Oxford University Press, 2000.

B. Davies, *Shadows in the Sun: The Experiences of Sibling Bereavement in Childhood*, London: Brunner/Mazell, 1999.

A. Dent and A. Stewart, *Sudden Death in Childhood: Care of the Bereaved Family*, Edinburgh: Elsevier/Butterworth/Heinemann, 2004.

D. Klass, P. R. Silverman and S. L. Nickman (eds), *Continuing Bonds: New Understandings of Grief*, Washington: Taylor & Francis, 1996.

B. Monroe and F. Kraus, *Brief Interventions with Bereaved Children*, Oxford: Oxford University Press, 2005.

J. W. Nadeau, *Families Making Sense of Death*, Thousand Oaks, CA: Sage, 1998.

G. Riches and P. Dawson, *An Intimate Loneliness: Supporting Bereaved Parents and Siblings*, Buckingham: Open University Press, 2000.

P. R. Silverman, *Never too Young to Know: Death in Children's Lives*, Oxford: Oxford University Press, 2000.

J. W. Worden, *Children and Grief: When a Parent Dies*, New York: Guildford Press, 1996.

Chapter 5: Death in Hospital

R. Bryant-Jefferies, *Counselling for Death and Dying*, Oxford: Radcliffe, 2006.

M. Cobb, *The Hospital Chaplain's Handbook*, Norwich: Canterbury Press, 2005.

P. Firth, G. Luff and D. Oliviere, *Loss, Change and Bereavement in Palliative Care*, Maidstone: Open University Press, 2004.

J. Green and M. Green, *Dealing with Death: A Handbook of Practices, Procedures and Law*, London: Jessica Kingsley, 2006.

J. Lugton, *Communicating with Dying People and Their Relatives*, Oxford: Radcliffe, 2002.

J. Schott, A. Henley and N. Kohner, *Pregnancy Loss and the Death of a Baby: Guidelines for Professionals*, London: SANDS, 2007.

J. Woodward, *Befriending Death*, London: SPCK, 2005.

Chapter 6: Contemporary Perspectives on Grief and Bereavement

M. Bradbury, *Representations of Death: A Social Psychological Perspective*, London and New York: Routledge, 1999.

D. Francis, L. Kellaher and G. Neophytou, *The Secret Cemetery*, Oxford: Berg, 2005.

J. Hockey, J. Katz and N. Small (eds), *Grief, Mourning and Death Ritual*, Buckingham, Philadelphia: Open University Press, 2001.

G. Howarth, *Death and Dying: A Sociological Introduction*, Cambridge: Polity Press, 2007.

S. Payne and S. Horn, *Loss and Bereavement*, Buckingham: Open University Press, 1999.

G. Riches and P. Dawson, *An Intimate Loneliness: Supporting Bereaved Parents and Siblings*, Buckingham: Open University Press, 2000.

C. Valentine, *Bereavement Narratives: Continuing Bonds in the 21st Century*, London: Routledge, 2008.

T. Walter, *On Bereavement: The Culture of Grief*, Maidenhead, Philadelphia: Open University Press, 1999.

Chapter 7: Changing Christian Beliefs about the Afterlife

J. Bremmer, *The Rise and Fall of the Afterlife*, London: Routledge, 2002.

P. Brown, *The Cult of the Saints: Its Rise and Function in Latin Christianity*, London: SCM, 1981.

C. W. Bynum, *The Resurrection of the Body in Western Christianity, 200–1336*, New York: Columbia Press, 1995.

E. Duffy, *The Stripping of the Altars: Traditional Religion in England 1400–1580*, New Haven and London: Yale, 1992.

D. L. Edwards, *After Death? Past Beliefs and Real Possibilities*, London: Cassell, 1999.

V. Harding, *The Dead and the Living in Paris and London, 1500–1670*, Cambridge: Cambridge University Press, 2002.

J. Hick, *Death and Eternal Life*, London: Collins, 1976.

P. C. Jupp and C. Gittings (eds), *Death in England: An Illustrated History*, Manchester: Manchester University Press, 1999.

C. McDannell and B. Lang, *Heaven: A History*, New Haven: Yale University Press, 1988.

J. B. Russell, *A History of Heaven: The Singing Silence*, Princeton NJ: Princeton University Press, 1997.

D. G. Rowell, *Hell and the Victorians: A Study of the Nineteenth Century Theological Controversies Concerning Eternal Punishment and the Future Life*, Oxford: Clarendon Press, 1974.

D. G. Rowell, *The Liturgy of Christian Burial*, London: Alcuin Club/SPCK, 1977.

Chapter 8: Resurrection and Immortality of the Soul

J. Clark-Soles, *Death and the Afterlife in the New Testament*, London: T & T Clark, 2006.

D. Davies, *Death, Ritual and Belief*, 2nd edn, London: Continuum, 2002.

D. Davies and A. Shaw, *Reusing Old Graves: A Report of Popular British Attitudes*, Crayford: Shaw and Sons, 1995.

D. Cohn-Sherbok and C. Lewis, *Beyond Death*, London: Macmillan, 1995.

G. D'Costa (ed.), *Resurrection Reconsidered*, Oxford: One World, 1996.

J. Davies, *Death, Burial and Rebirth in the Religions of Antiquity*, London: Routledge, 1999.

T. Peters, R. J. Russell and M. Welker (eds), *Resurrection*, Grand Rapids: Eerdmans, 2002.

K. Rahner, *On the Theology of Death*, New York: Seaburt Press, 1973.

R. B. Stewart, *The Resurrection of Jesus*, London: SPCK, 2006.

H. Thielicke, *Living with Death*, Michigan, Grand Rapids: Eerdmans, 1983.

N. T. Wright, *The Resurrection of the Son of God*, London: SPCK, 2003.

Chapter 9: Concepts of Heaven and Hell in the Modern Era

P. Badham, *Christian Beliefs about Life after Death*, Basingstoke: Macmillan, 1976. Reissued London: SPCK, 1978.

P. Badham, *Immortality or Extinction*, London: Macmillan, 1982.

P. Badham, *Religious and Near-Death Experience in Relation to Belief in a Future Life*, second series of occasional papers no.13, RERC Lampeter, 1997.

P. Badham, *The Contemporary Challenge of Modernist Theology*, Cardiff: University of Wales Press, 1998.

S. Davis, *Death and Afterlife*, Basingstoke: Macmillan, 1989.

Doctrine Commission of the Church of England, *The Mystery of Salvation*, London: Church House Publishing, 1995.

The Evangelical Alliance Commission on Unity and Truth among Evangelicals, *The Nature of Hell*, London: Acute, 2000.

M. Fox, *Religion, Spirituality and the Near-death Experience*, London: Routledge, 2003.

J. Hick, *Death and Eternal Life*, London: Collins, 1976.

C. McDannell and B. Lang, *Heaven: A History*, New York: Vintage, 1990.

N. Murphy, *Bodies and Souls, or Spirited Bodies*, Cambridge: Cambridge University Press, 2006.

G. Rowell, *Hell and the Victorians: A Study of the Nineteenth Century Controversies Concerning Eternal; Punishment and the Future Life*, Oxford: Oxford University Press, 1974.

Chapter 10: The Past, Present and Future of Burial

P. Bachelor, *Sorrow and Solace: The Social World of the Cemetery*, Amityville, New York: Baywood Publishing Company Inc, 2004.

D. Davies and A. Shaw, *Reusing Old Graves: A Report on Popular British Attitudes*, Crayford, Kent: Shaw & Sons, 1995.

D. Francis, L. Kellaher and G. Neophytou, *The Secret Cemetery*, Oxford: Berg, 2005.

J. Hockey, L. Kellaher and D. Prendergast, 'Of Grief and Well-being: Competing Concepts of Restorative Ritual', *Anthropology and Medicine*, Vol. 14, No. 1, April 2007, pp. 1–14.

R. Huntingdon and P. Metcalf, *Celebrations of Death: The Anthropology of Mortuary Ritual*, Cambridge: Cambridge University Press, 1979.

I. Hussein and J. Rugg, 'Managing London's Dead: A Case of Strategic Policy Failure', *Mortality*, (8)2, 2003, pp. 209–21.

L. Kellaher, D. Prendergast and J. Hockey, 'In the Shadow of the Traditional

Grave', *Mortality*, 10(4) 2005, pp. 237–50.

J.-M. Strange, *Death, Grief and Poverty in Britain 1870–1914*, Cambridge: Cambridge University Press, 2006.

K. Worpole, *Last Landscapes: The Architecture of the Cemetery in the West*, London: Reaktion Books, 2004.

Chapter 11: Overcoming 'An Architecture of Reluctance'

P. B. Bond, 'Architecture for Mourning', in Cope, G. (ed.), *Dying, Death and Disposal*, London: SPCK, 1970, pp. 85–98.

P. B. Bond, 'The Celebration of Death: Some Thoughts on the Design of Crematoria', *Architectural Review*, 14, 1967, pp. 303–4. Republished in *Pharos*, 33:3, 1967, pp. 62–6.

J. S. Curl, 'The Historical Problems of Designing Crematoria', *Pharos International*, 47:2, 1981, pp. 45–51.

J. S. Curl, *A Celebration of Death: An Introduction to Some of the Buildings, Monuments and Settings of Funerary Architecture in the Western European Tradition*, 2nd edn, London: B. T. Batsford, 1993.

J. L. Seaton Dahl, 'The Ideal Crematorium', in *Cremation in Great Britain*, 3rd edn, London: The Cremation Society, 1945.

D. J. Davies, *British Crematoria in Public Profile*, Maidstone: The Cremation Society, 1995.

D. J. Davies, 'The Sacred Crematorium', *Mortality*, 1:1, 1996, pp. 83–94.

D. Farthing, 'Defects in Crematoria Design and the Cremation Service: The Funeral Director's Point of View', Annual Cremation Society Conference, 1967, Report of Proceedings, 1967, pp. 13–20.

A. C. Freeman, *Cremation in Great Britain and Abroad*, London, 1904.

E. Maxwell Fry, 'The Design of Modern Crematoria', Report of proceedings of the Cremation Society Conference, Bournemouth, 23, 24 and 25 June 1964, pp. 39–43.

P. C. Jupp, 'From Dust to Ashes: The Replacement of Burial by Cremation in England 1840–1967', *The Congregational Lecture 1990*, London: The Congregational Memorial Hall Trust (1978) Ltd, 1990.

H. R. W. Orr, 'Crematorium Architecture', *Pharos*, 16:4, 1950, pp. 3–5.

A. Douglas Robinson, 'The Architectural Approach', Annual Cremation Society Conference, 1957, Report of proceedings, 1957, pp. 15–19.

R. Sudell, 'Planning the Garden of Remembrance', Annual Cremation Society Conference, 1953, Report of proceedings, 1953, pp. 17–23.

Chapter 12: Ashes to Ashes, Dust to Dust

K. Rahner, 'Death', 'Resurrection', 'Resurrection of the Body', in Karl Rahner (ed.), *Encyclopaedia of Theology: The Concise Sacramentum Mundi*, London: Seabury Press, 1975.

'Funerals', in Paul Bradshaw (ed.), *The New SCM Dictionary of Liturgy and Worship*, London: SCM Press, 2002.

M. Boyer, *Baptised into Christ's Death and Resurrection – Preparing to Celebrate a Christian Funeral*, two volumes, Collegeville PA: Liturgical Press, 1999.

T. Buckley, *A Catholic Funeral*, Chawton, Hants: Redemptorist, 2004.

J. Douglas Davies, *Cremation Today and Tomorrow*, Nottingham: Alcuin/ GROW series, 1990.

A. Franz, 'Everything is Worthwhile at the End? Christian Funeral Liturgy amidst Ecclesial Tradition and Secular Rites', *Studia Liturgica*, Vol.32, No. 1, 2002, pp. 48–68.

H. James, *A Fitting End – Making the Most of a Funeral*, Norwich: Canterbury Press, 2004.

H. Krech, 'Funerals – Dealing with the End of the Middle of Life: Consequences for the Ritual in View of a Publicly Tabooed Death', *Studia Liturgica*, Vol. 32, No.1, 2002, pp. 69–88.

T. Lynch, *The Undertaking – Life Studies from the Dismal Trade*, Harmondsworth: Penguin, 1998.

Chapter 13: Theology in Ashes

D. J. Davies, *Cremation Today and Tomorrow*, Nottingham: Grove/Alcuin,1990.

D. J. Davies, 'Theologies of Disposal', in P. C. Jupp and T. Rogers (eds), *Interpreting Death: Christian Theology and Pastoral Practice*, London: Cassell, 1997, pp. 67–84.

D. J. Davies and L. H. Mates (eds), *Encyclopedia of Cremation*, Aldershot: Ashgate, 2006.

K. Denison, 'The Theology and Liturgy of Funerals: A View from the Church in Wales', *Mortality*, Vol.4, No.1, March 1999, pp. 63–74.

H. J. Grainger, *Death Redesigned: British Crematoria: History, Architecture and Landscape*, Reading: Spire, 2005.

Brian Parsons, *Committed to the Cleansing Flame*, Reading: Spire, 2005.

Chapter 14: The Challenge of Green Burial

J. Diamond, *Collapse: How Societies Choose to Fail or Survive*, London: Allen Lane, 2002.

M. Eliade, *A History of Religious Ideas*, three volumes, Chicago: University of Chicago Press. 1978.

M. Eliade, *Patterns in Comparative Religion*, Stagbooks, 1958.

O. James, *Affluenza: How to be Successful and Stay Sane*, London: Random House, 2007.

A. MacIntosh, *Soil and Soul*, London: Aurum Press, 2004.

T. Merton, *Entering the Silence*, New York: Harper, 2001.

J. Sacks, *The Dignity of Difference: How to Avoid the Clash of Civilisations*, London and New York: Continuum, 2002.

E. Tolle, *A New Earth: Awakening to Your Life's Purpose*, Harmondsworth: Penguin, 2005.

C. Tudge, *The Secret Life of Trees*, Harmondsworth: Penguin, 2004.

Chapter 15: The Church of England's Common Worship Funeral Services

Common Worship: Pastoral Services, London: Church House Publishing, 2000.

P. B. Bradshaw (ed.), *Companion to Common Worship*, Vol. 2, London: Alcuin-SPCK, 2000.

R. Anne Horton, *Using Common Worship: Funerals*, London: Church House Publishing, 2000.

T. Lloyd, *Dying and Death: Step by Step: A Funerals Flowchart*, Cambridge: Grove Books, 2000.

T. Lloyd, 'Prayer Book Services Across the Anglican Communion: Funeral Services', in *The Oxford Companion to the Book of Common Prayer*, New York: Oxford University Press, 2006.

P. P. J. Sheppy, *Death, Liturgy and Ritual: A Pastoral and Liturgical Theology*, two volumes, Aldershot: Ashgate Publishing, 2003.

J. Lampard, *Go Forth Christian Soul: The Biography of a Prayer*, Peterborough: Epworth Press, 2005.

G. Legood and I. Markham, *The Funerals Handbook*, London: SPCK, 2003.

G. Rowell, *The Liturgy of Christian Burial*, London: SPCK/Alcuin Club, 1997.

Chapter 16: The Roman Catholic Experience

A. Ball, *Catholic Book of the Dead*, Huntington, Indiana: Our Sunday Visitor Publishing Division, 1994.

In Sure and Certain Hope, London: Geoffrey Chapman, 1999.

Into Your Hands: Planning a Catholic Funeral, Readings and Prayers, Mildenhall: Decani Books, 1999.

F. McCarthy, *Funeral Liturgies*, Dublin: Dominican Publications, 2003.

D. Messenger, *Ceremonies and Celebrations*, Melbourne, Victoria: Lothian Publications, 1999.

S. O'Malley, *In the Potter's Hands*, San Jose, California: Resource Publications, 1988.

M. Marchal, *Parish Funerals*, Chicago: Liturgy Training Publications, 1987.

The Order of Christian Funerals, London: Geoffrey Chapman, 1990.

The Order of Christian Funerals: Rites of Committal, London: Burns & Oates, 2004.

Chapter 17: Free Church Liturgies

D. Davies and A. Shaw, *Reusing Old Graves: A Report of Popular British Attitudes*, Crayford: Shaw and Sons, 1995.

G. Davie, *Religion in Britain Since 1945: Believing Without Belonging*, Oxford: Blackwell, 1994.

Chapter 18: Orthodox Liturgy, Theology and Pastoral Practice

Texts of the services

The most complete recent texts in English were published in 1999 by St Tikhon's Seminary Press, Volume III of *The Great Book of Needs*.
The provisional translation of Archimandrite Ephrem Lash can be found at www.anastasis.org.uk/funeral.htm
The Greek texts can be found in the *Great Euchologion*, Μέγα Ευχολόγιον, Astir, 1980 edition.

Modern discussion

N. P. Vassiliadis *The Mystery of Death*, ET . A. Peter, Athens: Chamberas Sotir, 1999.
Hierotheos Metropolitan of Nafpaktos *Life after Death*, ET E. Williams, Levadia: Birth of the Theotokos Monastery, 1996.

Chapter 19: Music at Funerals

A. Caldicott, 'Music at Funerals', *Funeral Service Journal*, Vol. 121, No.2, 2006, pp. 106–8.
P. Denyer, 'Singing the Lord's Song in a Strange Land', in P. C. Jupp and T. Rogers (eds), *Interpreting Death: Christian Theology and Pastoral Practice*, London: Cassell, 1997, pp. 197–202.
K. Lysons, 'Issues of Music at Crematoria' *Pharos International*, Vol. 70, No.1, 2003, pp. 44–7.
M. Page, 'Grave Misgivings', *Religion Today*, Vol. 2, No. 3, 1985, pp.7–9.

Chapter 20: Funerals in the Multicultural Metropolis

F. Dominica, *Just my Reflection*, London: Darton Longman and Todd, 1997.
J. Hockey, J. Katz and N. Small (eds), *Grief, Mourning and Death Ritual*, Buckingham: Open University Press, 2001.
D. King, *Faith, Spirituality and Medicine*, Haworth: Pastoral Press, 2000.
N. Kohner and A. Henley, *When a Baby Dies. The Experience of Late Miscarriage, Stillbirth and Neonatal Death*, revised edn, London: Routledge, 2001.
J. Mabey, *Words to Comfort, Words to Heal* (poems and meditations for those who grieve), Oxford: Oneworld, 1998.
C. M. Parkes, *Bereavement: Studies of Grief in Adult Life*, 3rd edn, Harmondsworth: Penguin, 1998.
C. M. Parkes, P. Laungani and B. Young (eds), *Death and Bereavement Across Cultures*, London and New York: Routledge, 1997.
J. Woodward, *Befriending Death*, London: SPCK, 2005.
The Art of Remembering, The Memorial Arts Charity, Snape Priory, Saxmundham, Suffolk 1P17 1SA. Video about work by letter cutters on themes of memory and loss.

Chapter 21: Characteristics of Scottish Funerals

J. Beech, O. Hand, M. Mulhern and J. Weston (eds), *Scottish Life and Society: A Compendium of Scottish Ethnology, Volume 9, The Individual and Community Life*, Edinburgh: John Donald, 2005.

M. Bennett, *Scottish Customs: From the Cradle to the Grave*, 2nd edn, Edinburgh: Birlinn, 2004.

D. B. Forrester and D. M. Murray (eds), *Studies in the History of Worship in Scotland*, Edinburgh: T & T Clark, 1984.

A. Gordon, *Death is for the Living*, Edinburgh: Pentland, 1984.

C. MacLean and K. Veitch (eds) *Scottish Life and Society. A Compendium of Scottish Ethnology, Volume 12; Religion*, Edinburgh: John Donald in association with the European Ethnological Research Centre and the National Museums of Scotland, 2006.

R. Scott, *Death by Design*, Edinburgh: Black & White, 2005.

B. Willsher, *Understanding Scottish Graveyards*, 2nd edn, Edinburgh: Canongate, 1995.

Chapter 22: Funeral Ministry in Wales

P. M. H. Bell, *Disestablishment in Ireland and Wales*, London: SPCK, 1969.

K. M. Denison, 'The Theology and Liturgy of Funerals: A View from the Church in Wales', *Mortality*, Vol. 4, No. 1, March 1999, pp.63–74.

H. James, *A Fitting End: Making the Most of a Funeral*, Norwich: Canterbury Press, 2004.

The Book of Common Prayer for Use in the Church in Wales, Vols I and II, Penarth: Church in Wales, 1984.

The Constitution of the Church in Wales, Cardiff: The Governing Body of the Church in Wales, n.d.

D. Walker (ed.), *A History of the Church in Wales*, Penarth: Church in Wales, 1976.

Chapter 23: Funerals in Northern Ireland

J. Boyse, *Works*, two volumes in 1 folio, London, 1629.

R. Craghead, *An Answer to the Bishop of Derry's Second Admonition*, 1697.

J. G. Davies (ed.), *A Dictionary of Liturgy and Worship*, London: SCM, 1972.

A. H. Dill et al., *A Short History of the Presbyterian Churches of Ballymoney, County Antrim*, Bradford and London, Percy Lund: Humphries and Co. Ltd, 1898.

A. R. Holmes, *The Shaping of Ulster Presbyterian Belief and Practice 1770–1840*, Oxford: Oxford University Press, 2006.

M. McDiarmid, *Joey Dunlop, His Authorised Biography*, Yeovil: Haynes Publishing, 2001.

R. S. Tosh, 'One Hundred and Fifty Years of Worship: A Survey', in R. F. G. Holmes and R. Buick Knox (eds), *The General Assembly of the Presbyterian Church in Ireland 1840–1990*, Coleraine: Presbyterian Historical Society of Ireland, 1990.

T. Witherow, *Historical and Literary Memorials*, two volumes, London and Belfast: William Mullan and Son, 1879.

Index of Subjects

Aberfan disaster, 21
Acts of Parliament
  1686 Act anent Burying in Scots
    Linen, 226
  1847 Cemetery Clauses Act, 119
  1857 Burial Laws Amendment Act,
    106
  1902 Cremation Act, 119
  1914 Welsh Church Act, 234–5
  1919 Welsh Church Temporalities
    Act, 234–5
  1945 Welsh Church (Burial
    Grounds) Act, 235
  2004 Civil Contingencies Act, 21
  2004 Human Tissue Act, 49
  2006 Human Tissue (Scotland) Act,
    49
afterlife, Christian beliefs about
  historical survey, Ch. 7
  Resurrection and immorality, Ch. 8
  Heaven and hell, Ch. 9
Alder Hey Hospital, 49
Alternative Prayer Book (Church of
  Ireland), 245
Alternative Prayer Book (ASB),
  158–60
Anfield, 25
Anima Christi, 5
Arbory Trust, 152
architecture, Ch.11
Arbroath, 231
Ars moriendi, 71
ashes, disposal of 105, 110, Ch. 10
  passim, Ch. 13 *passim*, 171, 241–2

'bad news', 22
Baptist churches, 72ff, 180–2

baptism
  and funerals, 128–9, 145–6, 180–2
Benedict XVI, Pope, 176–7
bereavement,
  attention from Catholic liturgies,
    160–6
  contemporary perspectives, Ch. 6
  in disasters, Ch. 3 *passim*
  'Dual Process model', 40
  and burial, 105–7, 110–2
  funeral rites role in, Ch. 15
  in hospitals, 51–2
  journey of, 160, 162, 214
  and parents, Ch. 4
  support, 10
Beveridge Report, 75, 107
bilinguality, 242–3
body
  burial of, Ch. 7 *passim*, Ch. 10, Ch.
    12
  embodiment, 96
  see also resurrection
Book of Common Order, 237–8, 246,
  247
Book of Common Prayer, 245
Book of Common Prayer (Church of
  Ireland), 245
*Book of Common Prayer of the
  Church in Wales*, 241
Book of Public Worship (Northern
  Ireland), 247
Bradford, 14, 120
Bridgend, 123
Bristol Royal Infirmary, 49
British Humanist Association, 229
Buffalo Creek flood, 24f
Buke of Discipline, 224

Roman Catholic, Ch. 12, Ch. 16,
226–7, 229–30
Scottish, Ch. 21 *passim*
United Reformed Church, 183–4
Welsh Church, 239ff
lay-led, 175
staged rites, 130, 161–2
thanksgiving trend, *see* personalization
Liverpool, 203
Liverpool Pathway for the Dying,
213
local government, *see*
municipalization
Lockerbie disaster, 21, 25
London, Ch. 20
London, Honor Oak, 119

Manchester, Blackley, 204
Marchioness disaster, 110
Margam, 108
Marie Curie, 213
memorial
roadside, 25
sermons, 174–5, 246
services, 15, Ch. 3 *passim*, 198
memorials
to the unborn, 175–6
memory, 83, 95–6
mind, 98–9
minorities, funerals for ethnic, 76,
108–9, 213–4, 216–30, 238
mortuaries, 48f
municipalization, 10f, 106, 171–2
music, 69, 192–3, Ch. 19, 228

National Association of Bereavement
Services, 159
National Association of Funeral
Directors, 12, 159
National Association of Widows, 10
National Funerals College, 206
Natural Death Centre, 13
near death experiences, 99, 152
National Funerals College, the, 206
neo–natal death, 175
Newport, 239
New York (9/11), 24

non–belief
non–believers, inclusion of at funeral
services, 173–4, 183–7

*Order of Christian Funerals, The
(OCF)*, Ch. 15
organ donation, 49f
Orthodox churches 105, 111, Ch. 18

Pentecostal churches, 111, 219, 238
personalization, 14ff, 165–6, 240ff
prayers for the dead, 70, 75, Chs 15,
16 and 18 *passim*, 181–2, 190, 197,
224
Presbyterianism, Ch. 21 *passim*, 246ff
promession, 155
Psychical Research Society, 74
psychological approaches to grieving,
55–8
psycho-social transition (pst), 58–9
punishment, eternal, 99–102
purgatory, 70–1, 108

Rapture theology, 85
readers, 237
Reformation (Protestant) 71ff, 160,
190, 223–4
remembrance, 25f
see also memorials
resomation, 155
resurrection
of the body, 2f, Ch. 7 *passim*, Ch. 8,
Ch. 12 *passim*, 241–2
of Jesus Christ, 2, Ch. 2 *passim*,
67–8, Ch. 8 *passim*, Ch. 12 *passim*,
176–7, 180, 195, 251
retained organs, 49f
Retained Organs Commission, 49
Rheinau Sacramentary, 160
ritual, 25f
see also liturgy
Road Peace, 10

sacred space, 25, 149–50, 151, 156
sacredness, 117
St Helen's, 207
SANDS (Stillbirth and Neonatal Death
Society), 10

Index of Names